Not the
Whole Story

LIFE WRITING SERIES

In the Life Writing Series, Wilfrid Laurier University Press publishes life writing and new life-writing criticism and theory in order to promote autobiographical accounts, diaries, letters, and testimonials written and/or told by women and men whose political, literary, or philosophical purposes are central to their lives. The Series features accounts written in English, or translated into English from French or the languages of the First Nations, or any of the languages of immigration to Canada.

From its inception, Life Writing has aimed to foreground the stories of those who may never have imagined themselves as writers or as people with lives worthy of being (re)told. Its readership has expanded to include scholars, youth, and avid general readers both in Canada and abroad. The Series hopes to continue its work as a leading publisher of life writing of all kinds, as an imprint that aims for both broad representation and scholarly excellence, and as a tool for both historical and autobiographical research.

As its mandate stipulates, the Series privileges those individuals and communities whose stories may not, under normal circumstances, find a welcoming home with a publisher. Life Writing also publishes original theoretical investigations about life writing, as long as they are not limited to one author or text.

Series Editor
Marlene Kadar
Humanities Division, York University

Manuscripts to be sent to
Lisa Quinn, Acquisitions Editor
Wilfrid Laurier University Press
75 University Avenue West
Waterloo, Ontario N2L 3C5, Canada

Not the Whole Story

Challenging the Single Mother Narrative

Lea Caragata and Judit Alcalde, editors

With contributions from the
single moms of the Trillium group

**WILFRID LAURIER
UNIVERSITY PRESS**

Wilfrid Laurier University Press acknowledges the financial support of the Government of Canada through the Canada Book Fund for our publishing activities.

LAURIER
Inspiring Lives.

Library and Archives Canada Cataloguing in PublicationLibrary and Archives Canada Cataloguing in Publication

Not the whole story : challenging the single mother narrative / Lea Caragata and Judit Alcalde, editors.

(Life Writing series)
Includes bibliographical references.
Issued in print and electronic formats.
ISBN 978-1-55458-624-0 (pbk.).—ISBN 978-1-55458-636-3 (pdf).—
ISBN 978-1-55458-637-0 (epub)

1. Single mothers—Canada—Social conditions. 2. Single mothers—Canada—Biography. I. Alcalde, Judit, editor of compilation II. Caragata, Lea, [date], editor of compilation III. Series: Life writing series

HQ759.45.N68 2014   306.874'32092271   C2013-905919-9
                                              C2013-905920-2

Cover design by Blakeley Words+Pictures. Front-cover image courtesy of Aviva Community Fund. Text design by Janette Thompson (Jansom).

This book is printed on FSC recycled paper and is certified Ecologo. It is made from 100% post-consumer fibre, processed chlorine free, and manufactured using biogas energy.

Printed in Canada

RECYCLED
Paper made from
recycled material
FSC   FSC® C103567
www.fsc.org

Dedication

This book is dedicated to all single mothers whose own stories echo those contained in this volume.

We hope that this book challenges many of the contemporary narratives about who single mothers are and why they are parenting alone, often in poverty. We believe that with a changed public discourse and better understanding, government, employers, educators, and citizens can create meaningful and valued places in our society for single mothers and their children—places where no single mother asks herself whether she would have been better off had she stayed with an abuser, goes hungry to feed her children, or knows what it is like to be both homeless and a parent.

Contents

Acknowledgements

Lone Mothers: Building Social Inclusion was a Canada-wide research program funded by the Social Sciences and Humanities Research Council of Canada. The five-year-long study investigated the experiences of lone mothers on social assistance as they coped with newly introduced work-for-welfare requirements amid a changing labour market characterized by growing precarious employment.

One of several spin-off projects saw the development of a pilot project for a group of 12–15 lone mothers who were brought together with a skilled facilitator to explore and develop their own competencies and expand their sense of agency. This project was generously funded by the Ontario Trillium Foundation and sponsored by Opportunity for Advancement (OFA), a highly progressive Toronto-based NGO that works with low-income women. Over a two-year period the group developed into a self-help/mutual support group that became very important in the lives of the women participants.

Joanne Green and Anne Rattray of OFA, Maria Liegghio and Judit Alcalde, who in turn facilitated the group, and MP Olivia Chow, who gave of her time to talk about organizing for change, were all important mentors for group members.[1] The women in the group were (and are) critical supports for each other. Their names should be on the cover of this volume, and it is one more injustice in their lives that, after much discussion, all of the contributors felt the need to write under a pseudonym to protect themselves and their families.

All of us who were fortunate to have had the opportunity to learn from the women of the Trillium group hope that this sharing of their stories will enable the readers of this volume to come to know these women, albeit in a

---

[1] The names of the group members whose stories are included here have been changed, as have the names of those mentioned in the stories. Initially most of the women wanted to use their real names, as they wanted to name and own their experiences, but over time they came to see that such naming might negatively affect others, including their children.

small way—their experiences of abuse and hardship but also their humour, their passion for social justice, their capacities for love and friendship, and their ongoing contribution to their communities, which are truly inspirational. As the editors of the volume, we wish to formally acknowledge their resilience—and resistance—as well as their generosity and courage in making their stories public. We have learned much through our work together.

Thanks are due to a number of people who have supported both the group and the development of this volume, including doctoral students who have provided editing, writing, and research assistance, staff at Opportunity for Advancement who helped with preparing and tracking honoraria, and the editors at Wilfrid Laurier University Press, who saw the potential of the volume and remained generously patient through its long execution. The reviewers used by the Press, too, managed both support and helpfulness in combination with thorough critique, always a delicate balance. I have avoided naming names only because the list is long.

Introduction

Lea Caragata

This volume contains 16 stories that we hope will cause readers to think about and critically examine the ways in which single mothers have been positioned in our society. The life stories told here are narrated by single mothers themselves—they are their own stories, told their own way, about their own lives. Each of us has multiple life stories; as we talk about our lives and ourselves, the story told depends on our own moods and contexts. Each of us selectively interprets our own histories and selectively tells and describes our own histories. So, too, is the case with the stories that follow. Each of the women had the opportunity to edit their stories after they had told them, and decide which elements of the stories they wished to keep and which they may not want to be publicly available. The guiding focus of each story was the woman's experience as a low-income single mother and as part of a research and community engagement project in Toronto, Canada, over a six-year period beginning in 2004.

These stories are a small part of a social research project titled Lone Mothers: Building Social Inclusion. Initially funded by the Social Sciences and Humanities Research Council under their Community–University Research Alliances Program in 2004, this five-year longitudinal research project sought to examine and understand the experiences of single mothers on social assistance. The project was important and timely because of two critical changes occurring in Canadian society that we believed would have a particular impact on low-income single mothers. I briefly describe work-for-welfare, or *workfare*, as it is commonly known, and changes in a labour market that is increasingly characterized by precarious work. These changes set an important context for understanding the current lives of the women you will meet in this volume.

It is perhaps important to add a note about our distinction between single parents and single (or lone) mothers. In Canada, about 80% of single parents are women (Statistics Canada, 2011), so the focus here and in our research is on women as single parents. Generally, single fathers are much better off economically, and, perhaps because their numbers are small, they are often highly regarded as they take on the task of single parenting. This contrasts sharply with the moral censure that is so frequently applied to single mothers (Little, 1998). With respect to the question of whether we describe women who are parenting without partners as "single" or "lone" mothers, we began our work using the words lone mother, because "single" was critiqued for its reference to marital status. Often, though, the women we were working with needed a translation of that term—they saw themselves as single moms. We use the two descriptors interchangeably.

Workfare and Precarious Work

In the last 20 years, welfare rules have changed across Canada (except in Newfoundland) for everyone, including single parents. These new rules require that people who are on welfare, or social assistance, be actively engaged in looking for work (Herd, Mitchell, & Lightman, 2005; Torjman, 1996). These programs have been called workfare or work-for-welfare, and although their implementation was contentious overall, a particular concern was the extension of these provisions to single parents (Evans, 1997; Gorlick & Brethour, 1998; Little, 1998).

Before these regulations there were, in most Canadian provinces, special welfare benefits for single parents, an acknowledgement of their need to be available more fully to their children (Evans, 1997). In addition to being exempt from job search requirements, single parents also received a slightly more generous welfare benefit because it was expected that their "stay" on social assistance would likely be longer than average (Gavigan & Chunn, 2007). Welfare benefits are set at low levels with an assumption that those relying on them will experience some level of deprivation. How much deprivation is thought to be a good thing—motivating the person to get off of the system—depends on the values of the time. The higher benefits for single parents recognized that a period of sustained deprivation would likely harm the family and negatively affect the life chances of the children. This latter point has been extensively well documented by studies that show economic well-being as a major social determinant of health (Ruxton & Kirk, 1996; Ecob & Smith, 1999; Marmot, 1999; Lynch et al., 2000). With the introduction of workfare programs single parents were expected to be actively looking for work, and the harsh benefit levels introduced applied equally to them and their families (Evans, 1997).

These changes began in 1995 in Ontario and around that same period in other provinces in Canada, classifying single parents with other employable adults as having a work obligation (Evans, 1997; Little, 1998). The Lone Mothers: Building Social Inclusion project sought to understand how single parents were coping with this change because the earlier Family Benefits programs (as they were called in Ontario) acknowledged, in effect, that the primary or custodial parent would need to be available for child care. The impact of the new workfare obligations on single parents was not clear, especially considering the lack of an accessible national child care strategy.

The other major shift, which began in the 1990s and continues in Canadian society and across the Western world, consists of profound changes in the labour market. At the same time that the social assistance system changed, requiring lone mothers to be actively looking for work, much of the Canadian labour market began to be characterized by what is now described as precarious work (Caragata, 2008; Evans, 2007; Vosko, 2002). This generally includes work that is low waged, without benefits, and outside both the standard hours of work and what used to be the standard employment relationship. This means work that is casual, part-time, and/or shift work at low rates of pay, most often contractual or structured as self-employment. This precarious labour market has grown significantly in Canada so that it now accounts for about one-third of Canadian workers (Vosko, 2002, 2005; Vosko, Zukewich, & Cranford, 2003).

For the many lone mothers who had relied on social assistance, these two changes plunged them into a new world. It became difficult to meet the needs and interests of their children while contending with uncertain and irregular child care, the loss of drug and dental benefits previously provided by social assistance, and inadequate family incomes even if they were able to obtain full-time work. More typically, work for single moms leaving social assistance consisted of part-time hours and split shifts because they had no reliable, affordable, and safe child care. After a few months of gruelling schedules marked by missed work due to kids' illness, or late arrivals because of slow toddlers and late buses, many women reluctantly returned to social assistance to face a system that pressured them to try it again.

Welfare changes demanding work accompanied by labour-market changes that privilege precarious work have combined in a particularly insidious manner. Jobs that can sustain a family with one less-skilled wage earner are hard to come by; thus, even single mothers who the system deems to have successfully exited social assistance seldom report significant gains in income. For too many welfare-reliant single moms in the present climate, with real opportunities for significant education and skill building foreclosed and a paucity of subsidized daycare places, the aspiration of earning a family wage is unrealized.

The women who tell their stories in this book do so with the hope that they will be less negatively judged by the reader, and that systemic and structural issues that cause them to experience the life stresses might themselves be addressed. At the very least, they hope that these issues will be acknowledged by the public and within the social systems and institutions wherein single mothers and their children negotiate their lives.

The Making of This Book

Lone Mothers: Building Social Inclusion gave rise to a number of pilot projects as we sought to examine in more detail the impact of the broad changes described on lone mothers and their children. One such pilot was a project funded by the Ontario Trillium Foundation that sought to examine the social and civic engagement of single mothers on social assistance.

Recognizing that for single mothers finding and sustaining paid work was a challenge, expectations in the welfare system were modified so that women could actively volunteer in their community in lieu of work. The intention was that these volunteer roles would build work experience and self-confidence, as well as social capital, so that over time those so engaged would become more employable (Social Assistance Reform Act, 1997: ch. 25). In the meantime, they would be making a contribution to their communities and would model such engagement for their children. Not surprisingly, many of the women that we recruited as participants for our research project had very little social capital, very few connections to the volunteer world, and limited opportunity to creatively think about and express their potential volunteer interests. The most common volunteer roles undertaken by the women we interviewed involved working in their children's schools. We imagined that the volunteering aspect of workfare expectations might have greater possibility for these women if they had an opportunity to be more creative and deliberate about the kind of volunteer roles that they undertook. It was with this idea that we approached and were funded by the Ontario Trillium Foundation for a project on community engagement and lone mothers. With Trillium support we wanted to explore with a select group of single mothers on social assistance whether with careful and strategic assistance they might become actively engaged in their community in ways that were more personally meaningful, thereby satisfying the expectations of the social assistance system but also enabling their own growth and development. This led to our beginning to work very closely with 8 to15 single mothers, initially all on social assistance.

Some of the group members had been participants in our research project, and some joined the group as a result of a snowball sampling process in which other people in the group said, "Oh, gee. My friend would be terrific at this. Could she participate?" We thus began a two-and-a-half-year process whereby what we describe as the Trillium group met about once every two weeks to talk about their social and community roles and about how we, the researchers, might facilitate these. Over the course of this period the Trillium group evolved and changed. Initially the women advised us that they weren't interested in merely mapping out an individual volunteer plan or program for themselves, which is what we had imagined they would do, and which was the basis of our proposal to the Trillium Foundation. With the support of the Trillium Foundation we changed the focus, and the group worked on their own individual engagement in the community as well as thinking collectively about advocacy and how they might challenge the public discourse about single mothers. It was this latter issue that really became the focus of the group. It is important to note, though, that despite the group's focus on broader social change, the work of the group and the group process itself contributed significantly to the growth and development of the participants. In the stories that follow, many of the women describe the ways that their involvement in this process contributed to change in their own lives. That many of the group members continue to connect with each other in meaningful ways is a testament to the power and possibility of such facilitated but self-directed group processes.

The Trillium group was facilitated by a doctoral student from Wilfrid Laurier University, Maria Liegghio, and then subsequently by our research director, Judit Alcalde, who is one of the editors of this volume. At a particular point I attended a meeting of the group and began to talk with the women about who they were and how they imagined that their own identities and life circumstances had contributed to their being single mothers.

I wanted to understand how and why they came to have the kind of critical reflections that I had heard them express about the social positioning of single moms.

This was a pivotal moment for the group, and the genesis of this volume, because it inspired several women in the group to begin to tell their own stories. The women claimed that taking part in the group was essential to their feeling confident about talking about their experiences not only as individuals but as illustrations of the issues that they believed faced single mothers. These included the negative public perception of single mothers as well as concerns related to abuse, education, work and work equity, parenting, and child care. These issues were all seen to cause lone mothers to end up trapped—whether on social assistance, in low-waged work, or on disability benefits. The group participants expressed concern that their individual circumstances were assumed to be the cause rather than a symptom of their status as poor lone mothers and that this deserved a wider telling. It was these moments in the life of a two-year-long group process that led to this volume.

This process and its effects warrant the referencing of the work of Paulo Freire (1970). In his seminal book, *Pedagogy of the Oppressed*, Freire outlines a course of what he describes as "conscientization" wherein a group of marginalized people come to see themselves and their experiences, through a guided group practice, against a larger social backdrop. In this way Freire describes the individuals being able to move away from the feelings of shame and failure by which both they and the larger society characterize their status. Group members come to see themselves and their own struggles, and they also see how these have been shaped and sustained by systemic and structural forces. The impact of these transformational experiences is twofold—freeing the individual from the often-paralyzing effects of self-blame but also engaging these citizens in processes and activities related to social change. Although we were familiar with Freire's work before our own Trillium group began, it is interesting to note that we did not think of or plan to engage the women in a process of conscientization as Freire describes it. It is a testament to the power of his work that our outcomes closely parallel what he describes. The women participants experienced their own growth and change, felt liberated from many of the negative labels and stereotypes they felt had been cast on them, and vowed to challenge the elements of the systems and structure that so perniciously castigate and marginalize single mothers.

Methodology

This work developed in the following way: Each of the women was provided with an opportunity to tell their story at a meeting of the Trillium group, and have it taped and transcribed verbatim. They also had an opportunity, if they preferred, to tell their story privately. Most of the women elected to tell their story in the group because they felt that the group was illustrative, emblematic, of their developing self-confidence and trust in each other. It was their work in the group that led them to have the confidence to see their stories much more broadly than only the telling of their own struggles; their stories are too often lone mothers' stories.

Each of the transcribed documents was returned to the woman who had narrated it, and she was given the opportunity to make revisions. Subsequently, we met with each of the women and through a process of interviewing, taking notes, and doing some additional tape recording, we filled in identified gaps in their stories and provided the women opportunity for further revision. At the culmination of a process of careful editing of the stories, we returned them once again to the individual authors to have them make final adjustments to the story. Our goal was to ensure that the women had significant time to think about the inclusion of their story in the volume and to ensure that the story told was the story each woman wanted to tell.

We have edited the stories, sometimes simply for clarity, sometimes to create a more typical narrative form. We have edited as well for grammar and to acknowledge the difference between verbal and written storytelling. We have also asked the women to include elements that aid in an outsider's understanding. We have taken great care to ensure through these processes that each story remains true to the woman's voice and that it is the story she wanted to tell. Moreover, as all of the narrators were given an opportunity to review the entire volume, we have tried to ensure that the overall message of this book not only tells the struggles of individual lives but also reveals and exposes the broader structural and systemic issues that shape these lives. We hope that if what are often seen as individual life circumstances are aggregated to highlight the common threads among them, we can better understand and improve our social welfare systems, our social service systems, and our judicial and legal systems such that some of the worst of the experiences related here might not happen in the future. These are the two objects of this volume: to provide a window into the lives of hardship and resilience lived by so many poor single mothers in Ontario and in Canada, and to frame what we believe are some of the significant public policy issues that, as an inclusive and civil Canadian society, we might wish to remedy in the interests of better and more equal opportunities for these women and their children. It is our thesis that it is truly the case that the civility of our society can be best measured by the life experiences of its most vulnerable members—in this case the lone-mother-led families we discuss here. Furthermore, a society lacking inclusion and civility will negatively affect us all.

This book has been long in preparation—not only the manuscript but the growth process in these women's lives that have enabled them to come forward with these remarkable, forthright, and disclosing stories. These are stories of hardship and abuse but also of growth and personal change—the latter through a process that has compelled these women to want to advocate for broader change so that other single moms might not endure the same hardships. Ultimately we hope that this is a hopeful book.

As Catrina said in a group meeting at the conclusion of this process: "The good part, the important part [of our telling our stories] is so maybe other people who are going through this can say, 'Okay, this is not going to last forever and there is hope. I can move on and change things. If these people were able to change things, then I can do it, too.' That's what was really, is really, inspiring. Like, okay, I'm not alone, and if she can do it, then I can do it, too."

In spite of having done extensive academic research with single mothers on social assistance, participating in this project has given both editors a much deeper insight into the lives of single mothers living in poverty. The women's words, their focus when telling their stories, and their powerful experiences are markers of the key areas highlighted in all 16 stories, but we come to know and appreciate these structural and policy issues in a very different way. We believe that this way of approaching the policy issues is a more honest one, less filtered through our academic eyes. It is also more raw and perhaps takes a risk in allowing the stories to be that—individual stories. But this process has powerfully given these women voice and that itself has been a remarkable aspect of this work. Each of us as editors is grateful to have been able to witness that transformation.

After completing a first draft of the book, we came together with all the women to share their reflections on the book and its process. For them, the book has had several benefits, including, as described previously, its potential to give other women hope and to create change. Another was the benefit that participation had on them personally. Catrina told us that telling her story was a healing process because, previously, every time she had tried to talk, people would not listen. This issue is a common one—women were not listened to, people denied their abuse experiences, and too often workers they encountered in the system failed to help. Telling their story, publishing this book, is their manifesto.

> It did happen and we need to know that it does happen and that we cannot allow this to continue.
>
> After I wrote the story I had this dream that I just was looking at these people and saying, "Listen. This is what has happened, and now I can tell you, so stop bothering me."

Telling their stories helped the women find their voice, and the book and its stories also reflect their growth. Many of the women said that they want the book to show other women that with supports they can move forward and create a positive life for themselves and their children. Their perseverance and strength in many cases is heroic as they combat addictions, protect their children from abusers, and get their children back when they had lost them, for example. Stacey reflects their common goals: "We want our children to know that we are trying to change things, we are trying to do something. In all our troubles, we have gotten something good out of this mess, but it doesn't need to be their mess."

Before proceeding to the stories that are the focus of this volume, I briefly highlight some of the systemic and policy issues that the group began to see more clearly and that are made apparent in the narratives that follow. I do so not because the stories themselves don't make these issues clear but because this book is about so much more than individual stories and we want to be certain that readers begin with this larger systemic framing.

Issues Shaping Poverty, Single Motherhood, and Social Status

Parenting and Single Mothers

Canada has more than a million single mothers (Statistics Canada, 2012a). It is one of Canada's fastest-growing population groups and, as previously mentioned, a group that differs significantly in most demographic factors from the very small number of male single parents. These circumstances suggest the need for inquiry about why it is that so many women are parenting alone and, beyond that, why many of them either are or become poor. What is it about our economic system, our labour market, our education and training provisions that might predispose women and single mothers to poverty? Why too, in spite of the rigorous attempts of provincial work-fare systems, has it been so difficult for single mothers to successfully exit social assistance? Welfare programs are sufficiently directive that it is no longer a question of whether or not a woman might wish to remain at home with her children and rely on social assistance. They are actively encouraged to be in the labour market, and yet it is extremely difficult for single mothers to achieve successful, sustainable labour-market engagement. Most often, single mothers leave social assistance for low-waged work that doesn't sustain their families. After a period of time they return to social assistance, often propelled by inadequate wages, overwhelming transportation and/or child care problems, a health issue, or children's needs that require more attention.

There are a number of important questions to ask with respect to why so many women become sole parents in cases of family breakdown, and why subsequently they become and most often remain poor. These significant issues are exacerbated by a pervasive negative social judgment that these women have created their circumstances through their own neglect, moral turpitude, lack of drive, and, ultimately, failure to appreciate their obligations as citizens, as Lawrence Mead (1986) might have described it. The view that the problems that these women face are of their own making is one of the notions we challenge here and through the stories that follow.

As a preview of the stories and the issues they raise, I highlight a number of these matters to help frame why it is that women become the partner that parents when relationships break up, why so many of these women remain poor, and why they are so vulnerable to continuing struggles and abuses as they negotiate being single parents amid the affluence of Canadian society.

Abuse

One of the dominant issues that the readers of this volume will quickly note is the prevalence of abuse in the lives of vulnerable women. This abuse takes many forms, but perhaps the most insidious, and responsible for shaping women's continuing vulnerability, are child sexual abuse, which we see in several stories, and the ongoing and too-common problem of women abused by their intimate partners. This latter issue is very significant as a determinant of the large number of women single parenting, which in turn is often the precursor to applying for social assistance. In spite of its prevalence, this issue is largely unacknowledged in welfare policy.

It is the case in many of these stories and in the research done by the Lone Mothers: Building Social Inclusion project that we repeatedly see women fleeing the economic and social security of a two-parent family in order to protect themselves and their children from physical, emotional, and sexual abuse. It is often in this leaving of an abusive partner that now-single mothers are forced to turn for the first time to reliance on social assistance. That an issue of this magnitude remains ignored reflects importantly on the ongoing struggles with regard to women's status as equal citizens. It remains a function of male patriarchal privilege that they can abuse women and at the same time so successfully castigate them for dependence and single parenting.

We believe this recurrent theme of abuse also underlies why lone mothers continue to be economically dependent and poor. In our research data, women who leave abusive partners are often ill-prepared to become economically self-sufficient, and this vulnerability contributes to the power of the abuser and/or is a direct result of the abuse experience. Because their post-separation lives include being mother/father/earner/carer to their children, the education and training necessary to their economic self-sufficiency is unlikely to be available and is certainly not supported through welfare job training programs.

We return to discuss this issue in more detail following the stories, but readers are forewarned that some of the stories contain painful and difficult recounting of abuse experiences. That so many women lived these experiences in all their varied horror compels us, I suggest, to consider how pervasive and gendered this phenomenon is and why in a seemingly civilized society it remains so unexamined and minimally exposed.

Employability and Earnings Equality

A factor related to the poverty of single mothers is, of course, their employability and their ability to be economically autonomous. Among countries in the Organization for Economic Co-operation and Development (OECD), Canada is one of the lowest spenders on education and training, and such spending fails to target issues of gender (Statistics Canada, 2010). In Canadian public policy, a policy of gender neutrality directs how we spend money on education and training. This has not always been the case nor is such targeting by gender uncommon among comparable industrialized societies. Canada's previous targets included moving women out of the traditionally female-dominated sectors of health, education, and social services into the better remunerated male-centred occupations of engineering, skilled trades, and computers and technology. We no longer have such initiatives. Furthermore, labour-market data reveal that while women are equally engaged with men in the labour market, this does not imply earnings equality (Blau & Kahn, 2000; Catalyst, 2012; Heisz, Jackson,& Picot, 2002; Maume, 2004; Williams, 2010). Canadian women continue to earn about 85 cents of a male dollar, and many women continue to occupy the lowest-waged sectors of the Canadian economy (Statistics Canada, 2012b). In fact, Canada is among the worst of its OECD comparator countries with respect to a gender wage gap (OECD, 2010). While many other industrialized countries have significantly improved their gender wage gap in the last 20 years, Canada has not.

As we have described, women face abuse in their intimate-partner relationships, and should they choose to leave those relationships, there are very few provisions for them to upgrade their skills and education to enable sustainable employment. These issues emerge again and again in the stories that follow. At issue here are a number of policy and service-delivery issues.

For single mothers on social assistance, getting work is meant to be enabled by training and upgrading programs sponsored by provincial social assistance systems (Social Assistance Reform Act, 1997: ch. 25). Data from longitudinal interviews done through Lone Mothers: Building Social Inclusion point to the poor quality of many such programs, which often teach such things as proficiency with Microsoft Office. Anyone with any labour-market familiarity can attest that this will not get someone work. Intensive education and training, including attending post-secondary institutions is usually prohibited while on social assistance. This means that the kind of education and training that could enable successful and sustained labour-market attachment requires a giant leap of faith—off of social assistance and in to the murky and precarious waters of student debt sufficient to cover both family living expenses (including child care) and education expenses. For many women such a move is more than a leap of faith; it is impossible because their own or their children's medical needs can be covered only by remaining on social assistance.

In previous policy eras, social assistance recipients could be approved for participation in university and college programs and could receive both social assistance and student loans. Under these provisions—which still partially exist in Newfoundland—single mothers were often successful in becoming teachers, nurses, and a host of other professional and semi-professional roles that enabled sustainable employment at an income level that could support a family. With the changing social values associated with neo-liberalism (Bezanson, 2006), benefiting from these two social programs—one income assistance, the other a loan—was seen to be "double-dipping," and the possibility of participating in both programs ended. With this went the real opportunity for single mothers to build the skills to economic self-sufficiency so touted by the neo-liberal welfare reformers.

Child Care and Child Support

Because Canada has no system of affordable, accessible child care, the simple fact of being a lone parent makes women vulnerable and labour-market "attachment" near to impossible. Women often have sole caregiving responsibilities for their children without any support provisions from the children's father. Even if a child's father provides financial support, the net effect is often zero for a lone mother on social assistance, as many welfare programs deduct an equivalent amount from the woman's social assistance cheque (Cumming & Cooke, 2009).

There is very little by way of public policy provisions that facilitate women's care of their children except in the province of Quebec (Cleveland & Krashinksy, 2001).This lack of policy support differs from a number of western European countries where there are extensive state-sponsored provisions to support parenting, including, in Norway, a transition benefit intended to ease the adjustment to single-parent status for a single parent and her children (Mahon, 2002). For the single mothers whose stories are told here, the absence of supports that recognize that these mothers are largely alone in providing affective (emotional) support and instrumental (eco-nomic) support for their family is readily apparent and a very real hardship.

Symptomatic of the values shifts that have occurred in Canadian society, the child care program planned by the previous Liberal federal government was scrapped by the Conservative government of Stephen Harper. Replacing it, with a framing of providing "choice," is a $100 per month child-care allowance that falls far short of average daycare costs of $700–$1,000 per month per child (Battle, Torjman, & Mendelson, 2006).

Immigration and Status Vulnerability

Another factor revealed in the stories is related to immigration problems and the particular vulnerability of women who immigrate to Canada with a partner who has gained employment here. Should that relationship break up, the woman's status is uncertain and they are at the mercy of their part-ner (CRIAW, 2003). Similarly, women come to Canada as refugee claimants or as part of family reunification provisions, and when relationships break down and they lose their attachment to someone with status, they become vulnerable (CRIAW, 2003). Such vulnerability is then often compounded by poor English, a lack of Canadian work experience, in some cases trauma experienced as a refugee, and the discrimination experienced in accessing resources. Many of the stories that follow reveal the defencelessness of women who are refugees and immigrants whose status is dependent on a partner.

Colonialism and Racism

The women's narratives also contain an important story about racism in Canada and the ways in which people "other" those not from Anglo cultures: First Nations women, women of colour, and others who are not seen to be "regular" Canadians. These women face discrimination and abuse at higher rates than do white native-born Canadian women and face increased public scrutiny of their parenting, of their reliance on social assistance, and more generally on their utilization of social services (Fleras, 2011). Issues of racialization also appear as women negotiate with the justice system, including family, domestic violence, and criminal courts. Racialized women find it harder to find and access appropriate housing, especially when they are single parents, and to move into the labour market in a way that might enable them to sustain their families. Although Canada avows a policy of multiculturalism and claims to celebrate diversity and racial equality, these are not the experiences of many of the women who participated in the Lone Mothers: Building Social Inclusion research. These findings are increasingly corroborated by other research(Collin & Jensen, 2009; Fleras, 2011; Picot, Hou & Coulombe, 2007).

The issues of racism that surface in the following stories, then, cannot be dismissed as individual and isolated experiences but must be acknowledged as very real problems that face racialized single moms. In addition, they face all Canadians if we are to confront the disjuncture between the myth of inclusive multiculturalism and the reality of racism.

Issues of racism are appropriately situated in the larger context of colonialism. The immigration and refugee settlement issues that arise in the stories often have their roots in colonization and the extraction of resources from the global South by the global North. The presumption of white goodness can be seen alongside its corollary of the suspicion-inducing values and practices of racialized African and Caribbean women. These issues are most often revealed as women engage with the formal judicial, educational, and service systems. As Abelev (2009) and others argue, these systems are rooted in Anglo norms. Other lenses, world views, and cultural practices that differ most often remain unexplored. The development in Toronto of both First Nations and Afrocentric schools with their transformed outcomes for formerly struggling students are a testament to Abelev's thesis and reveal the hegemonic power of our social institutions (Sefa Dei, 1995). As these narratives reveal, amid dominant-culture political and social institutions already overburdened with their own complex and bureaucratic structures, racialized and non-Canadian impoverished single mothers are unlikely to be fully seen.

Gender Inequality

These are stories about the experiences of women and their interaction with systems within which inequality is inherent. Furthermore, racism and colonialism, immigration and status vulnerability, issues relating to the care of children, employment and earnings inequality, single parenting, and abuse all intersect in the lives of women (Benoit & Shumka, 2009). While each of these are issues in the lives of some men, and while I am reluctant to essentialize, some aspects of these issues touch the lives of every woman. Thus, this book is fundamentally a book about gender and the myriad ways that our society permits and enables, through its almost invisible but ever-present patriarchal structures, the ongoing subjugation of women.

These six factors are repeated again and again in these women's stories, which are not only about individual struggles but detail major systemic issues that Canada has neglected to address. We hope that the stories are sufficiently compelling that readers feel that they begin to understand and empathize with the single mothers who have made their lives public to challenge negative discourse and flawed public policy. The effects of these keep single moms boxed in both in terms of opportunity constraints in their own lives and in terms of how they are understood by other Canadians. Theorists have argued (Sen, 2000; Fraser, 2000) that central to retaining an inclusive democracy must be discursive constructions that acknowledge and value the varied contributions of all social members. Single mothers, as sole parents and as contributors to their communities, warrant both recognition and respect for their status as citizens who are assets to our social fabric and whose life circumstances derive not simply from their own life choices but from a complex web of gendered values and social practices.

Format of the Volume

The layout of this volume is somewhat unusual because it tries to strike a balance between an academic enterprise oriented to a discussion of issues of gendered (in)justice and a way to make space for low-income single mothers who typically lack access to the world of publishing to narrate their life stories in ways that they hope will provoke new understanding while challenging a destructively negative discourse about who they are. Accordingly, it moves back and forth between a more academically reflective discussion and the at-times earthy and grounded self-storying of the lone-mother authors.

Reflecting this balance, one of the storytellers has written a reflective piece on the volume and the process of its construction. It might be seen as a lone mother's parallel to this introduction.

The stories then follow, organized by Canadian-born women, First Nations, and immigrants to Canada. After much deliberation we have chosen this way of grouping the stories because we see certain parallels among the Canadian-born women as well as among the lone mothers who are immigrants. In the latter stories issues of racism and colonialism are apparent, and a colonial legacy and its weighty costs loom large as well in the story of a First Nation woman whose story bridges these other two groups. Among the Canadian-born women, problems in the family of origin can be seen to set the stage for many of the issues and vulnerabilities our narrators relate as part of their complex life experiences.

As indicated, the stories powerfully speak for themselves. Our collective goal, however, is to draw their threads together and even more broadly to tie the issues raised to other research and policy discussions. For this purpose we have also summarized each story to enable an analytic appraisal of the issues raised. We felt that to do this to the stories themselves would be wrong, a betrayal of the simple power of their narrative. We hope that in using summaries of the stories for this purpose we respect the integrity of the authors whose voices are contained here. Accordingly, following the stories, the book makes a somewhat more academic turn. Concise summaries of the stories precede an analytic discussion that takes up the significant issues raised with reference to policy and service system issues. This chapter is written by both of the volume's editors. Judit Alcalde's contribution to this is especially important given her significant role in facilitating the Trillium group over more than two years and her very close personal work with its participants both through the group processes and in facilitating and sup-porting our co-authors through the narration of their stories.

A conclusion draws the book to a close, focusing on broader themes oriented to thinking about the implications of the deprivations and oppres-sion experienced by these women and by so many single mothers. It explores such shaping, discursive constructions as the moral construction of the single mother, ideas of freedom of choice, and the gendered basis of citizenship.

On the Process of Creating This Book and on the Stories That Needed Telling

Robin

I'd like to begin with an Acknowledgment of Country to pay respect to the fact that we are on Aboriginal land.

The Way I See It and Have Lived It

Lone mothers who are poor are all too often stereotyped into categories that only put them down. Women are often blamed for circumstances that could not be helped. Many of the problems that are described here are systemic, and the oppression that women and lone mothers feel is entrenched in patriarchy.

I don't know any lone mothers receiving social assistance who as small children dreamed lives like those lived by so many lone mothers. Childhood dreams do not imagine struggle, poverty, social stigma, and feeling worthless. They also don't include being on welfare, being trapped with barely enough to live off, but not enough to get off (the system). Until you are in the system it is hard to understand feeling fearful to speak up when you know that you really need to be heard.

The reasons some lone mothers seek help from social assistance vary. The death of a spouse, no work, job loss, exorbitant rents, abuse, mental health issues, minimal education, and no child care are but a few. Just as the reasons for applying for welfare are diverse so too are the women who need it, who come from many different beautiful pockets of Mother Earth.

The common denominators among such women exist in being a lone mother on social assistance, faced with struggle, fear, no security, and being stereotyped and categorized into low social standing.

It was these factors that brought a group of single moms and academics together to form the research and activism project Lone Mothers: Building Social Inclusion. It was a much-needed mixing of lived experience and theory.

When I first became involved with the lone-mothers group as a single parent on social assistance myself, I was skeptical and guarded. Shortly thereafter I realized the academics' intentions were pure—it showed in their willingness to go to great lengths to make us feel a part of the project. The idea was that together we could find ways to initiate needed changes to a social assistance system that was simply not working, especially for lone mothers. I'm glad I was a part of it.

We, the lone mothers, were given a platform to speak and be heard; for some of us this was a first. I started to find my own voice and have been using it to exercise my rights ever since.

The lone-mothers group introduced women to various ways they could be heard. Examples include conferences, newspapers, and conversations with politicians, TV, voting and elections work, and speaking before standing committees of the House of Commons and the Senate.

In the beginning many of us didn't even understand how the Canadian political system worked and some didn't know how to approach their MPPs, or they felt intimidated to do so. This changed because we educated one another by sharing our knowledge as it was gained.

There is a fallacy that exists surrounding lone mothers: that they live high off the hog and don't want to do anything other than sit on social assistance. That if they'd just stop being so lazy they'd succeed. This puts all the onus on the women while deflecting the responsibility society and government may have. This is a neo-liberal ideology and it is far from the truth. Anyone who knows how much a woman and child receive on social assistance can quickly deduce that no one is living high off the hog. There's barely money for meat! As for being lazy, one just has to look at the amount of unpaid labour lone mothers do. Many lone mothers are active in volunteering, and they are single-handedly raising their children and scrounging, planning, and managing as they try to make ends meet. If one has a chance to come close, to see firsthand what these lives are like, the fallacy of the lazy lone mother is dispelled. We hope our stories illustrate this.

Collectively, the women who authored these stories began a journey, meeting many times over the course of four to five years to engage in critical thinking and discussion about our own lives and the systems we were caught in. We hoped this process would lead us to some answers on how to make positive change. We also enjoyed good meals and one another's company. At times it was painful, but just knowing we were trying to find a solution to our situation made life a bit easier. It gave us hope that one day things would change for the better. Being together and understanding how much our own individual situations were shared by so many others helped us to stop blaming ourselves and boosted our self-esteem. Over these years we saw our children grow, and we rejoiced in one another's milestones. The ripple effect on our children was obvious; they intuitively knew we were doing something good.

Due to our many discussions we were able to recognize some key issues that led us to poverty and that keep us in it today. We identified that on a daily basis lone mothers must navigate within a society that allows us and our children to be treated "less than," simply because we are poor and women. That the skills, perseverance, and fierce drive it takes to succeed while in such a precarious position is monumental. Day in and day out, lone mothers often feel disassociated from society because so much of it is out of our reach. This existence wears a mother down; real breaks are rare if ever. Vacations, shopping sprees, back-to-school clothes, or even leaving the city for the relief and balance the country offers are rare if they happen at all. A lone mother often finds herself in a stagnant, dull, debilitating state that sucks not only our life energy but also our hope. Functioning daily becomes difficult; it is like having a headache, being tired, hungry, and lonely all the time, with no end in sight.

Most women on assistance see education as a way out or the road to a better life. Many lone moms who do escape the system are those that had the good fortune of getting an education before they became lone moms. But for those not so lucky, real education, the kind that opens new horizons and can take us beyond the world of part-time minimum-wage work is out of reach. In most provinces in Canada, lone mothers cannot receive welfare and student-loan support simultaneously. As a sole-support parent it feels like a very big risk to give up social assistance benefits, however meagre they are, and pay for all of the family expenses on top of tuition out of a student loan. Lone mothers who need drug benefits for themselves and their children are even less likely to be able to make such a move.

At present most educational courses being offered to single moms through social assistance cost the government ridiculous amounts, considering what is being taught. For the most part these courses lead nowhere.

Most employment obtained from these courses consists of hand-to-mouth jobs that don't even pay enough to cover child care costs—if one is lucky enough to find child care and a job based on a course provided through social assistance.

Even with a job, a lone mother's situation does not change radically. Most still find themselves poor and now largely absent from their children's lives. Adding to this difficulty are the jobs—insecure, often split shifts, evenings and nights, with no benefits and low wages . . . a dead end. Work of this type often results in single moms going back on assistance again because they have no safe child care or the costs of getting to work actually outstrip the earnings.

Single moms on assistance desperately want change; the money currently being spent on programs could be better spent on university or college courses that offer degrees. We want a hand up, not a handout: We want access to education that will lead to sustainable employment. We want education that leads to jobs that will see us get off, and stay off, social assistance. We want a better life for our children now and always. We would like to be able to contribute more financially to the society we live in. If we were able to do so we could play a stronger role in moulding the direction of our society the way we'd like to see it—fairer, more just, and inclusive. Then perhaps we'd finally feel a part of it.

Getting it out, that's what our stories are about: the good, the bad, and the ugly—our lived experiences, our realities. Our hope is that, in reading our individual stories, you will begin to see that we, as women, as lone mothers, are much more multi-faceted then we are given credit for. That we are strong and resilient, that we are human, that we are not bilking the system. Even if a few individuals are, we don't deserve the across-the-board stereotypes. We also hope that readers might see gendered injustice and join with us in advocating for positive change.

Finally, and very sincerely, I'd like to take the time to thank all of the people I was involved with on this journey. To all of the lone mothers . . . you're awesome, beautiful, amazing, and loved.

Shoshana, your patience and sensitivity gave me hope. Dawn, you are a gem who shines so brightly. Judit, you, to me, are simply amazing. Lea, your awesome determination and desire to understand rubbed off on me, and Maria, your strength was always evident.

Chi Miigwetch

The
Individual
Stories

The lone-mother narrators of this volume originally planned to use their real names. They were proud of the obstacles they had overcome and wished to "own" their own life stories. After extensive discussion in the group, the women somewhat reluctantly agreed to use pseudonyms—and to have the names of people in the stories changed as well. Many of the women agreed to this only to protect their children.

Sara's Story

I'm a single mom. I've been a single mom for 35 years.

I come from a little town on the island of Newfoundland. I grew up in a very small house with my mom, dad, and 16 siblings. I am the fourth oldest child. They were very hard times. We had a tiny house that had tiny bedrooms and was never very warm. My father was away most of the time and we kids had to do what we could. We cut, dried, and stored the wood for the wood stove. In the winter finding food was really hard. We ate whatever we trapped. My older sister had moved away so I was like the second mother. I learned to bake bread when I was 11, and from then on I did a lot of cooking as well as the cleaning and the laundry.

My mom was sick a lot, and she was really overweight. She did not like doctors and didn't go when she needed to. My father was an alcoholic and used to drink away most of his money. My mother never had any money to take care of us and became very abusive to us. I think my mom wanted to love us, but I don't think she ever learned how. She didn't have much of a chance. I never blamed my mom, although I used to get angry at her when she hit us. Sometimes it would seem like we had a little bit of a relationship and she loved us a lot, like when we played cards, but then the next minute it was like she hated us. My mom used to get my dad mad, and he would take his frustration out on us.

I remember one time when I was 12 or 13 when my mom got really angry at me. When my dad came home she told him I didn't listen, so they locked me out of the house for two days. I ended up staying under the house. When my brothers tried to bring me mittens they also got in trouble.

A few years later, when I was 15, I was a little bit late coming back from the store because I met a friend. I got a really bad beating from my father. My father was almost 6'5", 300 lbs., and had hands like bear claws. He liked to just reach out and knock us down. My father was a vicious person and I hated him. He beat us all. He used to beat my mom. He beat my older brother really hard. When he was sober we could talk to him, but he was not sober very often.

If my parents got mad at us, they took the food away. I remember my dad saying that there were certain cuts of meat that were for us and certain cuts just for him. His friends got the roasts. My father supplied the judge with moose and caribou. My father was buying the judge so we had nobody to turn to. He treated his friends better than his family, so they thought he was a great guy. When he beat us, we had nobody to turn to because they believed him.

In his younger years my dad worked with the railroad. After that he worked on a boat as a cook, and then he worked construction. My dad was a smart man, but he was a stupid man too. My mom was stupid to even stay. I said to my mom once, "Why don't you leave Dad? We can make it. We can plant a garden." My mom told me: "I can't leave your dad because I love him." As I started getting older, I thought I was going to meet a man who would beat me because he loved me. In the romance books I read I started to notice that the woman was always in love with the bad guy.

At a pretty young age, maybe as young as eight, I realized that my mother was not very old. As I watched her being treated the way she was, and not getting the care she needed, I thought, "I don't want to be like that. I don't want to be like my mom." She wasn't comfortable and always worried about what my dad would think. I was determined that I would find myself somebody nice and would not stay where I was.

When we turned 12 or so we all had to leave home, go out, get work, and then send money home to our mom and dad. My dad took me out of school in grade eight because my mom was sick and he said I had to take care of my mom and family. I started my first job when I was 13, going on 14, taking care of a little girl. When I was a little older I got another job and lived in the family's home. I worked for the family five days a week, and then on the weekend I cleaned everything at our home, cooked, and made sure that my brothers' and sisters' uniforms were ready for school. As long as I was contributing I was not a bad kid.

I remember coming home one time and saying, "Mom, I just got paid. There is some money. I am taking my sister and I am going to buy her a coat." My mom said I had to be back at home by nine because dad was coming home. While we were out I started to question why I had to be home at nine. When I got home at 9 or 10 my dad punched me in the mouth and knocked me down. I was angry, got right up and went out the door. He loaded the shotgun and shot at me as I ran away.

I ran to the place my sister was working. From a window I watched my dad looking for me and in a panic I wondered if he would kill me. All the time I was thinking how I loved mom and dad, but right then I didn't love my dad and was scared for my mom. I had to go back and let my dad know that I was okay. When I got home my mom looked at me and started to cry and hugged me. I didn't feel she meant it though. My dad came in and she had a big plate of dinner for him and he said to me, "Come here, sit down, and eat." He looked at me as I sat down and he started to cry. He said, "This won't happen again ever, but I need you to help your mom." I said, "We all help mom, but we can't run a household if you are going to kill us." I told him I was going to go away, further away than before, and my dad said that he knew I could get a job at the Mercers' store.

The Mercers needed somebody in the store and somebody to help in the house with ironing and other things, so they hired me. I was 15 when I started, and I worked there for a year. Mrs. Mercer was good to me. She would give me lipstick and earrings and little things because she knew I didn't have any of these things.

One day I was working in the store and I fell in love. He walked into the store and bought some gum. I thought maybe this was the guy I was supposed to meet. I was so lovesick that I used to actually get sick. Mrs. Mercer had seen what happened at the store and broke it to me that this man was married. He didn't look like he could be married, because he only looked about 20. At a distance I would see him looking at me, and one day I was walking home and he stopped and offered to drive me. I said no, but somebody must have seen me talk to him and told my father. My father went over and beat him. Then my father came to me and said, "I know you have been talking to that young fellow. You stay away from him. I am putting you on a train and you are going to work in Toronto."

My oldest brother and his wife were living in Toronto. I was turning 16, and my father put me on the train. I was meant to go to Toronto, stay with my oldest brother, look for a job, and send money home to my mom. Once I got to Toronto I pretty much had to fend for myself. My brother was doing his own thing, and after a while I didn't want to stay at his place. Soon I was on my own and I had to get out there, look for a job, and find a place to stay.

I stayed in Toronto for two years. I sent money home to my mom, but my father would still call and tell me, "That's not enough, you need to send more home." When I turned 18, I decided, "This is it. I'm going back home. I'll start a war but I'm going back home. I'm strong now." I think that growing up the way I did made me strong. And it made me tough. When I got back my father told me, "You can't come into the house. You're not welcome here."

After a while I found work in a hotel, which is where I met my late husband Jack. He was in the bar, and he was drunk. When I met Jack I was going out with a guy named George. George was a really nice guy, but there was something about Jack that I really liked. The day after I first saw Jack was my day off. I had to go to Clarenville to give my mom some roses for her birthday. George couldn't drive me because he had something else to do. Jack, who had arrived at the bar, overheard that I needed a ride and offered to take me. I will never forget that day. We went to Clarenville in his green Oldsmobile. My mom fell in love with him right away and told me that this was the guy for me.

We were going out for almost two years. One day Jack picked me up the hotel where I worked and took me down to visit his mom and dad. His mom was glad he had met somebody nice, but she told me he needed to go to university. I said I would try to talk him into it. Sometime later I asked him if he ever thought about going back to school. He said no, but said there is one thing he wanted to do—get married. I told him I would marry him if he went to university. So Jack started university, and I worked. I made enough money to put together a wedding. Mine was the only wedding my mother ever attended—she was so happy. She died when she was 45.

Jack finished university and became a school teacher and then a principal. I loved it, and he loved it. We lived in a trailer and we were happy. The second year that he was teaching was the only year from the time I was 13 that I didn't have to work. Jack said, "This is your year off." Those five years with Jack were the best five years of my life. We were doing okay until the car accident. I used to be scared when he drove. The day that he died, I asked him to let me drive, but he said, no, because the roads were dark and there were a lot of animals. The week before I'd threatened to tell his mother about how fast he drove, but that night he couldn't have avoided it. We hit a moose on the road and Jack was killed instantly. The funny thing about that night is that he thought we should stay home and have a nice night together. Something was telling him not to go, but we were driving my sister and her husband and he didn't want to upset them. The last words I remember was him saying were, "What are you guys laughing about?" My five years with Jack were a lifetime, and it all went away in a few seconds.

My life has gone through many stages. There were stages that I loved and some that I didn't love so much. I look at myself as being lucky because I met Jack. Even my dad changed toward me when I got married. He liked Jack. My whole family loved my late husband. I never had much luck in life, but that day I met him it was luck. After we got married I knew it wasn't for a long time—it was too good to be true.

So here I was, a widow at 23, and my life started to change all over again. I still hated my father and didn't want to be with my own family. After Jack died I stayed with his brother to recuperate. During this time I was drinking a bit. One day I was drinking and driving and almost hit a child. That put an end to the drinking. Eventually I left Newfoundland to come to Toronto to start a new life.

I met my daughter's father in Toronto. I did fall in love with Lucy's dad, but back then he was young and running around. I learned a lot from that relationship. He would often verbally abuse me and make threats. I guess he figured that he'd scare me and put me in my place. I stood up to him, and that's when I became a single mom. I've been a single mom ever since. I was striving and doing my best for my daughter and myself. There was nobody in Toronto that I could depend on. Lucy's dad had fathered her, but he wasn't around to help. I had no siblings with me at the time. The only way I could find to look after my baby was to apply for welfare. Taking care of my baby myself was the most important thing in my life. Marrying a nice guy, well, that was Jack, and that was gone.

When my daughter was younger I had to deal with social services a lot. Dealing with social services was a big problem because it often seemed that they did not really want to help. There are some people at social services who work for you and others who don't know why they're there and neither did I. Once I met with a guy who sat back in his chair and tossed peanuts into his mouth for the whole meeting. He asked what I wanted, and I told him all I needed was a drug card because I had no drug coverage. Then he asked, "Why should I do that?" and told me to get a full-time job. I explained that I had a part-time job, but he told me to only come back when I had a full-time job. I told him that managing my daughter on my own was a struggle, making sure there was food to eat, and that she was in school. But then I said to him, "You think you're wasting your time talking to me. Well, I'm wasting my time talking to you. I don't need your help." And I left. When I went to another social services office and explained what had happened in the first office, I got help right away.

I ran up against a lot of social services workers who wouldn't help. I could never get any help unless I treated the worker just like the worker treated me: with no respect. I found that if I treated them with no respect and they sent me off to somewhere else, then I would get the help I needed. Why did it work this way? I'd love for them to be able to answer that question. But that's the way it was for me the whole time I was in the system.

After a while I decided that I was finished with this social services thing. I couldn't handle the pressure and the degradation. They made me feel that, even though I was working part-time and taking care of my child, I was a nobody. I don't think that social services really help anyone. They forget they're working with us. I don't need them anymore, but even if I did need help, I'd go elsewhere.

I was dealing with social services a long time, but things did start to change a little bit for me. I finally got work and my daughter was at school full-time. I started talking with other people. I eventually went to work in a flower shop and I worked there for 15 years. I worked with an older woman who was from another country, and I learned a lot from her. She used to tell me about the abuse she suffered in her family. As my daughter started getting older and I started working, I started to get a little bit stronger. Finally, I told Lucy's father that I didn't want to see him anymore.

Over time I got involved with some women's groups, like Opportunity for Advancement. Talking to the women in those groups and associating with other women made me much stronger. I never used to speak up for myself. I was by myself and I never used to speak to anybody, really. But today I'm stronger and now I can talk to anybody. I let social services torment me over the years, but I wouldn't let that happen today. I think that when you find a group of women like we have (the lone-mothers group), it makes each one of us stronger. We all listen to one another's stories. Each story is different but the same in some way. Being together as a group makes us stronger. As a single mom, it's very hard to make it. So, what I've learned from my experiences is that single moms have to stick together, be a group, and help each other.

As a child I would write poems on little pieces of brown paper, torn from paper bags, because that is all we had around. My mom would find them, tear them up, and throw them in the garbage. Now I write children's poetry. I can relate to children. I have taken care of children and know what they are like. I can write just about anything. I have written a book full of poetry—I just need to get it typed up. I also like talking and am now comfortable talking in a group. I love teaching and writing and English. In school I always used to get an A+ on the stories I wrote. I only got to grade 12, which is not far enough to teach, but I would love to teach English and get kids writing.

Life was a struggle for me, but I'm not struggling anymore. I'm 61 now, I'm where I want to be, and I'm happy where I am. I have a good relationship with my daughter. I love her and my grandchildren dearly.

Martha's Story

My mom was a stay-at-home mom, and I really, really liked that she was there for me at lunchtime and after school. I thought my family was pretty big—three brothers and myself. My dad was always around. He was very important in my life. I made it clear to my husband that I wanted to have the option to stay home with my children when I became a mother. It didn't make sense that I would put my kids in daycare while I worked. I believed that my kids should come first, and work second. So when my husband and I separated, I thought it was important to be a stable, stay-at-home mom. In order to take my kids to school, bring them home for lunch, and be there after school for them, it meant that I couldn't work full-time.

I was the youngest in my family and had a very good childhood. I grew up in the York area of Toronto. It is a very old neighbourhood and it was a lot of fun. I would play outside until the streetlights came on and my mom prodded me to come inside to eat. I knew we struggled, but I never felt poor. I always felt that we had enough and that our basic needs were met. My parents are very old-fashioned and never talked about money.

My brothers are 8, 10, and 12 years older than me. We were very close despite the age difference. They were always home and often babysat me. We went to church regularly. Family and community were always very important to us. We always hosted Christmas dinner and my parents went to the same New Year's party for about 15 years. We vacationed up north every year. We didn't have our own cottage, but it was still a regular family vacation. I lived in the same house for my entire childhood. Even after I moved away from home I didn't move around much. I have lived in the same 10-mile radius all my life.

Although I had a mostly happy childhood, I experienced sexual abuse over a period of several years as a child. I had blocked out the abuse for years. My husband was stunned when I told him about the abuse, and it caused problems in our marriage. He didn't know how to deal with me because I would freak out when the memories came back. They were so vivid, and when they came back they were overwhelming. I am now in counselling and believe that the abuse I experienced holds me back in many areas of my life. I still lack confidence and I have serious trust issues with men. I also suffer from an eating disorder. When things are out of my control I turn to food to comfort myself. Seeing childhood sexual abuse discussed in the media and hearing famous people share their stories helped me realize the extent to which the abuse has affected my life. I truly believe it changed who I have become.

I struggle with confronting my abuser and am terrified to do so. It helps that I am seeing a counsellor, but I am a long way from being over the trauma of it. Fairly recently I had to face this person on the phone, and I was so stressed that I was physically ill for more than a day. I didn't realize how badly this contact affected me until I talked it through with a friend and tied my being ill back to the discussion I had had with this person. So this experience has affected my life in a very big way.

I finished high school but was pregnant by the time I graduated. I remember leaving one of my exams because I had to throw up. The father was my high school sweetheart. We had been together since before high school and started having sex when I was 15. We were together four years before I got pregnant at 17. I had not expected to get pregnant. Although we weren't practising what is now called safe sex, we were trying not to get pregnant. He thought he was sterile.

Abortion was not an option for me. It was not something that my family or I believed in. It was very, very hard to tell my mom about the pregnancy. She strongly encouraged me to put the baby up for adoption and threatened to kick me out of the house if I didn't. My mother was highly embarrassed by my situation. I went to a home for unwed mothers, mostly to please her. My mother is not open like I am and doesn't communicate well. She found it hard to talk about her feelings so we went to counselling for four or five months. She referred to herself in the third person throughout counselling so it was very hard to determine how she felt.

When I was still pregnant a good friend of our family took me out one day and said, "You know, you're agreeing to adoption because of your mom. You're 18 now or going to be 18 and this is your decision." Still, I went through with it and put the baby, my daughter, up for adoption.

It was very, very tough, going through all of this when I was only 18. My daughter is the light of my mom's life now, but at the time there were a lot of family issues. We hid my daughter's birth from her father because he did not agree with the decision to put her up for adoption. I didn't want him and his family to come to the hospital and cause problems. They found out anyway, came to the hospital and caused a bit of a ruckus. He actually got a lawyer and tried to fight for custody. The adoption caused a lot of problems between his family and our family. At the time it was very, very stressful but eventually we got through it and we healed.

As soon as my daughter was born I entered into a private adoption agreement. It was a very open adoption where I could actually see her, hold her, and bond with her. She and I left the hospital separately. After she was born I went back home. A couple of weeks after my daughter's birth, after much fasting and praying, I decided to get her back. I called the private adoption family, and I arranged for her to be returned to me. When I brought her home to my parents' place my mom said, for the first and only time, "Sorry. I think you made the right decision. I'm so glad that we have your baby here with us. She is our only granddaughter."

My daughter was only gone for two weeks. This was a hard time for my boyfriend and me because there was a lot of pain involved in my decision and he wasn't part of it. When my daughter came back to the house we talked things over and kind of got back together. Our relationship developed again and, within a few months, I got pregnant again. My first two children are less than a year apart.

I was not living with my boyfriend when our first two children were born. I believe strongly in marriage, and I didn't want to live together. I lived with my two kids at home with my mom. My first son was born in the spring and we got married that fall. I was only 20 when we got married. A few years later, in 1990, our second son, Jonah, was born. After two years of struggling and having low-income jobs I put my foot down and said I didn't want to work. I wanted to stay home with the kids instead. My husband wasn't very pleased with that decision. He became the sole breadwinner and he didn't like the responsibility. At least that's how I saw it. We separated in 1992, having lived together for almost six years.

We tried to stay together and tried counselling. In my opinion he was a little immature. I had all the responsibility of the children and he was not involved very much. Toward the end of the marriage he was present but not really there. When he left he took all the money out of the bank account and didn't even leave any food in the house. He really wanted out of the responsibility and to be a free man. I look back now and see that. I also know now that there was another woman, which I wasn't aware of at the time. It was a new concept to me that he would leave for another woman.

The hard work really began once we separated. The kids were young— seven, six and two—and I was happy to still be home with them. I didn't want to move. I wanted them to stay in their school and to stay in our apartment. I guess I wanted to keep the status quo. I was very involved in my community and I didn't want that to change after the separation. It is key for me to be well supported, well grounded, connected to the community, have a lot of women friends, have a lot of strength, and have a lot of shoulders to cry on. I was involved in a parent group and in a few different committees that were all supportive. They taught me a lot about who I am today. They also taught me how to get through the separation. For example, I learned how important it was to tell the teachers about what's going on so they know why your kids are daydreaming in class.

When my husband first left he visited once a week, and the kids stayed over every second weekend at the place he had with his girlfriend. After he broke up with his girlfriend he stopped seeing his children on a regular basis. In just a few months he stopped participating in their lives. This was really hard for us. I needed a break from three young children, and they really wanted and needed to see their dad. The situation was further complicated because his mother lives close by. It was very hard for his mother and I to get along because I would complain to her about her son. Over time we came to an agreement. We realized that I couldn't make my husband do what he needed to do but neither could she. We agreed that we wouldn't talk about him. His mother was actually more involved in my children's lives than my husband because she was so much closer then he was.

My husband's absence led to another difficult situation. Just before my youngest son turned three he started to have violent temper tantrums. For lack of a better word, he just went loopy. In my opinion his behaviour was caused by not seeing his dad on a regular basis. When my son was at my ex-husband's place he would have to be physically removed from my ex's arms because he didn't want to leave his father. We were in counselling for six years. We had a very, very good experience with our counsellor. Some months we would go to see him three or four times. If we couldn't meet him or I couldn't afford the bus fare to travel to see him he would come to our house. He was extremely helpful and became very involved in our lives.

Oh my gosh, it was very, very hard. Jonah never acted up at school, which in some ways was good. I was the one who always took the brunt of all his anger and frustration. He got very violent to the point that his counsellor said, "You could remove him from the home if you think that is best. You're the parent and you have to decide. It's up to you to call the police." I took a course that taught me how to physically stop Jonah from hurting himself and others. When he had an outburst I would put him in a "basket hold" and restrain him for 30 to 40 minutes. Sometimes it was as long as two hours. Finally he would fall asleep and I had time to recover from the episode. It was exhausting.

Nathan and Mary, my older two children, resented all the attention that Jonah got. I also struggled trying to explain to my mother-in-law what it was like when Jonah would have a fit. One time, when Jonah was about five and was under the kitchen table, holding onto the leg and refusing to go on the camping trip we'd planned, I asked my mother-in-law to come over to the apartment. She came and tried to talk to him. I think after that she kind of understood what it was like.

I had to fight both the health system and my ex-husband's family not to have him put on Ritalin. Jonah had bad behaviour, but it was contained to our home. He didn't misbehave at school. I didn't want him on that strong drug with all of its side effects when his problem was emotional, not chemical. People think a pill will fix things. I believe that a pill will treat the symptoms but it won't treat the cause. It was exhausting and very, very stressful fighting everyone who wanted him on Ritalin.

My husband had lost his job before we separated so we were already on welfare when he left. The cheques had been coming in his name and they had to be transferred into mine. In those days welfare workers used to come and visit you. When they came into our house they determined that my daughter and my oldest son couldn't share a bedroom anymore, so I shifted the kids around. I moved my daughter into my bedroom and my sons shared the other bedroom. It was a little difficult, but not too bad. Thankfully I have big rooms in my apartment.

Once the cheques started to arrive in my name, welfare became very invasive into my personal life. I was and still am very close to my ex-husband's family. It also happened that, at the time, quite a few of my husband's family lived in the same building as me. His mother, his aunt, his sister, and his grandfather all lived there, so there were a lot of reasons for him to be at our building other than to see his children and his wife. After being on social assistance for just a few weeks they called to tell me my next cheque was being held because they believed I was being fraudulent. When I had applied for welfare I had to give them my husband's licence plate number. I guess there was a worker checking the building's parking lot because they said that his car was frequently there. I tried to explain to them that my husband had other reasons to be in the building. My sister-in-law, who I happened to be with when they called, confirmed that other family members, including her, lived there and that my husband and I weren't together anymore. I told them to send a worker over immediately and I would show them that all his things were gone from the apartment and that my kids have shuffled their lives around to be in the bedrooms social assistance had told us they had to be in. It felt like big brother was watching. It was unbelievable that they would go to such lengths to make it hard for people who weren't abusing the system and who really needed it.

The kids were mostly sheltered from the stigma of being on welfare. They were at school and didn't really see any of the fights with welfare. But it was an ongoing fight with them to prove that I was legitimate, that the need that I had was real. Still they held my cheque many, many times for different reasons. Sometimes they held it because they claimed I didn't send in my income reporting statement. I always sent it in, so I'm not sure if they lost it or it was some other tactic. I started to fax and mail it in and then would follow up with my worker by calling right after I faxed it and telling them the date and time. I know it doesn't seem like a lot of work, but it just added to all the other things I had to take care of.

Being on social assistance felt like being institutionalized. At the end of each month I would wonder if the money was going to be there or not.

I wondered if I would be able to pay the rent or if I would have to ask my family for help. I also wondered if I would get the drug card. I have two sons with asthma. A lot of times the drug card would be late which meant I couldn't get the Ventolin they needed. I was very blessed because generally they were very healthy kids and didn't have a lot of illnesses.

I really pushed my kids to stay in school and get a good education. I had learned about the cycle of poverty and didn't want my kids to make the same mistakes that I had made. To me it meant being there for them after school and making sure they got their homework done. I'd feed them a healthy snack—feed their bodies, feed their minds—and then we would go out to play. My kids were all into sports and I think that played an important part in all their lives.

All this time I stayed involved in a community program in my community. Eventually I became employed part-time as a research assistant at the school my children attended. I was in this job for six years. I interviewed families in the community and it was really, really great. It was a really perfect fit for me because I did the interviews during school hours and I was already at the school to pick up the kids. I also did some public speaking to try to convince people to put money into prevention for at-risk youth. Our community had a reputation for youth getting into trouble. Working and my advocacy really had an impact on the lives of my children. I showed them a strong role model and the importance of volunteering in our community. The extra income, even if it was part-time, allowed my kids to have a better quality of life. They were able to do sports and things that kept them out of trouble.

Eventually my ex-husband started to work. He was paid in cash and it wasn't unionized. It was always challenging proving to social assistance that he was working at all. I would call him a lot to remind him that payments for the kids' sports were due, but nothing came of it. At one point he threatened that if I took him to court he wouldn't see the kids anymore. At the time I truly believed him but, in hindsight, he didn't see the kids anyway so I should have taken him to court much sooner than I did.

As my children got older I really needed a break and some time away from them. I'd learned through at a community program that before you're a mom or a research assistant you're a person and you need to take care of yourself. Taking care of yourself helps you to take care of your kids. I was terrified of seeing my ex-husband and fighting about money but I decided it was worth the risk to take him to court. I found a family support worker through the courts who was very, very nice. She walked me through the process and supported me throughout. Finally the money started coming. It was only $200 a month for three children, and that came off my social assistance cheque. So, it didn't really help and it wasn't worth all the stress.

My kids are now 25, 24, and 20. They are all doing well. My oldest son is in a master's program studying science. He's the brains of the family. My daughter worked for many years and is now in university. My youngest son is still living with me and is doing well. He doesn't have any memory of being violent and finds it hard to hear about it. He knows he gave me a hard time, but we are very close. Of my three kids I would say he is the most tender. I am proud of my children. I feel they have done well for themselves. It's definitely a success.

I went to school for a while and took an upgrading course to learn Microsoft Office. I got a full-time job in the customer service field. I was very proud to be working full-time. About 15 months into the job, there was a hostile takeover and the job became very stressful. The new owner and I didn't get on very well. I was so worried about my job and the environment there that I couldn't sleep. I tried to work really, really hard and ended up taking on some responsibilities that overwhelmed me. At some point my body just couldn't handle it anymore. I started having symptoms of a nervous breakdown. I kept missing work and eventually I was laid off. It would have been much harder if they'd fired me.

I was able to get EI (employment insurance benefits) and am now looking for work. I have always found jobs based on my volunteer work, so actually looking for a job is new for me. I haven't done my résumé and cover letters, so those haven't been sent out. So far I've only had a few interviews. It's all new to me!

My experiences have given me a pretty good understanding of the system. Yes, it has been important in our lives, but I can also see things that need changing. The drug card that is part of the welfare benefit is very important but it needs to cover more "good" drugs, for lack of a better word. My oldest son often had asthma attacks and was hospitalized quite frequently. His paediatrician prescribed a particular drug that wasn't covered by the drug card and it was $150 a month. I was able to ask my family to help pay for it, but I'm not sure what other people would have done if they didn't have that kind of support. Even then, getting this support put me in breach of the welfare rules because I should have declared that as income, and then the same amount would have been deducted from my cheque. This situation is a good example of how short-sighted the system can be, because taking this drug prevented my son from ending up in the hospital—which would have cost much more and been covered by OHIP.

Another issue with the drug card is that the pharmacist would hold the original drug card and only give me a copy. But I needed the original if I went to the dentist to get the kids' teeth cleaned or even to sign up for the parks and recreation programs. I found that running around very frustrating.

As I mentioned, I found it very frustrating that social assistance delved into my life in such depth. They made me use up money that I was going to use to go back to school. When I was eight years old an aunt left me money in her will. The money was put in a GIC that I reinvested when I came of age, not knowing I was going to get pregnant. I had a lawyer write to the social assistance tribunal explaining that I'd interpreted the will to mean that the money had been left for educational purposes only and was not to be touched. My plan was that, once the kids reached a certain age, I was going to use the money to go to university. At the time I was thinking of studying social work. My youngest was two and the others were in school full-time. I told social assistance how much I wanted to be in school. I told them I would go to school part-time. I figured by the time my youngest was four or five he would be in school half-time and I could go to university half-time. But going to school wasn't an option for me. The tribunal disagreed with the lawyer and we had to live off that $15,000 GIC until it was gone.

Another policy change to consider, which they do in Newfoundland, is to allow you to go to school and to be on social assistance at the same time. It would then be easier to get a better job to sustain yourself and your children and just have a better quality of life. I feel very strongly about this. Years after I lost my GIC I again thought about going back to school. I did the research and found three schools where I could become a massage therapist. I went to the resource centre, which was a new program at the time, and showed them my long-term goals. I showed them the three schools I had contacted and how much the program would cost. They said it was a good plan but they couldn't help because it wasn't something the system supported. I would have been in the massage program for a year and would have earned a massage therapist certification. With the certification I could have got a better job. But the social assistance system works to keep you on it because you don't have the skills to get a good job.

I'd also like to see employers take a more active role with single parents. Single parents are 50% of the population now. Their kids are important to them but they also want to work. I have read about some companies that have daycares on site. I think that would be fabulous. Part of the reason I was so involved with a community centre in my neighbourhood every day from nine to four was because there was a daycare on-site at no cost. I'm sure there would be some cost to employers, but it could be set up in such a way that employees would have their kids nearby.

Like a lot of single mothers, my experiences "on the system" have taught me a lot. The support has been critical to my life and to the successes of my kids, but there are so many ways that it made our lives hard and blocked my opportunities to get off of it.

Mary's Story

My name is Mary, and I'm 39 years old.

My mother abandoned my dad with three kids. I was the youngest of the three. My dad worked full-time as a construction worker and eventually ran his own business. My brother, sister, and I spent a lot of time in daycares and with babysitters. What I remember of growing up with my dad is waking up early at 5:30 a.m. I would make his coffee while my dad bathed and got ready for work. From about six or seven years old my dad would give me a list and some money so I could do the shopping. It was about this time that I also took over the housework. I remember doing dishes standing on a chair. While it wasn't always done very well, I tried. I wanted to impress my dad. As a boy, my brother just wasn't expected to help out, and my sister was too pretty. Putting her hands in dishwater just wasn't her thing.

My father was a good man. I felt he loved me as much as he loved my brother. Often, while sitting on my dad's lap, I would ask him why my mother didn't love me. My dad explained that she wasn't capable and that he loved me enough for both of them. No matter how much he said it, however, it was not enough. I couldn't understand—if a mother could not love her daughter than who could? There was always a sense of abandonment. I have been in and out of therapy and it is still something I can't get my head around.

Growing up in Kensington Market, across from the projects, was tough to start with. It was the sort of place that you either had to be tough or you got beat up. It made sense that I became a tomboy. I was always closest to my brother and my dad. My sister had a lot of behavioural problems when I was growing up and tended to be in and out of the picture. My mom played a big role too in forming how I thought of myself. In one drunken stupor she told me that I had been a mistake. I was so traumatized I decided then that I never wanted to be anything like the kind of woman she was. So, I took on the role of a boy.

The gangs or cliques started pretty young, maybe nine or ten. We stuck together so we didn't get hurt. There were no girls allowed in the gang, but I was not considered a girl because I could fight like a boy. And I fought. My sister had always been the pretty one, and I didn't get any attention from the other boys. It was only later, when I was molested, that I thought I had some-thing to offer as a girl.

Not too much later the drugs and alcohol started. When I was 12 and a half or 13, my sister, who was two years older than me, called me down to a bar. She stuck her finger into a bag of cocaine and gave me a sniff. I loved the way it felt! That little bit of cocaine made me feel confident and pretty. I imagined this was how normal people felt. I knew I had to be in a place where I could feel this.

We used to see my mom on the weekends. We'd visit her at my grandparents' house, which was about five houses down from ours and somewhere that I felt safe. My mother was often intoxicated during our visits. By the time I was 12 or 13 I was already doing drugs myself, and my mom would buy them for me. On our weekend visits we'd drink and do drugs together. It was that kind of relationship.

I had no attachment to school, and it held little appeal. My brother was sent to a private school that was paid for by a family friend while I slipped through the cracks of public school. In grade nine I still could not read and found out much later that I was dyslexic. Walking to school in Kensington Market people would offer me coffee and brandy. After two or three drinks I would say, "Fuck school!" and not show up. The year I entered high school I also started working at a bar after school, serving alcohol while wearing my high school uniform. At 14 years old, and still in grade 9, I dropped out of school. I figured that I didn't need an education because, hell, I was already working. At the bar where I worked I saw university graduates working as waiters and waitresses. I was waiting tables too but at the same time selling drugs and making more money than they were. What went through my mind was, "What were they doing with their education?" My God! I thought they were idiots, wasting all that time and doing the same bloody job I was. I remember one of the waiters telling me, "We can't get work right now but they can never take your education away from you. You know, that's something you'll always have." I didn't understand that then, but I regret it now, of course.

Around the time I dropped out of school I also left home. By the time I left home I was already doing a lot to survive on my own—selling drugs, prostituting, and fighting. A week after my 18th birthday I got my first cocaine trafficking conviction. My grandmother died shortly after the arrest. I was supposed to get two years in jail but I cried in front of the judge, who took pity on me when I told him my grandmother had just died. Instead of the two years he sentenced me to three months and warned me that if I didn't change my ways things would get worse. . . . And they did.

I fell in love for the first time a little before my 19th birthday. Up until then I had never had a boyfriend and the only relationship I had with men was working as a prostitute. I was just a piece of tail for the bigger drug dealers. I was pretty but I was tough, and they couldn't figure me out. I was 18 and a half and he was 34. He was from New York. I later found out that he was hiding here in Toronto because he'd shot some people while dealing drugs. He was the first person to tell me I was pretty and he wanted to live with me. I thought I was somebody now because somebody actually took the time to love me. And he must have loved me because he beat the living shit out of me all the time. If I hadn't known what abuse was before, I sure found out quickly. I'd really thought being in love would be a little bit more fun.

During the time we were together I was in and out of jail a lot. One time, after getting out of jail, I went straight back to Kensington and was hooked up right away by my boyfriend, my abuser. The next day I was too sick to get up for work so I got beat up and dragged out by him. That night when I got back I was coughing and fainting and told him he needed to get me some help because I could not get up. Instead he had men come in and fuck me while I was unconscious. I remember telling one man on top of me that he had to get me to the hospital. I can't recall how I got to the hospital, but I eventually did. I'd contracted TB while in jail and ended up spending a year in the hospital. For a while it looked like I was going to die, but a new medication saved my life. It took months for me to start eating solid food and by the time I left I was 22, weighed 84 pounds, and could no longer walk. Still, as soon as I was well enough to leave the hospital I went back to my life of drinking and dealing and misery. Although I had told God that if I got better I would change my ways, it's hard to change if you don't have the tools. And I didn't even know what tools I needed.

During this first relationship I found out that my boyfriend and best friend at the time had an affair and had children together. After they tried to convince me that nothing was happening and I was just crazy, I tried to commit suicide. Despite having used drugs for years and suffered through abuse and a near-fatal illness, it was then things really took a bad turn.

I started going with another older man who was a thief. We called them "boosters." I thought this guy was my salvation. He had on great clothes, stayed at hotels every single day, and had bags and bags of coke. We'd go to really high-end stores and just steal the hell out of them. He would make $700, $800 a day, you know, in like 30, 40 minutes. For several years I was the best-dressed bum on the street. We had no real place to lay our heads, but we'd get up in the morning and go to "work." We treated the boosts like a real job, but not exactly—more like we were self-employed! To make sure we could get a fix for the day, and some food, and somewhere to sleep, we would take orders of what people wanted and get paid when we delivered the goods.

During this time I didn't understand why God didn't just take me, why I couldn't just die and have it all be over. When I was 29 it all changed when I was raped again. It was a guy I was interested in and had flirted with in the hallways. He invited me up and we flirted some more and drank and made out. Quite suddenly his behaviour changed and he got very aggressive. After he raped me, he threw me out. I tried to block it out of my mind by going straight to the bar. It was a couple months later that I went to the doctor and he said I was pregnant. By that time, I had had about five or six abortions. I thought to myself that if I, you know, get rid of this baby, I might not have another chance. I don't know what was different this time but this was a baby who wanted to be born.

The guy I was seeing at the time, Mark, whom I hadn't slept with, talked me into having the baby. He was a drug dealer—I seem to say that a lot. But I thought to myself that I would have somebody to be with when I had the baby and I wouldn't have to do it all alone. At the time I didn't know Mark was here illegally. He told me he loved me, that I should keep the baby, go into rehab, and he would be the father of the baby. So I did. The baby growing inside me grossed me out. I didn't like that a little foot would come sticking out of my stomach. I had no maternal instinct, none, but in my mind I thought, you know, when you're pregnant, if you're a decent person you have the baby—and some part of me wanted to be that kind of decent person.

When I completed rehab and got sober, I moved in with Mark. It turned out that he was also a control freak and abusive. But in my mind, if you cared about me, the way you showed it and the way I knew you loved me was to beat the crap out of me. So it seemed as if he cared enough. If it upset him that much to put his hands on me, I must be special. Within three months of having my son I was pregnant with my daughter. I didn't want another baby and tried to get an abortion. Although I took to my son like a duck to water, my hands were full. I knew the relationship I was in wasn't going to last, as much as I wanted it to. In my mind you should have a daddy and I didn't want my kid to grow up the way I did. Mark convinced me not to abort his baby as he did when he supported me in having my son. So I had my daughter, and I'm really grateful today that I did.

Soon after my daughter was born, the immigration papers started to arrive. It turned out that Mark wasn't in Canada legally. He wanted us to have a baby and to be together because he thought it increased his chances of staying here. He tried to use me for status, which he never got. So he was deported to South America, and I turned back to drugs. For a while I cried and cried, wondering "Why me?" and thinking, "there's no way I can raise these kids."

After a while I decided to change my life and decided to take a course at George Brown as a mature student. Whoo!—they gave me all this money. But, instead of taking the course I took the $10,000 student loan, took out some credit cards, and moved my kids to South America to chase this loser who would beat the shit out of me and take my money. That was my great plan for my family.

Well, within the first three weeks of getting there, I was getting pounded. I started fighting back but it turns out you can't do that there because it's the man's word that counts. The police threatened to put me in jail. My brother flew down three separate times to try to smooth things over. Mark was always very charming, which most abusers are. While I was there he ripped up my plane tickets twice and maxed out all my credit cards. But of course I was lost in addiction and just could not cope. I couldn't make a plan to get myself and my kids out of this situation—or at least I couldn't stick to the plans I made.

I remember thinking during this time that I had done a lot of things in my past but that I wasn't a bad person. I wouldn't intentionally hurt people. I mean I'd broken the law to support my habit and I used to fight a lot but I never hit a woman. So I thought to myself, "Why is this happening to me? It isn't fair." I blamed everything on everybody else and didn't take responsibility for, you know, anything. I figured I had an excuse to be an addict. I was thrown away by my mom. I was raped. I had every excuse in the world. It wasn't until later, once I was in a rehab program, that I heard, and started to tell myself, that I have to take responsibility for myself and I have a choice.

In the end, the Canadian Embassy brought me back to Canada. By this time my kids were two and three, I was on drugs again and for the first time since having kids I got arrested. I used to do nine months here, four months here, six months here. I was a big chick, I was strong, so I never had a problem in jail. It was different this time. Something happened—my stomach hurt and I couldn't stop crying. When I used to put my babies to sleep and when their eyes were closed I would just smell them. You know when your baby sleeps and then their mouth is just opened a little bit? I used to stick my nose there so I could smell their sleepy breath. It was the most calming thing ever to me. I know I've been a certain kind of person all my life, but this is my purpose. Forget all of what had happened—these kids are why I've been put on this earth.

So I was arrested and looking at eight years for my crimes. In my first hearing after being arrested I had to sign custody over to my mom so the Children's Aid wouldn't get my kids. My mom was still doing drugs at this time, but I thought she would be a better option than Children's Aid. I was wrong. I stayed in custody because no one would post the $20,000 bond that was set. My mom stopped bringing my kids to see me and when Children's Aid visited they told me I'd never see my children again. I just couldn't accept that. The thought of not seeing my kids kept eating at me so when I came out of custody I went into rehab. I'd been in rehab four or five times before but could never make it work. I was in treatment for six months total—six months without my kids—but I got them back.

I was sober for a year and a half when out came the demon again. It was somewhat different this time. Because I love my kids I didn't do anything illegal to maintain my addiction. During this time we moved around a lot. We lived in four houses in three years. I'd start to think, "Shit, this house is messy. We'd better move." It's only a matter of time before a house gets that way when you're drinking. During this period I got off drugs but not alcohol. I found I could sort of manage to keep everything together and I didn't ever want to lose my kids again.

On and off, over the years, I did some construction work. I would work with my dad, who owned his own construction business. I trained the guys, set up rigging, and could do all that kind of stuff. I got to the point where I was good enough to supervise different job sites. Once I got a paycheque I wouldn't always go back to work. But I liked this part of my life because it was somewhere where I had some control. On the job site I could tell people what to do and they had to listen to me or they got fired. Six years ago though, I had a construction injury and my feet were crushed. Some of the boys had got high during lunch and they were laughing and we were carrying a thousand-pound freight elevator door. It should have been two-thousand pounds but we had sawed it in half. Anyway, they dropped it and crushed both my feet. I'm still not recovered, and have been told that I won't recover. So I said I was drug-free but that's not quite true because I'm on painkillers.

The injury is what landed me on ODSP. And although I'm grateful that ODSP gives me something to buy food with and puts a roof over my kids' heads, I found them to be the most disrespectful people—rude and uncaring. I've had so many blowouts with them I don't even go to the offices anymore. That works better for both of us.

I don't know when or if my circumstances are going to change physically, but I'm trying to do some small things. I have a part-time job, which helps, and hopefully I can get my kids into some more programs and things like that with the extra income. I recently found out that the doctors misdiagnosed my feet situation. They had thought it was arthritis that developed as a result of the injury but after doing an MRI the specialist determined that there were multiple fractures and I now have bone edema. The good news is that there is a surgery that might fix this and the recovery time is six months to a year. The hope is that the surgery will reduce 50–60% of the pain.

I want to do better for my children. Hopefully these medical conditions will be taken care of and I can do better. I only have a grade eight education, but I took my grade 12 equivalency and passed. I am going to have to do some testing to see what I am capable of. I am going to set small goals for myself, maybe a computer course, and then maybe an upgrading course. I have been swimming quite a bit and am starting to do a lot more reading. I would like to give back to my community in some way. It would be worth it if I could stop one kid from going down the path I was on.

I have been sober for eight months. I go to AA meetings. I find that I fantasize about patios and realize it's not about the patios, it's about the drinks. The disease will trick you that way. There is an AA program based on a spiritual program that I believe is changing my life. I have met a group of women in the meetings—thanks to the lone-mothers group that I started to go to. The women were nice and friendly and I realized not everybody is judging me or pointing the finger. There was no gossip, so I kind of saw that women were not too bad. You know, everybody was open, accepting, and funny, and it was a relief to finally be a part of something. I realized I had been really lonely because I had locked myself away for years with the drinking.

I also realized recently that I have a lot of anxiety about being a single parent. I have been doing it for 11 years and figured it would be better if I took away the booze. I laugh everyday with my kids. They have a great sense of humour and are so much fun. I still struggle a lot with depression but now I try to recognize when I am depressed and work through my feelings. My best friend died a couple of weeks ago, which was a perfect excuse to drink. But I got through my feelings without alcohol. I also do a lot of praying and meditation. I learned through recovery that I didn't like to be by myself. If there was activity around me I did not have to reflect on my own life. Now I enjoy the peace and quiet and can be by myself.

I am trying to get my life back. Eight and a half months ago I woke up every morning wishing I were dead. In eight and a half short months I don't want to die anymore. That's something.

Anne's Story

I was born in Toronto, in the west end. I have a fraternal twin sister and another sister who is two and a half years older. My parents divorced when I was five. My mother, who was a single mother, raised us until grade 10, when we were 15. When my twin and I started acting out in school, skipping out and getting in with the wrong crowd, my mother and father decided that it would be best if we moved in with him. We moved to High Park for Grade 11 to live with my father and his new wife. His wife was 20 years younger than him and she wasn't really great about the idea of having teenage kids move in. Things did not go well from the start. In either grade 11 or 12, while I was 17 and living with my father and stepmother, I started dating a man who was nine and half years older than me. My father told me to stop dating him but I continued to, so this gave my father a reason to kick me out.

I think I was an introvert as a child. I was known to be really shy and withdrawn. I would hide under the couch when people came over. This became much worse once my parents broke up. When I was nine I remember sampling some vodka from a bottle my mother kept in the living room. I remember really liking that feeling. When I reflect on this now, I think I likely suffered from concurrent disorders like anxiety or depression even before I became an alcoholic. The desire to numb all your emotions is what triggers alcoholism. You don't know how to live life on its own terms without a mechanism, and alcohol became that mechanism for me at an early age. My dad made wine, and even as young as 12 or 13 we were allowed to drink copious amounts. Early on I learned to live with alcohol as part of everything I did in my life. I think that for 25 years of my life I didn't really know how to live my own life. I don't think I ever really formed my own identity when I was an adolescent. I pretty much went from being a teenager living with my father to be being kicked out, living with a man I hardly knew, and working at an insurance company. Jumping into such an adult life was a shock. Whereas most adolescents take time to develop their identity, to decide where to go to school and what to take, and to hang out with their friends, I kind of skipped all that.

At the same the time I was kicked out, my older sister was taking a year off between grade 13 and university. She had a summer job at an insurance company and somehow she got me an interview. Sure enough I was hired and started climbing my way up the ladder. I started in a clerical position. From there I went into sales and started working for an agent. I decided that I liked the sales end of the business. I was always bright and am good at what I do. I worked my way up, getting my life insurance licence and my RIBO general licence, which is Registered Insurance Broker of Ontario. I got really good marks on my exams, always over 90%. Andrew, my boyfriend, had a good job as a flooring installer. We always had money and a car. Still, I was living this very adult life at 17, and I remember having anxiety at the time. But alcoholism is a progressive illness. It is a lot easier to function when you are younger. During this period of my life the drinking wasn't getting in my way. I did not really drink much during the week but left drinking to the weekend. By the time I was 29 I started drinking a bit more, adding Thursday to the days I would drink.

I stayed with Andrew for nine years. I got pregnant for the first time when I was 24, and we ended up getting married. I had my first son, Glenn, who is now 21. Shortly after Glenn was born I decided to take a year off work. Although things had been okay between Andrew and me in some ways—nice house in High Park and good jobs—we separated when I was 25 because I felt he was an alcoholic. Glenn and I went to live with my mother for a while because I was struggling with having an infant on my own. We lived with my mom until Glenn was about a year and a half, which gave me time to save money, buy a car, and go back to work.

When Glenn was two and a half, my twin sister and I purchased a town-house and moved in together. My twin and I are really close and life was pretty good then. We were about 29 at the time. My sister had stayed at home after I was kicked out, and she moved out when she was in her early twenties. By her late twenties she had separated from her first husband. Living with my sister was fun while it lasted but it only lasted a couple of years because she met somebody and I met somebody. She got married for a second time to a very wealthy man, but they divorced about 10 years later. You could write a movie about her life! Although we are very different we are still very close. She has never had any problems with addiction. She is wealthy. We were pregnant at the same time, and our daughters are only six months apart. Our relationship was a little strained the last few years of my addiction because it was really hard for her, as it is for most family members, to understand an addict when they are still using and to see how it affects the addict's kids. My sister was very generous with my kids and saw them a lot. Since I became sober three years ago we have become close again. We talk a lot, and she often helps me out.

Paul, the man I met when I was living with my sister, became my second husband. When Paul and I met, my sister moved out of the townhouse and he moved in. Around this time I was drinking more heavily and starting to experience blackouts. A blackout happens when you are wide awake but you don't know what you are doing. I was experiencing a blackout when I got my first impaired driving charge. It was February, my son was with my mom for the weekend, Paul and I were fighting, and I decided I was going to go on vacation. It was snowing out and I was flying down the QEW toward Niagara Falls when the car spun out of control. Amazingly, I wasn't killed. There were no cars around and I pulled over to the side of the road and thought I would get some sleep. This is how out of it I was when I was drinking. An OPP officer woke me up and took me to the Niagara Falls police station. One definition of addiction is that you are using a substance that causes serious consequences to your life but you continue to use it anyway. That describes my life at that point. I was starting to experience the negative consequences of my addiction.

My sister and I sold our townhouse, and Paul and I moved outside of Toronto. I was about 30 at the time. I became pregnant with my daughter, Melody, who is now 15. Eventually we also had my second son, Daniel, who is 10. Paul and I always had a volatile relationship. He had an anger management problem and was abusive. When you put a person like that together with an alcoholic it does not make for a very good relationship. Ours became a very bad relationship. He had a criminal record for assaulting his first wife. He had started abusing me as well. As a long-haul trucker he was away a lot but when he was home on weekends there was a lot of fighting, drinking, yelling, and screaming. The kids went through a lot. There was a lot of stress managing two kids, virtually as a single mom, with one in daycare and the other walking back and forth to school, while I was doing a 30-minute commute each way to work. So I was really, really busy and once you also consider the fighting on the weekends and my drinking to excess, my life was pretty chaotic. But all this time my career kept advancing and I was even promoted to manager of an agency.

By the time I had my second son, Daniel when I was 36, my relationship with Paul was really, really bad. Even though we were still together I always kind of felt like I was a single mom. Paul wasn't home a lot and when he was he really didn't provide much emotional support with the kids. In fact, because we fought so much, it seemed he just aggravated things. So, you know, it was bad. When Daniel was born, I thought, okay, I've had enough. I decided to take a year off because it was so exhausting. Even though I had a great job as a manager, and I was a little upset to leave it, I felt that I had to take a year or two off because I could not financially justify having three kids in daycare and after-school care. Even after-school care is really, really expensive. Once you pay for full-time daycare for one baby, for after-school care for two other kids, for lunch, gas, driving expenses, and everything else, you're almost losing money by going to work. When I was home with Daniel, my relationship with my abusive husband got worse. I found myself in this small town, not working, with a baby, a five-year-old daughter, an 11-year-old, and this crazy trucker coming home and screaming at me on the weekends. Finally, when Daniel was

16 months old, I had Paul arrested for the fourth and final time and had a No Contact Order brought against him. This time he was screaming the usual stuff at me while I had the baby in my arms. I was able to lock him in the basement and call 911 as he pounded on the door and screamed that he was going to kill me. I sold the house without him even knowing. Because we were not legally married I was able to do that.

My mom purchased a home in the same town we were living in, and we moved in with her a few months later. What I found as a single parent is that one income was never really enough. To raise three kids on one income was almost impossible. So, living with my mom helped us out a lot financially. Where else could we have lived in a five-bedroom house for $500 a month? I also went back to work in the insurance industry.

While moving in with my mom, to her beautiful five-bedroom house, sounded good on paper, it wasn't a good idea. She is a very negative, co-dependent individual. She can't stand alcoholics because her father was an alcoholic and was abusive. Her goal was that, as soon as I moved in, she would try to get me to stop drinking. Of course, if you tell an alcoholic not to drink, they end up drinking more. And that's what happened with us. My mother wanted to control my drinking and within a month of moving in she got Children's Aid and the police involved. I was threatened by Children's Aid that, if I didn't go for treatment, they would take away Daniel. I did a 21-day treatment program, all the time knowing that I was an alcoholic but not ready to stop.

For pretty much the next five years, until I went into my last treatment centre, I was just playing the system. I was in and out of treatment and in and out of AA, lying to the Children's Aid, lying to the courts. I had tried to stop and I thought I was going to end up living in treatment centres forever. Finally, in 2007 I reached my own bottom and got to the point where I couldn't take it anymore. Some of us don't reach our bottom until we are dead. By the time I walked into the residential facility in the summer of 2007, I was spiritually bankrupt and emotionally dead. I had reached the point of despair, where you can no longer picture your life with alcohol, but you can no longer picture your life without it either. You are basically just done.

The main problem I faced when I started trying to get help for my drinking was how to do that that while raising three kids on my own. I felt I was being told that, as a mother, I wasn't supposed to have an addiction problem. I still feel there's a lot of stereotyping of males and females. It's bad if a father has a drinking problem, but when a mother has the same problem it's a really different story, and it's completely frowned upon. That's how Children's Aid views it, that's how the criminal courts view it, and that's how the family courts view it.

I was caught between a rock and a hard spot. On one hand I had the legal system and the Children's Aid system telling me that I had to stop drinking and get better or I would lose my kids, my job, everything. On the other hand how was I going to get help? Where was I going to find the time to get help? How could I do what they were asking when I was the only one raising all three kids? What people don't seem to get is "How do you do both?" Even when I acknowledged that I was sick, an alcoholic, and I needed help, I also had to consider that I really, really love my children more than anything in the world. How could I look after them and get help at the same time?

For about six years I tried to do both. I went to two or three short-term treatment centres and was in and out of AA. I would think I was going to get better but really knew that I wouldn't. Every time I tried to get better I relapsed. My kids were going through utter hell and so was I.

I moved out of my mom's house in 2006 and got my own place with the kids. That year was really chaotic. I was in and out of treatment. I went to a residential treatment program twice. By the end, my mom had taken Daniel and my dad had taken Melody. Glenn was about to start university and was living by himself in the house that I was renting. When I went into treatment again in February 2007 I knew there was no way it was going to work and that I was going to relapse. I discussed this with my counsellor and she helped get me on a list for a residential treatment centre. I went back to my home, got rid of the house, and put everything into storage. My family had finally taken my kids when Children's Aid explained that they needed family members to help out or the kids would go to foster care. So, in the end, they were kind of forced to help me out. So, the kids were with my family and I checked myself in to the treatment centre for six months. By the time I checked in I had accepted that I had lost my kids. To me there was no point going on with them the way I had been because I wasn't being their mother anyways. I didn't want to go back and hurt them again and to hurt myself again so I decided to live in the treatment centre and see what would happen. I put myself into a six-month program. It was the longest-term facility I could find in Toronto because I wanted to make sure it worked this time. I didn't want to put my kids through any more pain, and I didn't want to go through any more pain myself. At one point I felt that if I couldn't get better then I would just live in these facilities for the rest of my life because I could no longer put my kids through this suffering. Saying goodbye to my kids was the hardest thing I've ever done—it's still very painful when I think about it—but I needed to do it. While I was in treatment I was there with other women who had the same problem as me. I needed to be alone in treatment to focus on my illness and really, really try to overcome it, which is what I did.

After the first two months, I was trying to go to more AA meetings in the evenings. I met this great woman who I asked to be my sponsor. I told her how desperate I was, how I had been trying the program and nothing was working. I knew I really needed to work the steps of AA. I really wanted to complete the fourth step. The fourth step helps you to let go of your resentments and anger, what really keeps an alcoholic sick. I worked really hard with her at night while I was in the treatment centre. The treatment centre was great for keeping me safe. It was also a great place to keep women away from the pressures of kids, family, and triggers, and keep them focused on their own recovery. As helpful as the centre was, I really gained my sobriety by working through the steps of AA with my sponsor.

While I was in treatment I noticed that I was not obsessing about or craving alcohol anymore. I also noticed that I was responding differently to people. It's changes like these that make people believe in the 12 steps of AA. I knew in my head that it was the 12-step program that was making the difference because nothing else I had tried could get me sober. Following step two, I came to believe in a power greater than myself. Once I embraced the spiritual program it was amazing how, all of a sudden, the desire and the obsession with alcohol went away. I still work really hard at staying sober. I go to at least three or four meetings per week, still work with my sponsor and stay involved in the organization. It took me five years in and out of treatment centres to get to where I am. It is a horrible disease. I feel now that, once you are sober, three years is nothing. The last three years have been like being reborn. For so many years before that I had never learned how to respond to my emotions because I was anaesthetized with alcohol. It's hard to explain to people who haven't been there, but everything is new. You are relearning everything from how to discipline your kids to how to talk to somebody on a date. So it is a lot of work.

After the treatment centre I went to a sober-living facility for another six months. While there, I was able to straighten out my legalities with Children's Aid and work on getting my kids back. During that period I also applied for and was approved for a disability benefit. A lot of people were surprised that I was approved because there was nothing wrong with me other than my substance abuse and depression, which was most likely caused by the substance abuse. Often, these don't seem to count as disabilities and people with addictions get stuck on welfare.

I got an apartment of my own in July 2008. Around the same time I also got my daughter back. She and Daniel had both gone to live with their dad because my family members had become tired of looking after them. The time that they were living with their father was very tough on my children because he continued to be abusive. It took me many more months to get Daniel back. Paul wouldn't release him right away so I had to go through the courts. When Daniel finally came to live with me it was mostly because Paul had been leaving Daniel alone and unattended every morning before school and was forced to release him.

So I've had my kids back for over a year now, and we're all doing really well. My eldest son, Glenn, is at university, majoring in business. He is probably going to do a master's at U of T; the sky is the limit for him. I've shared all my experiences with him. My daughter, Melody, is in high school and is doing well. She babysits from time to time, which helps out. My son Daniel is in grade four. I'm living sober, we're very happy, and life is great.

Some of the barriers I face now as a single mother are the same as they always were. I struggle to find time for myself and find time to get other things done while still looking after my kids. Melody is old enough to be left alone quite a bit, but Daniel still needs me around a lot. Another major roadblock I've faced is dealing with the system. I've had a horrible time with the Child Tax Benefit. They've held off paying me for the past year or so because they are reviewing some of the previous years when they question whether or not I had my kids. For the past 10 months I've made it almost a full-time job to try and get in touch with them, and the whole time I haven't been paid my $700 a month benefit. I have finally been approved and they have agreed to pay me back for months they withheld.

As far as ODSP goes, I have given up with them. I can't even describe how badly they treat people. I've often said to them, "It's a good thing I have a brain and can speak English because, if I didn't, I would probably be standing on a street corner without a cent." You need to know which benefits you are entitled to and constantly check to make sure you are receiving them. If I wasn't in the office every two weeks, jumping up and down and filling out more forms, I probably wouldn't get a cent. Even when you get your benefits they hardly pay you anything. The amount they give a single mother is completely ridiculous. I think their rent allotment is $700 dollars a month. There's no way that you can find an apartment in Toronto to house four people for $700.

I've had to supplement my income in other ways, mostly begging family members for money. A lot of people on disability, especially single moms, rely on family members to support them. The government knows this but they pretend that they don't. A lot of people wouldn't exist without family members helping them. Of course there are other ways to support yourself, sitting on the street downtown somewhere.

Even though I've had a lot of financial problems, I can honestly say that the last year has been the happiest of my life. I believe that's because I am sober. My children and I are content and happy. It's really hard to explain the difference in how they feel and how I feel. Of course money isn't everything, and I feel as long as I have my kids, we have our health, we're happy, and we have a safe, warm place to live, we can forge ahead. I also like to find support networks, like the lone-mothers group. I think it's important that women support each other and share each other's ideas and knowledge in various areas. I think women need that, and it helps a lot with the community and getting ahead as a woman.

I just graduated with honours from an intensive program in Addiction Studies. Unfortunately Centennial College never had their fast-tracked program approved to be eligible for the student loan program. I asked the disability benefit people if they had any funding for courses if I wanted to go back to school. They said no and advised me to get a student loan. I wondered, "How does this work then?" The college doesn't have funding for student loans, and disability will not give me any money because they think the college should have funding. I thought maybe I wasn't supposed to go to school. My twin sister, thank God for her, came up with the $730 per month I needed to go back. Now that I am looking for a job I notice that a lot of jobs require experience. I am applying to the odd job here and there and am going to volunteer. It's actually worked out well that I have this time to deal with my son Daniel. I've been having difficulty with him lately. Right now he is very defiant. He's going to go see a child psychologist because I think he developed a little bit of a personality disorder. He was really young, only five years old, when I was in and out of treatment, and his dad had issues with abuse. He went through a lot and I think it's coming to the surface now because of what I went through. At least now I feel like I have the resources and personal energy to take care of him, to try to be the mother I wasn't for so many years.

Madison's Story

I was born and raised in Toronto. My parents are in a different house now, just down the street from where we used to live, which is funny. They are both from Italy. My dad came here first to work. Later, he knew somebody who knew my mom, so he went back to Italy and proposed to her and they both returned to Canada. So there are five of us in the family—me and my four brothers. I have an older brother and three younger. I am the only girl, growing up with a traditional Italian Catholic background. It was tough being the only girl. My mom stayed at home raising us, you know, cleaning and cooking. She was always good at that. And my dad had developed his own small construction company. He still has it, and he is still working.

My mom was a typical mom, doing all that she could. She didn't have a driver's licence, and my dad was always at work. Like I said, I think it was tough being the only girl. You know, when I was young it was great—I was kind of like a doll. My mom would dress me up and all this stuff. It was weird because I was never into the clothes part, I was more the artistic type. So I remember asking my mom if I could get into dance classes and stuff like that. But because my dad was almost never home, my mom was alone with the five of us. It was too much for her to put me into anything. All we did was just go to school and church. When I was a teenager, that's when things started to get a little more difficult.

My first boyfriend was named Paul. He was the type of boyfriend my parents wanted me to have. I was 16 and he was seven years older. He was my neighbour's best friend. Before I could go out with him, I had to introduce him to my parents. So that's a little weird, because at the age of 16 my parents wouldn't even let me go out with my girlfriends. I think I realized afterwards that by introducing Paul to my parents and getting to go out, I was kind of using him. He was the only gateway to going out. Paul was a great guy—older, Italian, with a good job working at a Hospital, and from a Catholic family. Everything my parents would want for me, you know, to get married and have kids and all that stuff. And of course after meeting him, they both liked his attitude, so they approved of me going out with him. At first it was great because we got to go out to dinners and go see movies, go downtown, do things that I had never done, because my parents would never go out. They never took us to movies. They never went to restaurants. I never did anything beyond going to school. I started working part-time at Canadian Tire when I was 15 and I was still working there when I dated Paul. It was just up the street. I lived almost entirely within a few blocks; everything I did happened in these few blocks, including the friends that I could hang out with. But Paul made me see more of the outside world. I met people older than myself. I was going out, having a bit more fun.

I was with Paul for two years, and that's when things started going really bad. I realized that I loved him as a friend but that the passion wasn't really there. He was the first person I slept with, when I was 17. And when I broke up with him my parents just lost it, because I told them that I was too young to be with one guy. I had never experienced just going out with a group of friends, going on dates. I had my high school friends, and then I came home. I never went out after school. I was never allowed to go on those school trips—you know to Ottawa or Montreal or those little weekend or four-day trips. Basically my parents were really strict, but not abusive. Because I was the girl, it was that traditional thinking—you stay home, even though I showed them how responsible I was. I did well in school, I was always an A or B student. I worked part-time. I always listened and cleaned the house and helped my mom with my little brother. I changed his diapers and took him out for walks. Whatever it was that they wanted, I did, and I always showed my parents that I was a responsible person. But still, they never let me do things on my own. I always had to be overseen. They never trusted me. They lost even more trust when I broke up with Paul. They didn't respect me anymore. I even remember my mom calling me a slut because I wanted to date other guys. I remember it was my last year of high school and I was sneaking off to the library, not telling my parents even though we were doing projects, doing school stuff.

I always kind of liked this guy Adam. And I told him to come over to the library that was just up the street from where my parents lived. I was at the library with Adam and we were actually doing schoolwork. After, when we were leaving the library, I gave Adam a big hug to thank him for coming to meet me. So, unfortunately, my dad caught me giving this guy a hug. We were right out-side the library and my dad saw us. I had never seen him so aggressive and so mad. He slapped me in front of my friend, which was really embarrassing, and it was a bad slap, I felt the sting on my face. And then there I was, crying. I felt embarrassed. Even Adam was sort of scared—my dad's a big guy. He's not one you'd want to fool around with. I could tell that Adam was wondering, "Do I help her? Do I run away?" so I looked at him and said, "Adam just go. Just go, I'll be okay." So then my dad pretty much dragged me into the car. We drove home right up the street. Then right away he said to my mom, "Look at your daughter, she going out with other guys." He just made me sound like a really bad person, so of course I tried to explain to my mom that we were actually doing school work. Okay, yes, I gave him a hug to say bye to my friend. But my mom, I guess because of her traditional ways, always stands with my dad. It didn't matter what I said. They said, "You're not going out." They forced me to stay at home, and they would take the phone away from me if I was on it for too long.

I had a very free spirit, and my parents would not allow me to embrace that. So that was the turning point, when I became very angry with my parents. I was angry at my dad for being so aggressive toward me. Hitting me and yelling at me and calling me these names and stuff like that. And I was mad at my mom for taking my dad's side, never defending me even though I was a decent teenager. I needed to be able to live my own life. So I was really mad. I wouldn't talk to them. I just went to school. Once in a while either before school, or between school and work, maybe I would try to see a friend. However, I didn't bother much because I didn't want to get in trouble, I was scared. So I met this other guy, another Italian guy, a little older, working at Canadian Tire. I wanted to be able to go out again. I introduced him to my parents. Billy had a car and he took me out. I started drinking, but I wasn't the type of person to do anything stupid, like hard-core drugs or really heavy drinking. But when I started drinking, I felt a little older, I had more fun. Billy helped build my confidence and I became more outgoing. I had been so introverted because I never associated with anyone except for a few people at school. So I think I slowly started developing more of my own character. I realized that I'm not the type of person who can just sit at home all the time. And so Billy would take me out, to movies, and then we would go back to his place and have a couple of drinks. You know, nothing crazy, but it was good. I did like him.

Again my parents approved, because he was older, and Italian. You know, a nice guy, job, car, and more established so, again, they allowed it. This went on for I'd say less than a year. I think what happened was I started university. Although I did care about Billy, I wasn't in love with him so I broke up with him. Of course my parents thought that women were not supposed to break up with the boyfriend. You are only supposed to have one guy, one guy only. You're supposed to get married. Guys are going to look at you and find you have been with this guy and that guy and that's not right. This was why my parents were calling me a slut and saying, "You're not good for anything. People are not going to respect you." I just kind of ignored their comments. I was almost 19 and I had started university. I said to my mom. "I'm 19 years old. Give me a break."

Being in university was great because the hours are different so I could tell my parents that I was at school, which was true—I was always at school. I was in the fine-arts program and I was really proud of that because it was hard to get into because you had to have a portfolio. It was one of the harder programs because they had only very limited spaces. I was taking a painting class and a Photoshop class, and in the beginning it was all really good.

I was just kind of ignoring my parents. My mom was taking care of my younger brother. My dad was never home. My dad was your typical man who just worked, worked, worked! Which I give him credit for. He was a hard-working man. He had a small company and he was always able to provide good food. When I was 14 we moved into a nice big house. So my dad definitely was a good breadwinner. He brought home the money, and my mom was able to buy clothes and whatever. But when it came to his attitude . . . when I think back, still to this day my dad has never given me a hug. My dad has never said, "I love you." Dad has never said, "Madison, that was awesome." But when I was bad he always commented on that. I don't want to get upset about it now because it was a long time ago. When I think about it, I know you can't blame your parents all the time. And, I know that it's also true that as you get older you can't keep blaming your current life on your past. But the past also makes you who you are. And I think now, that maybe there were times that I was depressed. Or that one minute I was on top of the world and thought I could do anything, but then would think of myself as a quitter. Or just that I always got bored and wanted something else. I wonder if it was a lack of confidence in myself because I was never given confidence, given positive messages about myself.

So by going to university I showed them and myself that I could do it, I could do it on my own. When I told my dad I want to go to university. He said, fine, but since you're working you pay for it." Even though my dad had a lot of money, and a brand-new big house. But I didn't care, I took on the responsibility. It was a lot of money, it was probably thousands of dollars, and at the age of 19 it was a lot of money for me, but I paid for my school. So here I was, going to school full-time and still working part-time at Canadian Tire and meeting new people. People that had more worldly experience. A way about them, a confidence about them that I don't think I had yet. Because even though I can figure things out, even though I think I am smart enough, I never had that confidence. You know, ever. Even still to this day I still lack it. And so again, I was meeting these people and again they were kind of triggering this thing, this inner person I thought I had in me but was never able to show to my parents.

I started developing a close relationship with one or two guys. And this one guy, Rick, was a musician, he was going to university and was a little bit older. He was a great musician and I admired him for being so outgoing. We developed a good friendship. He had a car and would sometimes drive me to work and drive me home. He couldn't drive me right home; he would stop a couple of blocks away from where I lived, and then I would walk the rest of the way. Here I was, 19, working, paying for school and I still had to sneak around with my friends. And God forbid if they were guy friends. Right away my parents thought I was sleeping with everybody because I broke up with those two men they thought I would marry.

One time I came home later than usual, maybe two hours later. I got home at about 7 p.m. instead of at 5. I was tired: I'd had a long day at school and

I had gone to the university pub with Rick afterwards. I came home tired, you know kind of looking forward to doing my school work and stuff like that. But even before I could drop my bag, my mom says, "I can't take any more. You coming from school late, I know you finish at 3." Just yelling at me. Just going on and on and on. She says, "I don't trust you. I bet you are sleeping with all these guys, you know I don't like you going to university." I'm like, "Ma, I have the right to have friends. I have the right to go out. I have the right to see anybody I want, whoever I want, whenever I want." But of course their final argument was always, "This is my house, these are my rules." So my mom and I are arguing back and forth. I was saying, "Leave me alone, I am doing everything I can. I am a woman now. I am 19 years old, legally I have the right to do whatever I want." Finally, I said "Ma, I'll move out." She said, "Goodbye, move out, move out."

I slowly started looking for a place behind their back. I just couldn't take it anymore. I remember looking through newspapers and calling people. And, again, because of my anger and feeling fed up I wanted to find my own place, but because of my lack of confidence I couldn't look for a place too far away. I found this place. It was a house. It was near my work, near the university. But I wasn't sure; I knew I couldn't afford it. I didn't want to quit school and work full-time. I didn't want to do that yet. So then what happened was, my good friend Rick drove me home. I was already late, so he dropped me off just a couple blocks up the street and I walked home. I came home, I dropped off my bag, grabbed a glass of water and right away my mom started up again, "Where the hell were you? You're driving me crazy. I don't trust you. Who were you with? I should tell your dad to come pick you up because I don't think you actually go to school." My mom called my dad, because by this time I was yelling, "I can't take it. I'm moving out." So she saw me literally packing my bags. I said, "Ma, you know what, I have a place. I can go there right now and stay there. If this is what you want, if we can't get along like this. I've got to go. Either you're going to kill me or I'm going to kill you." I was just so angry and I could tell that my mom was just so disappointed in me and I didn't want that any more. My dad came home and he was yelling at me as well. "What's going on, what do you think you're doing?" So what happened was, I was about to call 911. My dad was literally holding me down. I said, "Listen I have the right to leave." And my dad wouldn't let me leave. My mom threw one of my perfume bottles at me. I remember it shattering. I was saying, "I can't take this anymore. I am too depressed. I can't concentrate anymore. All you guys do is insult me. You guys never say anything good to me, never." Then I was crying, she was crying, and I left the house.

So picture me running out of the house. I didn't even know where to go, I was just so freaked out. I was not used to going to many places. There's a hotel I remembered . . . I was on the bus and crying, and my shirt was ripped and everybody was looking at me, and out the window I saw my two brothers in the car. Before I knew it my brother was honking the horn at this bus driver and telling him to pull over. And I'm like, "Don't stop. Keep going. They are harassing me. Don't stop." "Are you sure?" he asked, and I said yes. Then what did my brothers do? My brothers cut in front of the bus and so the bus driver said, "I'm sorry I have to call the police." "Fine," I said, "let's get this done. Do what you have to do." A TTC constable came and a police officer came. They got my story. Unfortunately, they had to take me to the station.

I talked to another officer, like a counselling officer, to give them my story. I saw my parents coming and I guess they told their story. Finally they got us together with these two counsellor-type cops. The statement that my parents gave is that I hit my mom. I think that they did not want to make themselves look bad. I said, "Excuse me, I never hit my mom." So I was looking at my parents and they're looking at me and the counsellors asked me, "Can you go back home?" I said, "I can but I don't want to live there. I'll go back home to get my stuff." Then the cop said, "Look, she is 19, she has the right to go, she has the right to go anywhere she wants, do anything she wants. I understand when she's at your house she's not allowed to hit you or break things, or whatever." So I just sucked it up. I went home, grabbed my stuff that was in the foyer, went upstairs, and locked my door. And I said, "If you guys bug me, I swear I'm leaving right now."

For a couple of days I did not talk to my parents. I just hated them at this point. After about four days I just decided to do stuff after school. So I came home late and again my mom yelled at me, so I said, excuse me, and I went upstairs. I had been slowly grabbing boxes from the Canadian Tire and I started putting everything in my boxes. I called Rick and asked him to come pick me up. Not even an hour later he was at my door and helping me take boxes to the car. So my mom's screaming, "Who are you? What are you doing to my daughter? Why are you helping her like this?" So of course she called my dad. My dad came home and he's yelling at this poor guy too, but finally we just left.

After I moved out I swear I didn't talk to my parents for like a year. I tried to go to university and work part-time, but then I realized I didn't have enough money to pay the bills, my rent, and transportation. So I left university. I still regret ever so much leaving university. I didn't even finish the semester. I regret it because I think now my life would have been so different. I was trying . . . I wanted to be a teacher. I knew I had the potential. I had the grades.

I am the first female in all my family—and we're are talking about aunts, cousins, everybody—that's ever left the house without being married. My mom was the yelling type, sure, she put me down. But she was never physically abusive. My dad was a stern father; he was a little more aggressive. And again he put me down. I just couldn't take it. I realized this is why throughout my life I have a lack of trust for people. I have a lack of commitment. Because I see that my parents were not even nice to me, so how could a stranger be nice to me, if that makes any sense. One minute I feel like I'm on top of the world. I really do. Things are good. I feel great. I'm not stressed out. But the next minute I feel depressed, really depressed, because I don't trust anybody. I get angry for no reason. I lack confidence in just who I am. I never had the encouragement that a teenager should have.

So I started working full-time at Canadian Tire. And again it wasn't enough. So I worked part-time at Burger King two minutes away from the Canadian Tire. I felt better. I did. I didn't have to worry about my parents. My parents didn't know where I lived. It was difficult because I was closest to my older brother. I missed them, but at the same time there was a sense of relief. So I was working, making new friends, going out, being your typical 20-year-old. When I was 21, my parents found out where I lived, and they came there and harassed me. They even spoke to my landlords. So here I was, almost being harassed by my landlord. I remember one night coming home at around one in the morning—it was a Saturday night, I had been out with a couple of friends, and we had had a few drinks. My landlady literally knocked at my door and said, "We don't like you coming home so late." I tried to explain: "I pay rent, you have no say in where I go and what time I come home." They said, "We don't like your attitude," and stuff like that. I ended up having to move from there. Once again my parents caused trouble for me even when I wasn't living in their house. I moved to a crappy apartment not far away. I just couldn't go further away because I didn't have the confidence you know? All I did was move a mile or two away.

This was when I started to go to clubs. I loved to dance; when I was young I always wanted to be a dancer. So now I was going to these clubs, thinking, "Wow, we can go to clubs, dance any way we want, and have fun."

So I met this guy who convinced me to get into stripping. So I thought, okay, well I like dancing, I'm artistic, I think I have a nice body . . . I guess I have to admit, I was intrigued. . . . So I went out to the clubs and I met him— he was a DJ at a club. I saw the girls, and the girls had all this confidence onstage. Just beautiful. Men yelling at them, and because I had never been to a strip club before it was all new. So I thought I could do this. You know, it's good money. And that was the main thing. Canadian Tire and Burger King, like how far was I going to get? I knew for a fact that morally it wasn't who I was, not that I am dissing strippers. Luckily, back in those days it wasn't like strip clubs are now. There weren't lap dances. I haven't been to a strip club in years, but I'm pretty sure it was quite different then. It was like burlesque, with people tipping you onstage. There was the dancing and the stripping, but there was no touching. I thought that given I was artistic and had taken drawing at university where nude models had come to our class, that this wasn't so different. So the nudity wasn't a big issue, and of course the dancing seemed like a lot of fun. Because, like, wow there I was onstage, and I've always wanted to be onstage and dance. Now, I know this is totally opposite to what being onstage doing ballet and jazz dancing might be—here I was in a strip club. But it gave me a chance to dance. It gave me a chance to be free, and it gave me a chance to make good money.

So I worked at a few different clubs. Some of them were pretty seedy. Again no offence to the people or the places, but there were a lot of drugs, a lot of pimps. It tends to go hand in hand with stripping. But I was very moral, I had values. There are things that I would never do. I would never do the hard-core drugs. I was making good money. I was young. I had a great body. I had fun onstage, and people could tell. I worked really hard. You know—I've got the work ethic of my dad, I was very hard-working. I didn't go there just to work a couple hours, I'd work an eight-hour shift, five days a week. I worked hard for one or two years then I took a year off. Because what happens in that work, at least it did for me . . . you do get caught up. People buying you drinks, and you kind of lose yourself. I started to see myself as just this piece of meat. A lot of the men I met were generally nice. But then some of them would always say, "Hey baby, nice tits, what are you doing afterwards?" You know, they don't see you as a person. They just see you as this sexual thing. And even though one minute it gave me confidence because I was getting compliments and getting paid, in another way it also confirmed that I wasn't worth much.

In the end I think this really screwed me up when it comes to men. Still to this day, I don't trust men. I saw those pervert men coming in, most of them were married, had serious girlfriends, kids, and here they were trying to take me out. Not home but to a hotel. They acted like morons in front of their friends, like, Oh yeah baby you know what I want. And so I saw this over and over again. And it's how I started to view men. It was bad enough how my dad made me view men. You know, hard, stern, making me afraid. I had always felt the lack of love and encouragement and then here I was at a strip club. In some ways, I think I wanted to work at a strip club hoping that my parents would find out, just to piss them off. I didn't really talk to them for years. Briefly, a call here, a call there. But I began to think a lot of about what I was doing: "God, is this how men always see me? Is this my life?" So after six or seven years of working in Toronto strip clubs I met Steve. Steve was a DJ manager at a strip club and I fell head over heels for this guy. This guy, Mr. Con Man, sweetheart, swept me off my feet. I was, working in the bar business but I was becoming more a waitress/manager but still stripping, because in the end that was where the money was. So Steve was the manager and I was like the floater, bartending, waitressing, helping him out with the managing, and whatever. He wanted to leave Toronto to go out west, and he wanted me to come with him. So I thought, why not? What do I have here? I don't have much here. So we left. I was the one with the money. I was the one with the car.

We drove out west and at first it was great. You know, we took our time. We saw the country. After about a month we arrived, and right away he wanted to get back into the strip clubs. He met this guy who wanted to open up a strip club, and we started working for him. Steve was a manager for the bar, and I was the manager for the girls because of all the experience I had. So it ended up being pretty good at first. We were working at a bar/restaurant/cabaret.

Over time though, I figured out that the owner was a drug dealer. Here I was, trying to manage the girls, still stripping as well because that's where the money is. So I was stripping but I was always the one with the head on my shoulders. The owner was drugging up these girls, selling crack and coke and ecstasy and weed and everything under the sun. I was probably one of the lucky ones not to get into this kind of lifestyle. But I found out that Steve was getting into it and taking my money to buy crack and coke and drink. He made nothing compared to what I was making. It was my whole environment— everywhere I looked there were drugs and eventually, and unfortunately, I got a bit into the drugs too. It was stupid. I was thinking, Well, screw you, if you're going to spend my money, I'm going to do it a bit too. But again it was not really me. When I was high I always felt like an idiot, I just felt out of it, stupid. And so I stopped. Steve began to show a side of himself that I had never seen, being manipulative, taking my money. I had to sell the car. I had an RV too, and I had to sell that because I couldn't keep up paying for his crazy lifestyle. And I was babying him. Of course, being in love, you do whatever you can to make some-one happy. At least I thought that's how it would work, right? By this time, I had found out I was pregnant. So of course no more strip clubs. Don't even give me a joint. Don't even give me anything. But of course Steve was still doing drugs, and now he was doing it behind my back and I was asking him to quit.

Steve got in trouble with the law and I found out he had already been charged with possession in Toronto and that he left Toronto to hide. Out west he was charged with possession as well. So who paid for his lawyer? Me. We are talking about thousands of dollars. Finally I had had enough. I couldn't take it. I couldn't take the dirtiness of everything, so I came back to Toronto to have Zack. My parents and I weren't exactly on good terms but when I came to Toronto they helped me. I stayed at their place for three months, and I had Zack.

Steve flew down for the birth of his son. He stayed for a couple of weeks— he was being decent toward my parents, toward me, and toward Zack. But then he went back west.

I went back to Vancouver and tried it out for another six months. I couldn't take it; you know, he kept trying to convince me to do the drugs again. So I said, "Steve I'm out of here." He didn't want to come back with me because I think he was still afraid of the charges in Toronto. And so I came here with Zack, and my parents were nice enough to let me stay at their place.

I had some money saved but then I spent it in the first year and a half after Zack's birth. I was a single mom, by myself. Not working, obviously, because I had Zack and I wanted to stay home with him. I think a parent should have the right to stay home with their kid. Even at the beginning social assistance was very annoying because they asked so many questions. Where is your ex and this and that? And I didn't exactly know where he was. But I didn't exactly tell them everything about him because I think they could have found him. But I know for a fact he had no money. So it's like taking blood from a stone. There's nothing you can take from Steve.

From the time Zack was maybe two to the age of four, I was on social assistance. I was a single mom—Steve never came back. I just kind of pretended he never existed, you know, with social assistance and in my heart. Then Zack went to school and I had more of a chance to go look for work. I also started volunteering at the food bank. Because of my energy, because I am a quick learner, when there was an opening in the office, the person who was in the job and was being promoted encouraged me to apply. She told me to say that I needed the work and that I had been here for six months. She also told me she had confidence that I could do it. So I thought about it. I had always lacked confidence because I worked at crappy places like Canadian Tire and Burger King. And I worked at those bars, strip bars, and at a few restaurants here and there but there was nothing that looked good on my resume. The only thing that looked good was the fact that I volunteered at the food bank. I got to know the executive director. He knew my work enthusiasm, my team effort. I worked well independently and I got along with everybody. So I was able to get an interview, and I got the job.

Things were looking up. I was able to get off social assistance. Children's services were always there to help me pay for daycare, because my work hours were longer than the school's. Children's services was great—if I hadn't had good daycare I wouldn't have been able to do my job. I was at the food bank for four or five years. I did well there. But again something triggered me . . . you know life, you can't help but think about your past . . . you can't help think about what you could have been. . . . I ended up leaving.

Steve was back, but he was not really working. He helped with Zack a couple days a week. He was not doing drugs but his work ethic will never change—he's lazy. I was back on social assistance.

I was also having relationship difficulties. I think maybe it was just my lack of confidence in men being honest. John was my boyfriend at the time, and we were even engaged. I have known John for 15 years. He was around before Zack and before Steve. We were buddies, and then he became my boyfriend. We were young so it was just kind of like being my friend, being close, hanging out. And then all these years later, we moved in together. He helps with Zack, he supports me every which way. But I don't know what it is, even when I have something good, I don't think it is going to last. So I let it go before I even give it a chance, before it ends up being bad. When things are too good it's like I don't deserve it or something. And so I got scared, and I just let John go. We are not engaged anymore. It's probably going to be my little curse. John just moved out, so right now I'm on my own, living in a place where the rent is more than what I get. He still says, "I want to be your best friend. I will help you with Zack," and he is more supportive than Steve ever was. Zack sees John as his stepdad, as a cool guy, and John is decent person, and I want that for Zack, someone that a kid could look up to. I trust John. He's never done anything wrong to me or Zack. He's a hard-working guy. He's responsible.

I don't want to fuck up Zack. Excuse my language! Because, in the end he's the only person that I so much want to do right by. Even though I may screw up ten thousand relationships . . . that's my stupid choice. But I don't want to screw up Zack. It's bad enough I left his dad. But I know for a fact I had to leave his dad. For me to survive and have a healthy life and Zack to have a healthy life, I had to leave. I don't regret that—I don't regret leaving Steve.

I'm on social assistance again. I'm going back to school next week. I am excited about that again. I just have to remind myself not to quit, not to quit when I'm doing well. You know, sometimes I wish I could go to therapy or talk to somebody . . . that's why I think these projects are good. Like sometimes it feels good telling my story because you hear it outside of your head, if that make sense. It gives you a different perspective. That's why I don't mind telling my story. It's maybe not as dramatic as some people's, but I've gone through enough. I think some of these issues in my life will always affect me.

It's tough being a mom, its tough being a woman in today's time. Even through the stupid mistakes I've made, I think the only thing I do right, for the most part, is caring for my son. I'm lucky that I have my mom and John, and once in a while, Steve. It's not like I pawn Zack off, but I don't want to see Zack when I'm weak. So it does help to have other people in his life that really care about him. Because if Zack saw me all the time, we might have a destructive relationship, because you know how you take it out on people you're close with. You know, if you are upset, or angry, or depressed, people see it. And I don't want an eight-year-old to know that mommy is screwed up and she's depressed and almost wants to give up. He's just a kid. I think I feel bad that sometimes I don't always have the strength that a mother should have. He goes to school, I'll do his homework with him, and we have fun times. Yesterday we were playing in the park. But sometimes I get scared because I see the way his mood changes and I get scared that he probably gets that from me. One minute he's the sweetest boy, and the next minute he's getting mad at everybody because he lost a game. Maybe it is just the way kids are, but I can't help analyzing it.

I think with today's complicated life, you almost have to be perfect. And sometimes you're just not. And I feel bad that I'm not necessarily the perfect girlfriend. I'm not necessarily the perfect co-worker. I'm not the perfect mother sometimes. But when I have to do something, I do it. I love my son. He has grounded me. I guarantee if Zack wasn't in my life, if I hadn't gotten pregnant, I probably would have been some burnt-out stripper on drugs. So in a way he kind of saved me. Now, it's my turn to be there for him and save him when he hurts his knee, loses a baseball game, or gets mad at a friend, or just needs me. Zack has helped me. I was living my life day by day, and I still have that attitude. I don't think about the future, but I know we need a future. I want a family. I want a house. I want a home.

Stacey's Story

My name is Stacey, and I am 49 years old. I am the youngest daughter in a family of six. I was born in Toronto and am second-generation Canadian. My grandparents were from Barbados and Saint Kitts.

I never knew my grandparents. My grandparents met in the islands and came to Toronto to start their family. Apparently my grandfather used to take me around when I was young, but I don't remember him. My grandmother died when my mother was still quite young. As I understand it, they had five kids, and after my grandmother died my grandfather couldn't handle them all on his own. At some point the kids ended up in Children's Aid for a short period of time. My mother's oldest sister got married and was able to take the youngest. My mother and her brothers went out on their own.

Once my mother was out of Children's Aid and on her own, her brothers and her youngest sister stayed with her. My mother got married but didn't have any children with her husband. She wanted kids, though, and went on to have six kids with three different men. My mother didn't stay with any of those men and actually outlived them all.

I didn't meet my own father. He died before I was born. The one man I remember coming around was American and the father of my older brother and my sister. I have been told he used to beat my mother viciously. For as long as I remember, my mother has had burns on her nose. For a long time I didn't realize they were burns. Later in life I found out that he used to put cigarettes out on her face.

My mother was 37 when I was born. She used to call me her "change-of-life baby." I didn't know what I'd done or what it meant that I had this name, but I decided I was either special or inadequate. One of the only things I know about my father is that he was a really good man. My mother had her third child, my sister, with my father. They were apart for six years while she was with the American. During that period of time she had two more kids. My mother and father got back together afterwards and had me. As far as I know my father must have truly loved my mother. So, maybe I am her change of life in a good way.

The other thing I know about my father is that he was a heroin addict. I only know bits and pieces of the story, but I get the sense that he would work as hard as he could and then he would use. The story I've been told is that he was either not using or trying not to use, and one day a friend came by and said, "Let's do this." My father took the same amount of drugs that he normally would, but I guess his system wasn't used to it, and he overdosed.

My mother was seven months pregnant with me and in the next room when this happened. She found him with the needle still in his arm.

I can't find out much more about my father because he was an only child and adopted. I don't know what he looked like but I think that I look like him. I think I have his nose and his chin, and maybe some of his sense of humour. I don't think my parents took many pictures. I think my mother was camera shy because of the burns on her face. I don't even know how my mother looked as a young woman. When I look at my older sister I get a sense of what my mother would have looked like.

I don't remember anything before I was six. At six I remember being in a fire that I started. My mother was out drinking. I wouldn't say she was an alcoholic, but she was a binge drinker. People came over on the weekend to gamble and drink. I remember the Five Star Whiskey bottles. I would take the star off and stick it on the fridge. There were a lot of stars on our fridge. My mother was out that night and I was home with a friend of mine. I don't know what I was thinking but I lit a candle on the gas stove and put it on the windowsill. I proceeded to look out the window and my clothes caught on fire. Back then they didn't tell you "stop, drop and roll," so I ran. I ran all over the place. My girlfriend hid rather than get help. Thank God the landlord's daughter was home and heard me. She came and put the fire out. I still have some scars as a reminder. I don't remember my mother coming home. I just remember going to the hospital and my mother coming to see me there. I never blamed her.

We always lived in a house, which I loved. I remember the house we lived in on Hamilton Street. I was a little tomboy and played a lot at that house. Even though my mom drank, she was the sweetest, kindest, gentlest woman you would ever want to meet. This sadly wasn't true when she was drinking, though. The rest of the time she was quiet and loved politics and reading. We grew up on welfare, and although we didn't have much, she always made sure we had enough. Our furniture didn't match. She always darned our socks. She stayed home and there were always three meals. She made big meals and I felt loved. Even though I felt loved, I knew my mother had issues because her mother had died at such a young age and she had been in care. When she drank she would get mean. We would hear her sobbing and then she would turn on us. She would smash dishes and then, at two o'clock in the morning, she would tell us to clean up the mess.

When I was young we didn't go to department stores very often. Simpsons-Sears was a big deal. We had merchants come to us with stuff. Someone would come to our house through the week, lay clothing out on the bed, and we would choose. We also had people come around the house to sell us things like linens and drapes.

My mom ran a tab at the corner store. She would write a list of what she needed and I would take it to the store. The store would write down what everything cost and at the end of the month, because we were on social assistance, my mom would pay the bill. She was very good at paying and so we never had bad credit. My sister, who worked at a bank, took care of my mom's finances. My other sister did the grocery shopping. I didn't do anything. I was the baby, you know, and just ran in and out of the house.

When I got older we moved to Regent Park. One of my sisters thought it would be easier for my mom. At first I hated it. I didn't like living in the projects. There were a lot of community events, which was good, and after a while I got used to it. I lived there with my mother until my early twenties. I moved out when my brother and his six kids moved in because of a crisis.

Up until grade 11, I did pretty well in school. In grade 12 I started to smoke weed and started getting lazy. I also hung around with people who didn't go to school. Once I began to skip school my grades went down so I decided to leave. I never completed grade 12. I probably would have only needed to go back for about six months to finish. I never did and that's something I've always regretted.

I started working as an inserter at *The Globe and Mail* newspaper. I worked from midnight until six in the morning putting the flyers and things into the paper. I was about 23, and it was my first real paycheque. I was dating a boy who also worked at the paper, and I stayed at his place on the weekends. When my brother moved in with my mom there wasn't much room in the house, and my boyfriend said, "Stacey, you might as well just stay here." That was my first taste of living on my own.

My boyfriend and I were together for six years. Things were pretty good when we were together. He was from the American south. He had blond hair and blue eyes and his parents were prejudiced. At the beginning of our relationship it didn't matter that I was black, but once they realized we were engaged it became a problem. We decided to call off the wedding. During the last year we were together I got into some heavy drugs, crack cocaine. When we broke up I just kept going with the drug use.

I met my daughters' father during this time. We were together for two years before I got pregnant. We talked about having children and I figured that at 32 it was time. I was using drugs the whole time we were together. When I found out I was pregnant I tried my best to stop, and did cut down a lot. There were times that I still used but I told myself that if I ate right everything would be fine. Eventually I stopped using and ended up having a beautiful daughter. The real problem was that her father was also a drug addict. He was much more involved in drugs at that point than I was. He couldn't handle the responsibility of having a child and left the relationship.

My family supported me while I was pregnant and helped me get my own apartment in Flemingdon Park. After the baby was born her father came back and we tried to make it work. He was still doing drugs and I started using again. I used drugs as a coping mechanism. I made sure my daughter was bathed, dressed, and put to sleep and then I would use. In my mind that was all right. It was my way of de-stressing. When my oldest daughter was about 18 months or so I got pregnant again. I had my second daughter, and their father left again. Now I had two babies in diapers, was single, and doing drugs. I continued like this throughout my daughters' childhoods.

Before my first daughter was born I had worked for an insurance company and then an insurance broker. When I found out I was pregnant I quit the job with the broker so I could stay home with my daughter. I think that staying home was important to me because my mother had always been home with us. I grew up with a stay-at-home mom, and I thought that is what you did. My daughter was my world and I wanted to be home with her. I was the one who was supposed to take care of her, so, I went on social assistance. I needed the support and I needed money and didn't see any other way of doing it.

My mother was alive to see my sisters and brothers have children, but she died of cancer when I was 28 so she never got to see my daughters. My children have a grandmother on their father's side but she is so religious it scares me. I don't have any contact with his side of the family. Thank God I have a strong family. My sisters and brothers have been great aunts and uncles. My oldest sister acts like the grandmother and her boyfriend acts like the grandfather for my daughters.

I struggled a lot with the drug addiction, especially being single with two children. I used to babysit the children who lived down the hall so I could have money for drugs. I would try my best not to use but there was always some reason to go back to it. I tried to be a good mom but drugs were how I coped. They're how I got through my day. I didn't understand the disease of addiction then like I do now.

My addiction lasted for 20 years. During that time I got myself into some really bad scrapes. By the time I left Flemingdon Park, I was getting slapped around by some of the drug dealers. That's when I knew things were taking a turn for the worse. My family thought I needed to move so I got a place at a housing co-op. It was one of the best moves I've ever made. I'm still there. One of my sisters lives just down the street and another lives just up the street. For the first year and a half I was in the co-op I still did drugs. After getting into a few more scrapes I decided to go into treatment.

I have been in treatment three times. The first time I went into treatment I still lived in Flemingdon Park. I thought I was ready and the only thing holding me back was that I didn't have anybody to watch my children. A good friend of mine who lived in Hamilton said she'd take them. Everything went well with the children, but I didn't commit to the program as I should have. Everyone was on my back to go to treatment so I really did it to shut them up. I was clean for the first three months. A girl I knew from treatment offered me some stuff and I figured, "I've been clean three months. Why not?" My addiction slipped back into place and stayed that way for another couple of years.

The second time I went to treatment it was my decision to go. I understood addiction better by that time and knew I needed to join a group, go to the 12-step meetings, and get a sponsor. All those things made a huge difference because I now had a support system. I had people I could talk to and places I could go to discuss the things that were bothering me. I was clean for nine months and had one relapse. I put myself back into treatment again. The third time I was in treatment I did a day program and I have been clean ever since.

I think the real turning point for me was one night, after I'd been using, I went into my daughter's room to give her a kiss. She woke up, looked at me, and said, "You've been doing it again." Then she started to scream at me, "Why are you doing this Mommy?" At first I just wanted her to leave me alone so I could do more. Then I had a moment of clarity. I saw that one daughter was shutting herself down to the point she would leave the house any chance she could get. My other daughter was full of anger. That's when I realized what I was doing to my children. My girls were 12 and 13, and that night I decided I'd had enough.

I've been clean and sober almost four years now. I'm in a program and I help other women with their addiction issues. I have been working on myself diligently. One promise I made to myself is that I wanted to go back to school and become somebody. I always wanted a career. Whether I was doing drugs or not, I always volunteered my time. I helped teach at the kids' schools, worked in the kitchen to feed the homeless, and did some art work. I enjoyed just giving back. When I got into recovery and started to share my story, I found that a lot of women came to talk to me and to confide in me. Often they'd say that they liked what I said and that it made a lot of sense. I was very free with information. All I could do was talk about my life. I couldn't tell them how to continue on their journey but I did tell them what worked for me. That's when I got the idea that maybe I should go into addiction counselling.

At the time I had a really good worker at social services. She had been tough but supportive when I was honest with her about using. When I told her about trying to fight my addiction she told me she was trying not to have a cigarette. Here she was trying not to smoke cigarettes while I was trying not to do crack. She tried to show me that she understood. So I told her about my dream to go back to school. She said I needed my GED. I knew I wasn't ready to get the GED. In reflection I didn't like that the social services agency pushed me into something I wasn't ready for. They didn't understand where I was with my addiction and that after being in treatment I needed time to rediscover who I was. I needed a good year to go to my meetings and build a solid foundation. But I didn't want to be punished for not doing what they wanted me to do. I kept trying for my GED and kept quitting. I saw them putting out money for something I didn't want and asked myself why couldn't they pay for something I did want.

I went to George Brown College and registered through the mature student program. Social assistance was fine with the decision. However I couldn't get a student loan because I'd already spent $17,000 of OSAP on crack cocaine. So, I have bad credit that was coming back to haunt me. I discovered I was able to get bursaries through the college. They would pay for 80% of two courses and pay for books. Social assistance would pay the rest. I'm able to go to school and be on social assistance because I'm at school only part-time. The arrangement helps me a lot because I don't owe anybody anything, except OSAP.

I've finished my first year of college. It took me the whole year, from September to September. I go to school every Monday from noon until 8:30 p.m. I have due dates, when things have to be handed in, and from just that one day of class I am swamped with work. It's a three-year program. When I'm done I get the same certificate as everybody else. I'll have the bursary again for my second year. I think they see that I'm serious and honest and that this program is what I want. I will be off the system. I'll have a career, and I'll say thank you very much.

My kids now have part-time jobs. They are working for the city as summer camp counsellors and both are still in high school. My oldest daughter talked about going into social work but recently has shown an interest in music. I am not sure exactly what she wants, but I know that both of them will be going to college if I can help it.

There are not many college graduates in our family. We've all lived on social assistance. My mother was raised on it, I was raised on it, and my children have been raised in it. My two sisters and my brothers have all got off of it. As adults they have always worked and haven't been on the system since they were growing up. I'm still on the system at 49 years old. By the time I'm 51 or 52 I hope to say I'm a career woman.

The good thing about working in the field of abused woman and as a youth advocate counsellor is that there is no age limit. It's about helping others, and I enjoy being able to help other women. I understand these women because I've come from a place of poverty and been in quite a few abusive relationships. I share my story and tell them they can succeed too. I say it is possible but you have to believe.

I believe anything can be accomplished if you put your mind and your soul into it. I stay on that path and don't let anything get in my way. With the clarity that comes from being clean, I've been able to accomplish quite a few things. I got involved with a speakers bureau. It's called Voices from the Street, and they gave me my voice. They bring people in to talk about government policies, poverty, homelessness, and housing. It helps marginalized people have a voice and believe that we can make a difference. We go to Queen's Park or other public places, get up on the podium, and speak about our experiences. Through Voices from the Street I'm learning about policy, how governments work, and a how effective a strong voice can be. I've joined some other agencies. I'm a member of "the 25 in 5" anti-poverty network and have helped out there by telling my story and advocating for policy change. I've also been on the news as I try to get public attention focused on poverty. I try to stay busy and speak out whenever I can. One of my goals is to go to schools and talk to children who are going from grade eight to grade nine. I feel that's a big transition and when things can start to get confusing.

I'll talk to anybody. I am not ashamed of my past. I use my past to help me with my present. I have learned to turn things around. I used to be scared of what was on the other side of my addiction so I would continue doing what I knew, even if it wasn't good for me. I was in a cycle of abuse and poverty and a lot of unhappiness. I didn't know how to handle these things but at least I knew what they were.

In recovery I learned not to be scared but to ask myself questions, go through my issues, and deal with my emotions. Through that process I get answers. I've also learned to let go. I still have my struggles—I have anger and pain—but I don't stay in them long. The real difference is that I can turn things around more quickly, learn from my mistakes, and move forward. Doors have been opening and things are working out. I do believe that things work out the way they are supposed to. I have good people in my life and make sure I keep good people around me.

I feel I was born to be a single mom. It was all I knew from my mother. Even in her weak moments my mother had to be a very strong woman to raise six children without a man. I always wondered what it would have been like to have a father. I didn't want my children to grow up without their father but that's how it happened. Quite recently my daughters' father has come back in their life. I don't trust him fully. There are a lot of lies and deceit. He still has a lot to learn.

Raising two children was hard but I was always there for them. I wasn't the type of addict mom who took off, even though it would have been easy to do. I used in the home when they were sleeping. Later I used when they were at school or as soon as they'd left the house to go to the store. I knew using was wrong, and I tried to hide it, but in my mind I justified it as stress release. Of course I was stressed; I brought additional stress to my life through addiction.

People used to tell me I was a good mother. I often thought, "If only they knew what I was doing." Money was always an issue. When I'd spent the money for rent, groceries, and hydro, I'd break into my kids' piggy banks or try to sell anything I could that was valuable in the house. If I gave my eight-year-old daughter money to hide from me I'd wake her up in the middle of the night and demand it back. Christmas and birthdays were very important moments for me. I don't know how I did it but I always made sure they had gifts. I made sure not to spend that money on drugs. That was the one time when I could actually hold on to money and I don't know why because otherwise I spent it all. It got to the point that I had to ask social assistance not to send me my cheque but to pay my rent for me. Thank God I asked and they were able to do that.

My children and I were like the Three Musketeers. Wherever you saw me, you saw them. Even though I was in my addiction, I tried not to neglect my motherly duties. This was pretty difficult sometimes but I made sure to provide for my children, even though I went without. We went to community events and I made sure that my children were involved. Being involved in the community was a good way to get free services for my children. I joined places where I didn't have to pay for my children to participate in day programs and summer camps. I liked them to participate in programs that focused on solidarity and togetherness. The only times I was away from my children were when I went away for treatment. Even while in treatment I made sure I saw them every weekend.

There's a lot of good and bad in welfare. Social assistance got me through. Since being on the system I really haven't done anything underhanded, like work on the side. The winter clothing and the back-to-school allowances really helped and I felt it when they were taken away. The baby bonus is also a big help. My oldest daughter is about to turn 18, which means that $350 will be coming off my cheque each month. It seems that I've always had timing on my side. At least sometimes, it works out that when something bad is about to happen something good happens too. At least that's the way I look at it. My daughter is comfortable with getting a part-time job and going to school. Once my daughter starts making her own money, there will be less coming out of my pocket. I have two more years before the next $350 comes off for my younger daughter, when I'll have stopped getting the baby bonus. Hopefully I'll be working by that time. It doesn't make it easy that the system stops these supports when kids are only 18—I would like to be able to provide more support to my daughters to make sure they go to college.

The other thing that worries me right now is that I am in co-op housing. What I like about co-op housing is that you are included in all of the decisions.

We go to meetings and decide whether the rent goes up or down. The government was involved when the co-op was set up. Once the government lease is up, which will be in two or three years, it will pull out of the co-op. The problem for me is that my rent is subsidized and the government is set to stop subsidies in three years. My neighbours aren't on subsidies and won't want their rent to go up to subsidize me. When the subsidies stop my rent will probably go up to $1000 per month. I hope I can afford it, but we'll just have to see how it goes. Again, I hope I'll be working in three years.

The one thing I am still working on is my anger. After getting clean I needed to get rid of the shame and guilt brought on by the things I had done while drinking and doing drugs. Some of the things I had done didn't reflect the person I was, but the addiction had brought out a type of person I could be. I was raised with morals and I was raised knowing how to do the right thing. Understanding that my disease caused this behaviour has brought me to a place of peace and serenity. Although I got rid of the shame and the guilt I still had a lot of anger. Often I would have outbursts with my kids. At one point one of my daughters said, "I don't know why you went to anger management—it doesn't seem to be working!" Kids can be a good reminder of what we need to keep working on!

When I came out of treatment I tried to change how things were done but my children resisted. My sponsor helped me to understand that I was the one who had to change, not them. My kids can push my buttons like nobody else. They are the only ones who can get me really angry. We are normally close and loving, but we get on each other's nerves too. They argue and call each other names. When things got heated I used to be the sort of person who would attack, following you around, getting in your face. I've had to learn how to step back. Relaxing, taking a deep breath and going for a walk are some of the techniques I am just learning. I have learned that I can't control my kids' actions but I can control my reaction. After an outburst we do come back together and say, "I'm sorry." It doesn't mean that they don't piss me off and it doesn't mean that I don't piss them off, but we come back together in the end. The three of us have been through a lot together.

Right now I'm just looking forward to my life. I'm usually very positive, and I know positivity has a lot to do with how my life is going. My daughters haven't had problems with drugs and alcohol. They are good-looking girls but they are not boy crazy. There haven't been any pregnancy scares. They do come and tell me things. We have very good communication. I have learned to turn things around for us. I had been living in fear but have learned so much about myself through recovery. One good thing about being in recovery is that it's like having a free psychiatrist. When I go to meetings I can sit down, analyze what's going on in my life, and talk about things that are important to me. It's freeing to know I can go to a meeting everyday and there are people there who are just like me. They understand what I am talking about and don't shake their heads asking, "Why did you do that? Why did you do that?" I now know that I have a disease and that it's something that I will have to take care of. It will never leave me, and I will die with it. I also know that I don't have to be a using addict. I can be a recovering addict, a loving mother, and a supportive ally.

Robin's Story

I was born in Toronto in the late 1960s, during the month of February. My mother is Algonquin First Nations/Irish, my father is Scottish. I have a sister who is 16 months older.

My parents were kind and loving toward my sister and me as best they knew how, resulting in a lot of love and a lot of neglect. My parents had volatile tempers toward each other, they simply could not get along, and both had issues with alcohol. There was a lot of fighting and yelling between them, so it was no surprise they were divorced before I was two. I can't recollect an amicable time between them; the only thing they seemed to see eye to eye on was how much they despised each other.

I grew up feeling torn between the two. My mother would tell me that my dad's support payments were always late and my dad would claim otherwise. Regardless of who was right, there are some things kids don't need to hear. But everyone learns by living.

A recollection I have of my mother and alcohol: I recall sitting in smoke-filled bars with my mom while she got drunk and I drank Shirley Temples. I'd mimic her while looking at pictures of all the pretty drinks on the paper place mat before me. When the bar closed I'd have to coax her to leave. Often she'd start yelling and I'd have to diffuse the situation. On our way home there were times she'd have to urinate outside because she wasn't going to make it home. I'd guide her down a lane and watch over her protectively. I was 11.

The next morning I'd be exhausted, but I'd still go to school. I hated being at school—it was a horrible place for me. It was not a place I felt safe to speak with anyone about my issues. No one questioned my lateness or the dark circles under my eyes. No one felt it worthwhile to explore my below-average grades. Rather I was judged by the students and by the teachers. I was labelled and eventually expelled. I never shared what I was going through and no one asked. I recognized early on that life was not always fair.

A recollection I have of my father and alcohol: My father often worked out of town, far away, and for extended periods. When he was in town my sister and I became excited. We missed him so much and would count the days until we'd see him. An arranged meeting place would be set up; it would always be away from our home to avoid any possibility of my parents crossing paths, usually the old Pape subway, which had "The World of Cheese" attached to it back then. My sister and I would pace back and forth on the sidewalk. Occasionally we'd stop, squint, shield our eyes from the glaring sun while straining to see if that car coming close was dad! But it wasn't . . . on average this went on for more than two hours. Eventually he'd show up and we'd happily jump into the car and tell him we loved him. I usually always smelled alcohol on his breath. My sister and I put up with it because he was our dad and we loved him. We also desperately needed the clothes he'd be buying us that day.

As an adult I'm able to recognize that both my parents had issues with alcohol. They both put my sister and I in danger many times because they could not control their drinking, it controlled them. I'm also aware they're regretful and wish things had been different. Understanding the past does not change it, but it helps me have a healthier future.

My maternal grandparents were wonderful. I loved to spend holidays and summers with them; they were absolutely the *Leave It to Beaver* type with my sister and me, our solid foundation. The grandmother I speak of is not biologically related to me; she is German and my grandfather's first wife whom he had three daughters with before he left her and met my biological grandmother, who was Aboriginal.

When my mother was three my grandfather went back to my German grandmother, whose own kids by then were all grown and no longer living at home. He asked that she take him back, along with his child, my mother. She did, and together they raised my mother.

The age gap between my mom and her siblings was vast; they could have been her parents. The family dynamics were messed up, out of sorts, in an era that was epitomized by the white middle-class nuclear family.

My Aboriginal grandmother, or òkomisan, went through a lot at a very young age. Diagnosed with tuberculosis at the age of eight she was placed in a sanatorium until she was 16. I can only imagine how terrifying and lonely that must have been for her. She was away from her family, culture, teaching, and ceremony. It is being looked into to see if she contracted TB from the residential school she attended. Upward of 150,000 Aboriginal, Inuit, and Metis children were removed from their communities and forced to go to Christian schools to be assimilated into Western European culture. TB ran rampant in these schools. As a young woman my òkomisan liked to have fun. I can't blame her, considering how the first part of her life unfolded. She became reliant on alcohol and as a result at times gave my mother vodka in her bottle to help her sleep. I don't believe she realized the harm it could potentially bring . . . it wasn't methodical. Unlike assimilation.

My mother had a caring heart when it came to people. She would often invite people to stay with us, believing she could give them a hand up. Most of the encounters were great. We had artists, actors, and singers all visit. My mom really believed in these people and felt exposing us to them would be beneficial and broaden our horizons. For the most part everyone was a positive influence on my sister and me with the exception of one woman.

She'd given birth to a son that was disabled due to active heroin use during pregnancy and lost custody of him. It killed her; pain and trauma were her life. She was sexually abused as a child and ended up molesting me. I was about 11 years old the first time I remember being inappropriately touched by her. I never told my mother until I was an adult—she was crushed and surprised, she'd suspected nothing.

Soon thereafter things changed for the better, my mom's partner moved in with us, and life suddenly became fun. There are some people who never bear biological children, but by all accounts, hands down are the best parents in the world; that was Kathleen to me.

I loved my mother's partner; she was my "other" mother, she was positive and made me happy. We had a nice place and nice things. I remember thinking, Wow! Now we have food in the fridge of all types, all the time. I was introduced to different cheeses and exotic vegetables. Shark meat, artichokes, and dandelion soup are some I remember. Life was healthier, a direct result of my mother and Kathleen taking care of my sister and me, pooling their resources together, and my mother trying not to drink.

I really liked the ballet, and Kathleen had friends who did as well, so she arranged to have a friend take me regularly. This meant a lot to me because I use to fall asleep at night listening to classical music while choreographing ballets in my head.

Kathleen also taught me about different forms of art as she herself was an artist. From Maxfield Parrish to Andy Warhol, abstracts and mosaics. This combined with all the paintings I witnessed being done by our Aboriginal visitors such as Simon Paul-Dene and John Turo cemented my love of art. I admired how Kathleen spoke out about abuses in society. She would not tolerate racism or homophobia; she was an organizer and an activist. She inspired people and made them laugh. Kathleen made me look up every word I couldn't spell in the dictionary before she'd discuss it with me. She was also the first person in my life to make me believe that one day I could go to university.

Around this time my mom made a drastic choice that proved to be one of the best she'd ever made and switched us from public school to an alternative school. Wandering Spirit Survival School was the first First Nations School in Toronto. Staff at the school were well respected in the community. Many were dedicated teachers and carriers of knowledge. They passed indigenous knowledge on and taught Aboriginal world views. They were paving the way back to our roots. This period of my life remains the fondest memories I have of attending school ever.

With my mom, Kathleen, and my sister life seemed to be going well. . . . Then my world changed again. When I was 12, I experienced a life-altering event. My mom and I went to pick up some takeout food from a restaurant.

While driving we were followed and accosted by three men in a car who made sexual gestures toward me with their fingers and tongues. I still remember thinking how odd it was and how gross. After all, these were grown men. We managed to get away from the men only to have them enter the restaurant we were at. They continued their intimidation, so my mom called the police, then Kathleen. She rushed down within minutes. As the men got up to leave they brushed up against my body; one of them pushed me up against a wall and grabbed me in private places. My mom and Kathleen followed the man who'd pushed me up against the wall; they didn't want him to get away with it.

As they followed him, he called them dykes, niggers, fags, one racist derogatory comment after another. Meanwhile I was alone at the restaurant by the phone waiting for the police; they never showed up, even after I called an additional three times. I ended up flagging a police car and they drove me in the direction of my mom and Kathleen. When I spotted them I saw they were following the man who had pushed and grabbed at me. He was walking quickly toward a group of police officers who had congregated on a corner. I told the officers, "That's the man!" Then I watched as he flashed something to the group of police and they let him walk on by. I was confused and couldn't believe they were letting him get away. It didn't make sense to me.

We went to the station to have a report written up, it took all night, and the police officer typing the report kept making mistakes or did not include pertinent information. My mom and her partner were adamant and demanded it be written properly. I don't feel the full scope of what happened was ever typed out. It turned out that all three of those men were Toronto police officers. The case took over four years in court. During this time my mom started her own business—a record store. She soon had to close it down because the alarm was mysteriously set off night after night. I was also watched and followed from school often. This form of intimidation made me paranoid. I could not concentrate, I became very depressed, and I developed an ulcer. I became afraid to go to school, and coupled with all the court dates I had to attend, I missed a lot of school. I failed grade seven and by age 13, I sought relief from the realities of my world by smoking pot.

Our lawyer was wonderful, he fought long and well. He's now a Supreme Court judge. When I was 16 years of age the courts finally made a ruling—all three plainclothes police officers were demoted to desk jobs.

I never got my day in court with the police officer who grabbed me, who grabbed a visibly young girl in her private parts; he committed suicide by hanging himself. Nor did I get a day in court with any of them. They were protected from the get-go. I wasn't. From age 11 to 17, I was sexually assaulted several times by strangers who were charged and found guilty in court and sentenced. For many years I wrestled with the whys: Why was I such a target? Such a victim? Why did adults target me? What did I do? Was I too nice? Today I now know that it had nothing to do with me. I was a child; it was all them. They were very sick.

The next bit of info I realize is quite personal. Understandably most people would not feel comfortable sharing it. I choose to share my story with the understanding that anyone who tries to treat me badly today, based on who I once was, is certainly not someone I need or someone I'll allow in my life today.

I left home at 16, I tried cocaine and crack, did some illegal things. By 17, I was a single parent who was also an uneducated, messed-up, traumatized, lonely teenager. I wanted a better life for my daughter, so I went back to school; things were good for a while. I found a really good alternative high school called Contact. It had supportive teachers and street workers who stuck by me through everything for years.

At 19, I met a man and fell in love. By 20, things were not as good, I was using cocaine again with him. At 21, I gave birth to our son. My relationship with my partner became codependent and abusive. I cut my mom out of my life as her addiction to alcohol had taken its toll on me. She had also ended her relationship with her partner Kathleen, whom I stayed in contact with. I was a functioning cocaine addict for many years. I always had food for the kids and a roof over our head. But cocaine ended up getting the better of me.

At 22, I was raising kids with an abusive partner, and had developed a cocaine addiction. In a desperate move to earn money in the hopes of using it to leave with my kids, I imported cocaine from Jamaica. This resulted in my arrest in Miami, Florida. I spent six months in the Dade County Jail, then was sentenced to three years in a maximum security penitentiary in Broward County, Florida.

My daughter's grandparents took custody of her and my son's grandparents of him after my partner proved he could not care for them. This was one of the most painful periods of my life. I faced all my worst fears: being away from my children, poisonous snakes, hurricanes, bee stings. All control was taken away, phone calls were limited, letters were pre-read, and no physical contact of any sort was allowed.

Prison in the States is not about rehabilitation. I came out knowing more about crime then when I went in. The US prison system exacerbates and breeds mental illness as well as reliance on the state.

The guards freely raped and beat the inmates with no repercussions. Pregnant women were taken out for abortions in secret at night. I witnessed many, many crimes by the guards. Women died because of their neglect, and the guards felt justified in their actions because we were just inmates to them, who deserved to be punished above and beyond what the judge had deemed sufficient. One memory I have is of a woman in her 60s in a push wheelchair having difficulty getting back into her dorm. It had to be 100 degrees out, and she appeared disorientated. The captain instructed us not to help her; he said she was faking her illness. All day long several times I passed by her, I desperately wanted to help, but I couldn't. She baked in the hot sun and begged us for help. This memory is etched so deep. I hate what she went through; it's not right. I knew that if I tried to help, the captain would put a stop to it, toss me in solitary confinement, and still leave her helpless. Everyone knew the captain would never let us help her. She died later on that night. The captain came to our dorm and told us we had better keep quiet . . . or else.

My first job in the pen paid me 13 cents an hour. I served food to the inmates; shifts were often 12–14 hours. My second job was groundskeeper. I picked up all the garbage and dumped the ashtrays. Although I was in the hot sun all day long, 12–14 hours, I liked it more than flipping hundreds of burgers over a huge, industrial, hot stovetop. My third job was working in the garden; this is where I was able to get veggies and herbs to add to my food, making life in the pen just a bit easier. We were not allowed to take any of the food we grew back to our dorm, so I ate raw turnip in the day and snuck chives back to the dorm in my work gloves when my shift was done.

The entire prison was so oppressive. It was ridiculously hot and dry. Red ants bit my feet all over. Bush fires in the everglades regularly sent black ash through the air. Lightning struck with extreme force and hurricanes touched down many times. I realized there was no real help, or protection, it was only an illusion.

Most of the women I met in prison had the worst kind of upbringing you could imagine. They lived the kind of lives that in no way nurtured them or prepared them for the world. I began to recognize the majority of women I was incarcerated with were raised in poverty. They had little education, experienced racism, and most had been raped at one time in their lives. Drugs, homelessness, and loss of children were common.

Prison is not a safe place in general, on many levels. One such unsafe place, right from the get go, was that upon arrival women were required to undergo a physical exam. Week after week I'd hear women express concern over their pap smear test results. They'd come back with irregular cells being found. Next they'd be told another procedure was needed to collect more tissue. It was very obvious that a disproportionately high amount of black and Hispanic women were going through this. Shortly thereafter . . . BAM! They'd lose their uterus. I started speaking with new prisoners about this and warning them—we called it the "uterine conspiracy." It seemed a crazy concept, but we knew it wasn't. I saw it for what it was, a form of government-regulated birth control, a sneaky form of eugenics, a way to ensure that this population would never again procreate. I started to relay my findings and fears via letters home and was quickly pulled in and interrogated for a full day. I was threatened and told that I had to keep my mouth shut or else. These threats came from the captain who let the woman die in the sun and from the scariest, meanest, most off-balance, female sergeant ever.

Trying to keep busy and utilize my time I took six months of classes and enjoyed encouraging everyone to give the classes a try. I wrote my GED exam and scored in the top 2%. They hung a photo of me in the education department of the prison—that has always seemed odd to me. I also completed a six-month drug rehabilitation program to deal with my dependency on cocaine. After serving my time I was sent back to Canada. While serving time I corresponded with a man back home named Bob. He wrote to many inmates and helped to keep spirits up. When I got home he found me housing, and my children were returned to me.

For over a year, things were good except . . . everything felt surreal. My senses were all off; they were still in prison mode. I was disassociated. I needed supports I didn't even know I needed. I went into prison a confused, messed-up person and came out at times worse, except that I wasn't using. The cocaine was but a symptom of my real issues.

Eventually my son's father found me, and he had been clean for nine months so I decided to give us another try—big mistake. We were way too co-dependent. I could not have a relationship with him without the cocaine and vice versa. What had previously taken me years to lose I lost in three months and also found myself pregnant. I had another child. Within two years, I lost all of my children. Alone, traumatized, addicted to cocaine with a man who was abusive, and my kids depending on me like never before, I called a rehab centre and went through a 21-day program. Once finished I packed up all my belongings and moved out with a female friend. I was done with the cocaine, the abuse, and him.

I did whatever I was asked to do by the Children's Aid Society (CAS). Random urine tests three times a week, anger management classes, parenting classes, relapse prevention, and more. My boy's father refused to do any classes and managed to give a non-existent address to the courts and CAS for years. Yet he was granted visits the same as I was. The CAS worker I had was the most negative, judgmental, passive aggressive, least supportive person I have ever met. The worker told my mother their intentions were to adopt my youngest son out. She also said that statistically I had pretty much zero chance of making it, that I'd be lucky to make a year off of cocaine. At this point my mother left her job and the province she resided in and moved to Toronto so she could help out in whatever way she was able. I will always be grateful to her for this—always.

I have nothing good to say about the CAS. They made every step of the way much more difficult; they were all about blaming and shaming. They did not work with me, they worked against me. I attribute the way I am today on myself, my creator, and a multitude of loving beautiful people that have come into my life. If the CAS had had it their way, my son would have been adopted out to strangers.

After jumping over many hurdles and really working on myself, my son was eventually returned to me. I also began the reconciliation process with my older kids; today, 10 years later, we are still working on our issues. They are my inspiration, my pride, and the loves of my life!

It's been 10 years now since I have touched cocaine. I know this was my downfall drug; I can never ever touch it again or I'll be in trouble. Three years after getting off cocaine I started working with the lone-mothers group. By doing so I found moral support and purpose. Helping others helped me.

Four years after getting off cocaine I did the bridging program at the University of Toronto. I have been attending part-time ever since. My major is Aboriginal studies, influenced largely by my years at the First Nations school. Next came my health: I made lifestyle changes and started to exercise, losing over 70 pounds. Six years after getting off cocaine I quit smoking cigarettes and began to meditate.

Seven years off cocaine I was hired to work as a relief counsellor at a woman's treatment centre. Then while still attending university I started college at night and studied addictions counselling.

Nine years off cocaine I was hired as a hepatitis C support worker at a community centre—it's a great job working with amazing people. It has been 10 years now, and I'm glad I made the choices I've made because for me there was no other way.

In terms of finding closure, I have tried a few ways. I found a law firm who took on my case from my childhood pro bono, but after realizing how difficult the information would be to find, in part because it was not stored on computer and because so much of it was missing, the firm backed out. If one day I have the finances to pay for my own lawyer I may pursue it again. So today closure comes in the form of knowing I did not deserve to be abused. I am learning to forgive so that I can let go and move forward. To me, forgiveness is not saying what was done to me was okay, or that I'll forget it. Forgiveness to me is releasing myself of resentments I may have, because they weigh me down like a ball and chain and keep me in a negative place. When I am able to forgive I move out of a dark place.

My eldest kids are both in their 20s now and doing amazing considering what they went through as kids. My daughter is almost finished university and my son is working in the food industry. Our relationship is strained but progressing. I love them so much, always.

Today I believe I am well on my way to becoming the person I was always meant to be before I was tampered with as a child. I'm no longer held down by judgmental pointed fingers chastising me. I don't just answer questions, I question the answers. I'm all for comforting the disturbed and disturbing the comfortable. I believe rocking the boat is always a great way to get people thinking and shifting.

Changing how I am in this world took a lot of courage and determination. I'm living proof that with the right types of supports, encouragement, and programs life often heads in a better direction. With daycare I can work, which allows me to eat healthy and nourish my brain, thus enabling my ability to succeed in university, which teaches me how to think critically and better understand the world around me. I consider myself lucky, because not everyone gets to go to university even though they should.

Chi Miigwetch to the Creator.

Emily's Story

Until I was seven I was under the care of my grandmother and grandfather in a small village in Eastern Europe. Even though my grandmother was 61 and had a serious heart condition, she began taking care of me after my mom divorced my father. I was only one and a half years old and that she took care of me is a very special part of my life. She really saved my life. I know just how important she was because much later in my life, when my mother was angry, she told me that she had thought about putting me up for adoption. That didn't happen—because my grandmother took care of me.

My mom was working in a city very close to the village where I grew up, and although she claimed to have visited me every week, I really don't remember her visits. The only memory I have of her visit is helping with laundry. As a child, I felt happy and free, and I keep the memory of these feelings with me as an adult. During this time I felt safe. My grandmother was loving and caring, and she never would have laid a hand on me. The whole village talked about how special she was; she never would have hit or hurt her kids or me.

Part of my childhood is very painful for me to talk about. The painful memories from this time in my life still affect me as an adult. Although I was happy and free when I was with my grandmother, and I was very close to her (she adored me and was very kind and taught me lots of things), I still felt like something or someone was missing. There was a void or an emptiness in me—maybe it was not having my own parents. Then, when I was ready to start school, when I turned seven, I went to live with my mom in the city where she worked. I was to live in a new apartment and to start school in grade 1. It was difficult for my mom and I to connect and bond with each other. I remember trying to please her to get her to give me attention.

I remember that in the first couple of years my mom put lots of effort into my education. Because of that, I was very good at school, both in grade 1 and grade 2. In my country, although education is very important, it is very difficult for kids to get an education. I tried my best and I was almost always the best in my class. One time, however, my mother went to a meeting with my teacher and she heard some remarks from a teacher about my work in school. I had made one mistake in a dictation—this was in grade 1 or 2. My mom came back very angry at me and she beat me, even though it was only one mistake. I missed one letter in spelling a word. My grandma came right away, the very next day, to stand up for me. She said to my mother, "Don't touch this child anymore." The message my grandmother gave to my mother was that she hadn't even raised me and cared for me so she sure didn't have the right to hit me.

From that point on, my mom did not do anything to me and we started to build our relationship in a good way. I was nine when my mom decided to remarry. She was pregnant and married the man who became my stepfather. Not long after the marriage, he became psychologically abusive and controlling. My sister was born when I was 10 years old. My stepfather continued to be abusive, and this affected me. I was worried all of the time; I was always scared and I felt that I could not talk freely. I was walking on eggshells. Although he didn't physically abuse me, I was stressed and I did not know what to expect or what might happen next—things were unpredictable. He emotionally abused my mom, and I was a witness. For one year, my mom spent her time at home caring for my baby sister, and after that she put her in daycare and started working.

I lived at home until I was 19, and after doing well in school and graduating from high school I went off by myself to a technical university in another city. I found the program difficult—many people drop out—but I finished and I was glad. This was a big achievement for me, I now recognize. At the time, however, I was very tired. I was overwhelmed with school work and with my emotions. I didn't care for myself very well. A year after I graduated I met my (now ex-)husband. At the time, I was depressed and anxious. I had low self-esteem despite my academic success. I was working at the time, and he and I got to know each other over the course of a month before we started dating, although I don't think I knew him well enough. Three or four months after we met, we started to live together. Now, I think that's too fast, and I wouldn't do it again. If I have another chance, I will take longer to get to know the person before moving in together.

At the time, however, it felt nice to have a romance. I fell in love with him and it felt good to show him off to other people. He presented himself well in the beginning, and seeing a man who was caring and helpful to women was a new thing for me. He was very physical with me—always hugging—so I thought that he was really in love with me. Now I see that this was a sign that he was a controlling person and did not have healthy boundaries. After I became pregnant with my first son I gradually began to recognize other signs of his controlling nature: he started to criticize my friends, my aunt, and my parents, and almost anyone I related to in my life.

When my first child, a boy, was born, my ex-husband was very happy and very proud to have a son. He was not involved much in our son's care. I was the main caregiver, and it was difficult for me to take care of my son on my own because we lived far away from our families and my son was very active. My husband was always busy, not at home, and had many excuses for working long hours.

His behaviour changed toward me at this time. He started criticizing my cooking, my style of dressing, and sometimes mocked my intellect. He did not directly call me names but insulted me subtly. I finally confronted him, "Why did you say that to me in front of those guests?" but he just claimed that he was joking. He tried to avoid the truth. We lived like that for several years before he started to push me to come to Canada, because his family and many of his relatives live here. Finally, after my second son was born he convinced me to come here. I wouldn't have recognized the abuse for what it was if I had stayed in my home country, because he never physically abused me. After moving to Canada, I was able to see that he was verbally and psychologically abusing me. I am still in counselling for this and I have learned a lot. After moving to Canada, he became even more abusive, becoming physically abusive (pushing and shoving in the apartment), and even more verbally abusive. I felt so isolated. His family and extended family were already in Canada, but I was alone without family support. He did not let me see people other than his family members. Any social events revolved solely around his family members. Even after finally making some friends in the area where we lived, he would not let me see them or talk to them. All I did was take care of my kids and spend all of my time with them and him.

When we first came to Canada my second child was two and a half years old or so, and my oldest son was eight. My husband's family began indirectly but strongly disapproving of me and the way I was raising my kids. They were even judgmental and critical toward my children. This gave my husband the confidence to become even more abusive toward me. The abuse became worse while we worked as the superintendents of a building. He never let me work in the office because he wanted to be in control of everything—especially me. My boss was happy with my work and so was I, but I couldn't even go down to the office—I had to do work from my apartment. If I picked up the phone, he was on the other side of the line in our office listening in on my conversations. Sometimes he even closed the line or shouted, "Don't talk with nobody!" while I was on the phone. It was things like that, 24-hour control. I can't explain it more clearly than that.

I managed to maintain one friendship from my home country, but even when she called, he would get on the other line and listen to our conversation. He would interrupt and start yelling to my friend, telling her, "Do not call my wife anymore."

Every day, I had to get the kids up and take them to school, feed them, help them with homework, take them where they needed to go. My husband didn't do anything—he was never happy; all he did was shout and complain. I was so very stressed at that time, and he kept making it worse. He would do things like wait until I had fallen asleep and then wake me up by shouting.

He would say, "Why are you asleep? We have to talk," and things like that. He wanted to restrict my knowledge about Canada and life here. I didn't know about shelters, or even abuse, until one day when I spoke with one of the tenants in the building who spoke Russian, and luckily I speak Russian. I was in a crisis situation when we started talking. I really didn't know what to do. I opened up to her and she told me that I was in an abusive situation. My English was limited at that time so she explained abuse using a dictionary.

My husband's behaviour worsened and he became more dangerous. He was even brainwashing my kids against me by saying things like, "women are nothing, they are garbage and your mom too." I don't know how or why I survived this situation. I started to feel very strongly that he was planning to take the kids from me. He started threatening me and at the same time he was having secret phone conversations with his brother. I began to think he was going to take my oldest son away, so in October 2005 I talked to a woman who was one of the tenants, and she helped me out. She advised me on my legal questions and over the course of two or three days I began to plan how my children and I would leave my husband. I decided that I would go to school and pick the children up there in a taxi and take them with me to a shelter. This was very difficult because my husband was watching me all the time. If I was on the first floor of the building, he would show up in the first-floor lobby. If he didn't see me in the apartment he would look for me and find me right away. I felt constant stress from being under his control. If I went to the mall to deposit cheques he would ask, "Where did you go?" "When did you get back?" He asked these kinds of questions either out of his own insecurity or to get a sense of whether or not I had someone helping me. I began to realize that I was really in a very dangerous and unsafe situation.

Soon after talking to the tenant, I was able to escape to a shelter with the kids. When the shelter heard my story they suggested that I lay charges against him because of his abusiveness toward me. He found me in the shelter and the police came to take him away. I decided not to lay charges—I just wanted a safe place for myself and my sons. Over the next three years, I dealt with the legal system—family, immigration, and criminal court—all at the same time. This was very stressful and took lots of energy and was very overwhelming for me and my kids. The positive thing is that over this time my English improved dramatically and I was able to communicate verbally my needs and concerns.

Even though for these three years, my sons and I stayed away from him, he continued to abuse us by trying to manipulate and control us. The second month after moving from the shelter to our own apartment, he found out where we lived and showed up in the schoolyard where the kids would play. I was with my youngest son, and he tried to abduct him. We reported the incident to the police and he was charged again. The police took our case very seriously and offered me the option of leaving the province or installing an alarm system in our apartment for a period of a year. We stayed and lived with the alarm system, but we were still living in constant fear for our life and our safety. This had a big impact on both my kids' mental health and mine. In 2008, my ex-husband was finally deported. I finally felt some relief from the constant feeling of not being safe. I finally felt like he was not around so he could not hurt us.

I learned a lot during the three years after I left my husband and before he was deported. My kids finally felt safe, but they had still been witnesses to years of abuse, and this affected them. My oldest son, who was 11 years old when we separated from his father, started acting out. My other son was five and a half when we separated, and it was becoming difficult for me to manage them. I was depressed as well, but with help from the shelter both my kids and I received counselling. We went to family court, and I received temporary custody from the first day on through the two-and-a-half-year battle for final custody. Despite everything he did to us, he still felt he could get custody of the children, and he wanted me to pay him support.

During the custody battle, I worked most closely with the children's lawyer, a social worker, and my lawyer. The children's lawyer was unhelpful and almost always unprepared. She was paid to attend all of the hearings, but she did very little work on our behalf. After talking with my sons she would twist their words when she repeated them in court. My sons told her that they did not want to see their father, but when the court date came, the lawyer said, "My position is that they have to see their father. The kids want to see their father." When I asked my sons about this, they said, "No, Mommy. This isn't true." Finally, my son decided to write a letter to present in court. He explained in his letter why he didn't want to see his father. This situation was harmful for my children—they should not have had to be involved in these court procedures.

Beyond that, after I had explained to the lawyers and the Office of the Children's Lawyer that it was very important not to release any information about where we were or where my kids were going to school, the children's law-yer was careless and mentioned my children's school in front of my husband and his lawyer during a meeting. The next day, he appeared on the playground with the plan to abduct my son. Because my ex-husband was in violation of a previous bail condition, he was arrested.

We were in a very, very unsafe situation. Even though we moved to a new place after having stayed for a long time in a shelter, one son stopped talking and the other son was feeling totally overwhelmed from all of the stress. I was also in the middle of family court and criminal court and immigration. We all suffered for a long time.

It is very hard for women who go through this kind of process to succeed without proper help. I was very lucky because I received a lot of help from the shelter and from the police. Despite that, my kids and I remained traumatized. Even six years after leaving my ex-husband we are traumatized, and we are still going through counselling and recovery. I hope one day we will all fully recover. I still have flashbacks and I can't believe all I have been through since December 2002. I can't imagine how we survived living with my ex-husband. Surviving after that was not easy either, because dealing with the legal system here is difficult.

I have recently finished dealing with immigration. We were accepted as refugee claimants for reasons of spousal abuse. This has not been an easy process. Although my case was expedited in 2006, it was postponed six times before June 2009. I had to prepare myself mentally and work through the process with my lawyer, who helped me a lot. My kids have been affected by this process as well, but since it has been finished, it has been like a new safe life for us. We are still struggling from the impact of our past, but taking life day by day in our road to recovery. We really appreciate the chance to live a safe life in Canada without having to struggle with abuse.

Catrina's Story

I was born in Central America and I came to Canada on my own in my late teens. Before I was born, my mom had a good job where she worked as a representative for different companies. She worked at promoting the companies, which meant things like going to parties and events to talk about the company. She had two children, my half-sister and half-brother, with her first husband. He owned a company but he didn't have a good relationship with the employees, and he was murdered right outside the door of their house. My mom was quite young, about 38, when she became a widow. Then she met my dad.

My mom had me when she was 42. It was not a planned pregnancy. My dad raped my mom. He used to drink a lot and would force my mom to do things that she didn't like. It was not easy for my mom. The children from her previous marriage didn't accept my dad. They didn't accept me either. My mom had to give up her career at some point to take care of me. We moved around a lot while we were living with my dad. He sold security items like extinguishers and bulletproof vests for the police. He would sell and install security cameras and then train people how to use them.

My dad gave the impression that he was the perfect guy. Everybody liked him. He had a good job, he made a good income, and he seemed honest. But he was not nice to my mom. He had a mistress and he was away a lot of the time. He had a previous family, so I was his 13th child. He was really abusive to my mom and he abused me sexually when I was a child. That really marks you. I think I was three or four the first time that I remember him abusing me. I have completely blocked the memories because they are too hard. I first told my mom about the abuse when I was about eight and she said, "No. No, it didn't happen." I have been exploring some of these issues in therapy here in Canada.

The day my dad left, I was seven years old. Even though my mom said that she left my dad, that is not how I remember it. I remember my dad saying, "Well, if you're not going to do what I want, then see you." He made sure to take everything with him. He left us without any money. He emptied my mom's bank account and he cashed all the insurance money.

After my parents separated, my mom and I went to live with my aunt, my mom's twin, for a while. When we had to leave our house I lost almost everything that I had—my clothes, my toys, and my dog. My dog was everything to me because he was a gift from my grandmother.

We had no money so we even had to ask my aunt and uncle to help us get to their place. Two of my cousins mistreated me. I became a Cinderella of sorts because the law in my family was that the small ones serve the older ones. So, I cleaned a lot and did all the dishes for six or seven people.

Two or three months after my dad left, my grandmother, my dad's mom, died. She was my best friend. I knew I was safe when I was at her house. She would share all her memories and her treasures with me. I have never met anyone as amazing as her. She left me the house in her will, but because it was in my name and I was underage, my dad sold it.

On top of everything else, after a few years my mom had a nervous break-down, which affected her physically as well and she was hospitalized. She was in her fifties, was having trouble getting work, and was desperate. She had some surgery and in the process lost some memory. She could recognize my brother and my sister but not me. When she saw me she'd ask, "Who are you?" It was pretty traumatic. While she was recovering I bounced from house to house. I went from one aunt's house to another aunt's house, to my sister's house, and to the neighbour's house. I moved around for four or five years until my mom was able to get on her feet again.

During some of those years I had to live with my 24-year-old sister. Living with her was like a punishment. She was really abusive and always beat me up. One time she ordered a pizza with mushrooms. I didn't like mushrooms so I took them off. It was probably the stupidest thing I could have done. My sister made me eat an entire can of mushrooms. Another time there was a big hole in the wall. Her boyfriend had made it trying to install the phone. Even though he told her it was his fault she still blamed me. If she didn't like my behaviour she would beat me up or not give me any dinner.

Sort of like my Dad, my sister gave the impression of being really nice, so many people didn't know what she was like. As people got to know her they distanced themselves from her. For a while, she taught at the same school that I attended. She was always keeping an eye on me and made me change schools a lot so I couldn't keep friends. It seemed that I was always saying goodbye to the people who were taking care of me. People who were not part of my family were the ones who really cared about me.

Thanks to one of my mother's brothers we were finally able to settle in a house when I was about 11. It was one of the first houses in the neighbour-hood. It was a really nice house. The one really annoying thing about the house was that the construction workers who were always around would often make remarks to my mom as she walked me home from school. That lasted about a year.

I got my period when I was 11 and my mom told everybody. It happened on the day we celebrate childhood back home so it was particularly embar-rassing and horrible. After that I started to develop really fast. I started wear-ing a bra when I was 12. People soon started making remarks to me. They are really sexist back home and don't hesitate to comment on how you look. Putting up with that kind of attention was hard.

Most of the time, my mom did not like my friends. I have a lot of gay friends because I feel I can hang out with them and they don't want to touch me. My mom hated that my friends were mostly gay. My family is quite prejudiced. They are prejudiced against people who have darker skin, which, when you think of it, was really stupid because a lot of us have darker skin. And they were very prejudiced against gay people.

People used to say that I was adopted, that I didn't belong to my family, because I was not afraid to speak my mind. For example, I was not afraid to tell people about what my dad did to me, whether they liked it or not. I was about 15 when my mom finally started to believe me about the abuse. She only started to believe me when my siblings told her about other things my dad had done. My sister disclosed that my dad had tried to get close to her and had made pretty disrespectful remarks. My mom also found out that my brother had had a confrontation with my dad because of the way my dad treated my mom.

Growing up was not easy. Although I didn't have a nice childhood there were a few good things. A couple of summers I went with my aunt to another region where she had a big house. There were lots of kids my age there. Those summers were heaven. My aunt, who was my mother's identical twin, also helped me out at school. Most of my family was successful which meant that I had to succeed in school. If I were to get three A's and a B they would ask, "Why the B?" If I got a low mark my mother's twin would pretend she was my mother and advocate for me to improve the mark. This actually worked for a few years. It was only at my graduation, which they both attended, that the school realized they were twins.

My mom and her sister looked exactly alike. They had the same hairstyle and bought their clothes in the same place. The only difference was that my aunt chose a good guy and my mom, unfortunately, chose two bad guys. My uncle, my aunt's husband, treated me like his little jewel. He didn't disrespect me at any time. He was like a father to me. He was the one who took care of me when I was sick. He went to my presentations at school. He was there if I needed somebody to talk to. He was also the one that later helped me come to Canada. So I have a really, really deep appreciation for him. Of course his affections came with a price and made my cousins very jealous of me.

Things got better for me in high school. I started working and became more independent. I needed to work so I could pay for my high school, otherwise, I couldn't have gone. I was interested in doing drama or working in radio. I was very interested in studying and travelling—whatever would take me out of the town I lived in. I tried to get out of town to study many times but I never got the permission. I saw my friends travelling to other places to study while I was stuck where I was. Once I had an opportunity to travel to the US for camp but my mother had to turn it down because she couldn't find my dad to get his signature for my passport. Most official documents require a signature from both parents in my country, unless one parent has full custody. Not having my father's signature even caused a problem went I went to enrol in school. I missed a lot of opportunities that could have changed my life if only my dad had left something saying that my mother had custody of me.

While I was still in high school my mom was diagnosed with Hodgkin's, which is a type of cancer. The doctor told us to make arrangements because she only had one month left. It was the craziest thing. Everybody started to prepare for the funeral. They started to talk about who would take care of me because I was not 18 yet. My family told me to stop studying and take care of my mom. I didn't want to leave school, so I was considered a bad daughter. My mom is still alive. She was diagnosed nine or ten years ago and survived against all odds.

When I was 14 and 15, I had a nice body. I was sort of skinny but with a lot of curves, which drew a lot of unwanted attention. I tried to wear looser clothes but there was not much that you can hide when you have to wear a school uniform. I was also a tomboy and climbed trees while wearing my uniform skirt. That drew even more attention, which was not to my advantage. I got asked out a lot but I said no. My mom had to approve the guys that I really wanted to go out with. She wanted me to marry a foreigner with blue eyes and would introduce me to people she knew through work.

I met my daughter's father when I was 16 and still in high school. He was 18 and we met through a friend. He gave the same sort of first impression as my dad had. He was very enchanting and everybody loved him. His family welcomed me. He was going to school and studying to be a doctor. My goodness, he was my prince.

When I first went to his house it was always a mess, which I thought was weird. His dad was a retired military colonel and an alcoholic. He didn't seem normal to me. I was told that he had some mental health issues after he finished his service. I hoped it wasn't hereditary. His mom was a nurse. When I first met his parents I thought they were a nice family and that maybe this was the man I was going to marry. Marriage meant I would get out of my house. As I got to know them I realized that they had a lot of issues.

We started dating. At some point we were alone at my house. I think my mom was at the hospital for treatment. We were watching a nice, romantic movie, *Titanic* or something like that, when he started going beyond what I accepted. Much later my psychologists helped me put a name to it, which is date rape. At the time I didn't label it as rape. But I told him that it was really disrespectful because I didn't want to go all the way. Some touching was nice but all the way not so nice. I wanted him to keep his space, but he didn't, and I ended up pregnant.

I was shocked when the doctor told me that I was pregnant. It was worse when I got home. The secretary at the clinic knew my sister and told her the results. My sister told my mom. When I got home my mother seriously beat me up. She slapped me, threw me to the floor, and stepped on my belly. It was all I could do to try to get her off me. She wanted me to have an abortion but that was not an option for me. I thought that the situation wasn't the baby's fault. I felt strongly about this and had even been in the anti-abortion club at school.

My boyfriend and I did not know what to do. I wanted to tell somebody what he had done, but he convinced me that no one would believe me because people saw us together all the time. He also said that my mom was kicking me out and they were going to make me have an abortion because I was under-age. I was 16, almost 17. He suggested that we leave and go to another city. I figured we might as well move. My mom was kicking me out and my aunt didn't want to talk to me. Nobody else in my family had opened their door to me. In their eyes it was the worst thing to ever happen in my family. They called me a whore and other names. It didn't matter that I was a victim. They focused on what I had done, being pregnant, underage, and not married.

My boyfriend and I left and went to a city where we didn't know anybody. The first night we slept in the bus station because we didn't have money for anything else. I had some money saved from my part-time job. We rented a hotel room for a couple days and then moved to a little room. The room was not a place I would have chosen to live. The people in the area were quite scary. We only had one key, which meant that I would be locked in the room all day long. My boyfriend didn't want me to socialize with anyone.

My boyfriend had worked before we moved. Once we moved he wanted me to apply for a job but I refused. I told him, "I'm pregnant and not because I wanted to be. Nobody is going to hire me because I am underage and preg-nant." It took me a couple of hours of yelling that I wasn't going to work to convince him, but I stood my ground. So he found a job. I later found out he had an affair with his supervisor. When he was working I was alone, isolated in the room we rented. We didn't really have many things. I soon started to grow out of my clothes. I couldn't even call my mother because we didn't have the money for the long-distance costs. I started to become quite frustrated as well as scared and lonely.

Once my boyfriend got a job, because he was the one bringing home the food, it became whatever he said goes. He would bring home whatever food he wanted or whatever he could afford. I remember eating eggs for three months. Every meal would be egg with this and egg with that. I had to do the laundry by hand. The clotheslines were on the roof, so I had to carry heavy buckets of wet clothes up and down the stairs. Once my belly got bigger that became quite scary, but I had no choice. There was one bathroom for all eight rooms in the building. Having to share one bathroom, especially being pregnant, was impossible. I was not taking proper care of myself during this time because my boyfriend was scared that I would talk to a doctor on my own. He might take me to the doctor once a month or so, if and when it was convenient for him.

I couldn't go out if my boyfriend wasn't at home. At one point a friend tracked me down but I wasn't allowed to see him. My boyfriend yelled at me, hit me, and accused me of cheating on him with this friend. I think that this was our first real confrontation. From then on I could tell when he was going to be upset. He got very upset if I spoke my mind. He was used to his mother doing everything his father said and he expected exactly the same from me. He would hit me if I didn't clean because, being pregnant, I'd been throwing up all day. He also hit me if I told him that I wanted to be able to see other people while he was at work. I wanted to have a father for my baby and hoped that he was going to change. As things went on he started hitting me and shouting at me more often. He did change, not for the better, but for the worse.

After a while we went back to our home city. His parents had convinced my mother to start talking to me. After visiting with my mom, who needed some time to think about things, we went back to his parents' house. As soon as we got to his parents' house his mom and dad went in the bedroom. His dad started hitting his mother. We could hear her screams as he beat her. I think his mom had disclosed something to my mom and his dad was upset.

It was a wake-up call for me to see where my boyfriend's behaviour had come from. Just mentioning his mom's beating to him got me in more trouble. He did not hit me while we were at his parents' house but he would give me a look that meant, "You better shut up or you know what is going to happen to you." For the entire time I stayed with his parents I wasn't allowed to be alone. If I wanted to go anywhere, even just down the street, I had to be with somebody in his family. It was worse than being in prison.

Finally, I left with just what I had on me and took a taxicab to my mom's. My mom felt she had no choice but to take me back. After I left my boyfriend, his parents made my life hell. They knocked at our door every day saying, "Come back, come back." He promised that he wouldn't shout anymore, that he wouldn't hit anymore, and that he'd find a better job.

The baby came two weeks before she was expected. When I arrived at the hospital his mom was already there. It took me almost half an hour to convince hospital staff that the baby was coming right then—until my water broke in front of them. It was a holiday so there were only student doctors at the hospital. I told them that my obstetrician had already told me I would have to have a C-section. Still, they kept me in labour until they decided to do an emergency C-section. Then they almost killed me because the anaesthesiologist did not do his job well. My brother told me later that the doctor had told my family that they had to choose between the baby and me. My brother almost hit the doctor and said, "Listen, I want both of them alive!" Thank God I made it alive.

I lost all sense as soon as they took my baby out. The next thing I knew I was in a room with seven other women and there were babies crying. My mom could not afford to get me a private room and she could not take me home because I had had the C-section. At one point my mom left to get me something decent to eat and I had gone for a shower. When I got back to my bed my boyfriend's mom stormed in and grabbed my baby. I said it was okay for her to see her granddaughter but that I wanted my baby back. She responded, "No, I am taking it." At some point my mom came back and got into a physical confrontation with her. The poor baby just kept going back and forth from hand to hand.

The police were nowhere to be found. It just so happened that the security guy from the hospital was the cousin of my boyfriend's mother. It was even harder to get help because my boyfriend's mother was a nurse and she was in uniform and said she was taking the baby for a checkup. At some point some of the other mothers in the room helped remove his mother. We waited until she left the hospital and then, even though it had only been a day and a half since I had the C-section, my mom and I took the baby and left. We went out the back door and went to my aunt's house to hide. I was in hiding for six or seven months. I couldn't go out at all and even the doctor had to come to us.

Things got really complicated because I was underage and I did not have any legal rights over the baby. We had to register my daughter almost in secret. We arrived really early at the registration office to have her footprints taken. A lawyer had to explain why my dad was not there.

Both my boyfriend's family and my family made my life hell until I came to Canada. His mom's behaviour scared the hell out of me. I was told that not only did she have everything for a baby, including a crib in her room, but she had bought a doll that imitated a baby. I had to move from job to job and I had to move my daughter from daycare to daycare because his family would find us. If members of my family, except my mom, knew where we were, they would tell someone who in turn told his family. My family told me I should save myself the trouble and give my daughter up for adoption.

No matter how many times we moved, and the instability we suffered, my daughter's father would find us. I knew he kept a gun in his car. One time I returned from grocery shopping and I took the baby into my mother's house to sleep on the sofa. When I came back out to get more of the groceries he was there with a gun. He told me that I had to return to him or he'd kill me.

I said, "Okay, I'll do it. Just let me go grab the baby." He trusted me to go back inside because he knew I was afraid of him. Inside I grabbed my bag, grabbed my daughter, and escaped through the window. I went into the neighbours' backyard and asked them to call the police. They didn't think the police could help but they did take us to the bus station. My cousins were able to pick us up from there and take us to their house to hide. At that point I'd lost everything. I couldn't return to work or to the house where I was living. My cousins were the ones who really helped me. They kept me in hiding and sent me some of my stuff. They rallied to get us some money and kept providing things for my daughter and me until we came to Canada.

A friend of mine told me she had a cousin living in Canada. By this time I had turned 18 and could finally get my passport. Of course it was more complicated to get my daughter's passport because we didn't have her father's signature. The process was difficult and expensive but we got it.

When we arrived in Canada we didn't know anybody other than my friend's cousin, and we didn't even really know her. We went to stay at her house but after the second week she told me couldn't help anymore and that I should go find a shelter. I figured that if the shelters here were like shelters at home, I would rather live on the street. After we left her house I rented a room. We only stayed there about a week. During that time someone stole money from me and the guy in the next room kept bringing girls back for sex. So I was afraid. I went to St. Christopher House and I asked if anybody spoke Spanish. I told them that I needed help, and they helped me to find a shelter. And, thank God, once we moved into the shelter things started to get a little bit better.

I had come here as a visitor. I couldn't apply for refugee status right away because I was afraid and didn't know how to do it. Also, I had very little English. When I arrived in Canada I couldn't understand a word. Once I was at the shelter I was able to start the immigration process. Eventually I was granted refugee status based on the abuse I'd suffered by my father and the father of my daughter. It was a long, painful process. I did not have my refugee hearing until after my second child was born. A lot of the delay was caused by the fact I didn't speak English and I had a hard time filling out my personal information form. The first lawyer who transcribed my personal history did a terrible job so I had to get a new lawyer and fill out the form again. I had to tell my entire story detail by detail and gather evidence that was quite difficult to come by. Sometimes I had to choose between groceries and paying the lawyer, so we relied on food banks a lot during this process. At the hearing the judge made me talk about a lot of things that I didn't want to mention. I begged the court, saying that I didn't want my children to go through the same hell that I had gone through back home. Our refugee claim was granted and after a few years we got permanent residence status. The process was really painful because I had to repeat everything twice. By the end I felt like, "Just finish with me and get over it. How many times do I have to tell you that this happened?"

Around the time I moved into the shelter I met the father of my second child. I was quite vulnerable and scared and he was good to me. He was understanding and said he would help me. Then I got pregnant and he said, "Oh. Good luck." He disappeared, and welfare and I both had a hard time tracking him down. When I was pregnant I had to study English even harder because there was nobody to advocate for me. I didn't see the father of my second child again until I bumped into him at the mall when his baby was three months old. He still didn't believe the baby was his, but he came to see us a few times. Soon afterwards he told me he was being deported. I don't know where he is now but I have some limited contact with his mother.

After a while, I moved out of the shelter, got child care, and went back to finish high school. I had started high school pregnant and I finished high school pregnant. I studied really hard and also worked. At the time I was on welfare so whatever I earned in my part-time work they took, which was really frustrating. It seemed that the only point of working was to get Canadian experience.

While I was still pregnant I met a lady through the community centre who said she didn't have any grandchildren so she would like to adopt me and the baby that was coming. She was really supportive and still is. She helped me get things for the baby and she helped me start going to prenatal programs. One day she invited me to her house and I met her son. He is about 18 years older than me. We started going out and got into a relationship. Things were going fine and everybody was happy. I was not planning to get pregnant, but that's how I ended up. He and his family welcomed my baby, which made me feel quite good. He did not want to get married, and thank God we didn't because I later learned that he has mental health issues. No one told me he had been depressed for many years. It didn't really click for me why, at his age, he was still living with his parents. I didn't know he was growing and smoking marijuana. The day that I told him that I was pregnant he quit his job, rented an apartment and started a grow op.

We moved in together two months before the baby was born. For the most part we were happy. He liked the children and the children liked him, although my oldest daughter didn't quite accept him. Neither of us had a job at this point. I was supposed to be in bed because the pregnancy was a high risk, but that wasn't really possible because I discovered that he was really lazy. He liked to have things clean and tidy but left things everywhere and refused to pick up after himself. He would also smoke in the house and I'd have to tell him to go onto the balcony because of the children.

Things started to get difficult. After the baby was born I had postpartum depression. I was really close to getting postpartum psychosis. The medicine did not work. It made me feel more suicidal so I decided to stop taking it. Children's Aid had to get involved. They got involved the first time when they learned that he was expected in court on marijuana charges. They started keeping a really close eye on us and would be at our place at least once a week.

I finally had to leave him because he started to get really paranoid. He would play around with taking his medicine which was not good for somebody who has depression. He would be paranoid, get too anxious, or sleep all day. He started to show that he was not really responsible. Many times the daycare called me to say that no one had picked up the kids. He was supposed to have picked them up but he was sleeping instead. He also started to become really abusive. He told me that I was "just an immigrant and don't know anything." I hadn't known about the racist part of him before. He didn't hurt me but he threatened to. He told me many times, "If the kids weren't here I would beat you up."

The day that I left him I had to call his parents for help. He wouldn't let me out the door and threatened that if I left he would kill himself or that I wouldn't see the kids again. Once his parents came I was able to get out and went to stay with a friend. Even his parents stayed at a hotel that night because they were afraid of him.

The abuse continued when, a month later, he assaulted his mom and me when we were picking the kids up at school. He pushed his mom and he pushed me and threatened to hurt me. Fortunately the kids were still inside the daycare. He was going through a real mental breakdown. He left messages that he would hurt my daughter and that he never wanted the baby we had together. I had to go into hiding. I could not believe this was happening again. I came to this country to escape abuse! So thank God we were able to get a restraining order. Children's Aid intervened and they now watch that he doesn't step out of line. I feel backed up by the police here and know that if he threatens me again I could call for another restraining order.

His family was supporting us. They have been nice. His dad passed away recently. We are missing him a lot. His dad would sometimes intervene so there wouldn't be a fight. His dad was really supportive of the children. My daughter particularly misses him because he paid the same kind of attention to her that my uncle did to me. So now my children don't have any grandfathers. Earlier this year I found out that my father died. In his last words he had the nerve to say that he forgave us all for what we did to him. Thank God he's dead and won't do any damage to anyone else.

I feel sad that my children don't have a grandfather because none of the men I have chosen in my life has been the right one. After three children with three different fathers I think I am done with men for a while. I just want to focus on the children and myself. I'm also scared that somebody might try to abuse my oldest daughter or any of my children. I'm very overprotective. Even though my children are really small they know what is a good touch and what is a bad touch. Still, I monitor it all the time. My daughter is upset with me because we had to leave our country and she believes that she needs her father. I don't have the guts to tell her what her father did to me.

As a result of how I grew up, I had a deep desire to please everyone and to be accepted. Only now, at 28, am I learning to be assertive and say what I want and don't want. After all my experiences I believe I am wiser and a little bit more careful. I am also starting to have respect for myself and see myself as a human being who is going to make mistakes but who also has the strength to overcome them and be a good mother.

Lucy's Story

I am single parent, not really by choice, but I had to leave a violent husband. It was the hardest thing for me to do, because I come from another culture. Coming from Africa, we are taught that you are supposed to stay with your husband. It doesn't matter what happened. Your family is supposed to be this—a mom, a dad, and children. So when I came to Canada, I was really surprised to see how many people had what I called, in those days, broken homes. But then it happened to me, and the biggest difference between the country where I came from and here is that I had a choice. I did not have to stay in a violent marriage. It took me forever to leave that marriage. But when it started affecting my children, it gave me strength to leave. It was hard because I don't really have family here.

I lived in the countryside for about seven years, but most of my childhood was in a big city. We are seven children, and I was the first. My dad was a businessman. He still is a businessman, actually. He runs a corner store. I guess it would be called a corner store in Canada, but back home we call it a general store. I had no social life—my life was school and the store. I worked at my dad's store from an early age. It's a family business, so being the first born, that was my life. At age 10, I started working at the store. By the time I was a teenager I would be left at the store by myself sometimes. Sometimes there was one employee, but I would be handling the cash. We did not have a cash register, so I had to do everything. That is one of the reasons I really love math. We had no calculators or cash machines and you obviously did not want to lose money. So that was a really good experience and my favourite subject was math.

All seven of us are really close in age—maybe a year and a half between us. Being the first born, I was the boss. The second eldest in the family is a brother and there were lots of fights. It gave me a sense of responsibility because when all my brothers and sisters were out there playing or learning how to braid hair or things like that, I was working at the store. In a sense I thought I was hated the most because I thought my parents only loved my brothers and sisters. Now when I look back I don't look at it that way. I was close to my brothers and sisters, especially the ones that are close to my age. My closest sister is one of the younger children and now lives in England. When she was a baby, I used to take care of her. I haven't seen her in almost 20 years, but we talk on the phone. She has been in England for about 15 years. When I came to Canada we would talk on the phone and email each other. Raising kids in a foreign country, we have that in common, so we have become very close. My other siblings are all back home and it's hard to communicate with them. One of my brothers passed away, which was really sad because we were really close, but now I am in touch with his children through Facebook.

My mom and dad both ran the store. My dad started from nothing, really, really nothing—no education. He just worked really hard. One of the things that my parents instilled in me was the value of education. We all believed and still believe that education is the only way out of poverty. At first we were really poor and then with the store we could get food from the store, and things got better. My parents really instilled how important education was even though they weren't educated themselves. In my country, it's not a given that you go to school; you need to know somebody or have a lot of money. We didn't have that really, but my dad would do whatever it took. We all did standard seven, and once you did that you went to high school. Everybody in the country does the exam at the same time. It was a really big deal. Luckily, in my case, when I did my exam, I did really well and got accepted into a really good all-girls secondary school. My dad was really proud. I remember him taking me to buy a uniform. It was just so wonderful. I was really excited. Most people if they didn't pass very well had to pay a lot of money to get into a private school. In my country, private schooling is not a good thing. Going to a private school means you did not do well enough to be in a good government public school. It was easier for my parents that I got accepted because they did not have to work extra to find a good school.

Even when I was 11 or 12 I had no social life. I would go from school to my dad's store. I did my homework there. I was able to make friends, but I had no time to visit with them. School was a whole day thing—you weren't even allowed to go out for lunch. When school was over, which was usually around 4 or 5, I would go straight to the store. It was a long day, oh my.

I really liked sciences; I liked math and science especially. I was in this class and we were learning how to sew—oh, I hated it so much! And next to this class was the physics lab. Physics was my favourite subject and sometimes I would sneak into the physics lab and think this is torture, why do I have to be in sewing. Now I wish I had paid attention to the sewing so that I could sew some of my kids' clothes! Things have changed now in my country, but in those days you had to do history and other subjects and they all had to count toward A-levels. I didn't do very well in geography, history, sewing, and cookery. Even though I did really well in science, those other subjects affected my marks. Even if you are like an A student in some subjects, they look at all your marks and that really affected me because I really wanted to go to a good school. So, I went to a college and took building science, the closest I could get to engineering. When I went to this school, I was the only girl in the

Building Department. This was a boarding college and it was really wonderful. At one point, they took the top eight students in this college and eight students from a community college in Toronto and they did an exchange. It had something to do with Canada World Youth. Luckily I was one of the top eight students and I was able to come here and that was my first taste of anything other than country life. I had dreamed that there was something more out there. In those days, everybody wanted to go to America—people's dream was to go to America. Even my dream was to go to America, but the exchange was with Canada and I was very excited to be able to go.

I had been warned that it was cold, but I thought how cold could it be? It was January 1986, one of the coldest Januarys. They had given me a coat and I thought this really cannot be so bad, there is no way. So I refused to wear that coat. My uncle had also given me a coat, the biggest coat he could get in a warm country. I decided to wear my uncle's coat and not wear the other big coat. When I stepped outside, I felt like I had stepped on a live wire and been shocked. That is what I felt—my bones were cold, I was so shocked. So, I stepped back inside and got the other coat. They said it was very cold, so I thought it was like a very cold day back home, like 15 degrees.

I came here and we stayed four months. Everybody was placed with a family. We slept in their house, but during the day we met with the exchange people, we did volunteer work, and we went to school at the college. I volunteered at a woman's shelter and I remember thinking, Wow, you mean there is poverty in Canada? I couldn't believe that there was poverty here; it was quite a shock. Even when I went back home and I was telling people, they couldn't believe it. People back home don't really believe there can be poverty in Canada.

After the exchange program was over and I went back, my counterpart from the exchange program came to my country. She lived with another family because I went to a boarding college. The exchange program was important for me and at the end of it, my mind was made up, I wanted to come to Canada. I finished the building technology program. After that I worked, but you almost had to literally sleep with your boss to get a good job, to stay working. It was 1987 and it was bad economic times, and if women had a job it was like they were taking a job from a man. I actually got assaulted by a man at work because I was his boss. I remember he just assaulted me; he beat me up so badly. Some of the other workers were cheering him on and some others took him off me. This was a period when I thought I would rather not go to work, it was so horrible. I thought about going to work in my dad's business. But I didn't really want to do that, I was grown up, I was trained and educated, I didn't want to just live at home. It was really tough for any woman. So I just kept thinking I want to go to Canada.

We were Christian but in my culture, there were many Muslims. I remember one of my Muslim friends, she was so smart, she was one of the top students, but when she finished school she got married to a man she didn't know. I felt so sorry for her and I remember talking to her about it and she was crying. In a way for us, it was like wow, growing up was freedom. However, culturally this wasn't really true—here was this smart woman being forced to marry someone she didn't know and I was being told that I was taking a job from a man—and even being beaten up for it.

Being assaulted was not a good experience. It took my dad having to pay the cops off to get this guy. This experience made me feel that this was not the place for me. I came back to Canada as a visitor and I stayed for almost a year. I helped the family I was staying with and went to school part-time. This was not what I really wanted either, so I went back home. My dad is a wise man, and before I left he said, "Remember you have a home here." While I was in Canada there was a guy that was taking advantage of me and I didn't really know how to deal with it. I was all alone in a strange culture and so I thought about how my dad told me I would always have a home, so I realized that I didn't have to put up with this. So, I went back to my country and moved back home. I'm not sure if it has changed now, but at that time in my culture, unless a woman was married she was like a child, still under her parents' care.

I still really wanted to come back to Canada, so I applied to come to college. They told me that I couldn't come to university because I did my high school in another country. So I applied to whoever would take me, so I could get a visa. I was in my early 20s and I came back as a business student. I went back to the same community college I had been at for the exchange because I already had a history there and it was quite familiar. It was tough because my parents were paying for my school and it was very expensive. They actually had like a fundraiser. Neighbours and friends donated money for me to come to Canada. In those days, visa students were not allowed to work. Given that I was a girl, people were telling my father that he shouldn't be wasting his money on a girl. Luckily my dad did not think that way. Among my siblings, the girls are the ones that have gone on in education. My sister is a social worker and she is doing her master's in international social work. My other sister is a teacher back home. My brothers . . . there are so many problems back home and boys . . . when they get frustrated they drink a lot, so it is actually the women in our family that are more successful.

My mom—I felt as if she did not care much about me, but I realize now when I look back that this wasn't really true. She had seven children. I am the eldest and she had to take care of the others. I was really close to my dad and I would be at the store all the time. She knew I was being cared for by my dad and she had no extra time for anyone who didn't need it.

It was a pretty good childhood, particularly after the age of 10. Before that, there had been abuse from relatives. My parents didn't know anything about it because you didn't tell your parents about these things. I remember I would have been five or six. What would happen was that we lived in the country for a little less than 10 years and whenever my mom was going to have another child, I would be sent to stay with these relatives. They abused me. They were distant cousins, two brothers. It is so sad—it affected me in so many ways. I remember that when I first went to school there was one teacher who paid attention to me without wanting sexual favours—all I had to do was be a good student. In a way it seemed so easy—I was a good student, so that was something I could do. I used to think abuse is what happens to all girls. It was a terrible feeling. I told no one—one of the guys said if I told, they would kill my mom. So I couldn't tell, I had to protect my mom. I am actually right now getting some counselling about that. At least I can protect my kids so that this does not happen to them—still, I find there are some thoughts that I need to talk about. I feel like my mom didn't protect me. I felt like, why did my mom leave me with these people? One of the people I was left with had actually been in jail for rape. I don't really want to get into it; it is still painful and I am dealing with it now. So, the reason we moved is so we could all help in the business but for me this was like—ahh, I am away from these guys and I am saved.

When I moved to Canada, I was living near the college, renting a place with a couple of people. Financially, it was really tough. I had to do some babysitting and I took advantage of my math knowledge and would tutor people. It was still hard because school fees were so high and my parents could not afford to send money. At college, I was doing civil engineering technology but because I wasn't allowed to work, it was impossible for me to pay fees and so it was impossible for me to continue to go to school. I was also trying to change my status, but I didn't want to go back home, so I went to Atlanta and from there I applied and got landed immigrant status, but it was still quite tough to get work. I worked with this company doing office work, but the boss was really taking advantage of me again and I thought wow—even in Canada. I also did babysitting, but this was the only job I could get.

I met my husband here in Canada. I was babysitting and took the kids to a basketball after-school program. He was teaching basketball and that is how we got to know each other. I was totally smitten and so was he, so we got serious and were married, but I somehow knew there was something that was not right with him. He told me about his childhood—he had a bad, bad childhood. He is Canadian, many generations. He grew up in Halifax. It was quite tough for a Black person growing up in Nova Scotia. His family came generations ago from America, escaping slavery. So, we all have baggage and I thought, I am going to save this man.

So, we got married and the fact that this guy was so in love with me, it was flattering. However, it was too much, he was very controlling. There was a time I couldn't even call friends. It got very bad and I was feeling so trapped. First of all my parents did not approve of me marrying a foreigner, I was supposed to be marrying a nice man from back home, so I didn't have my parents' blessings and it's not like I could turn to them for help, or so I thought. I was very isolated because I had lost all my friends because my husband wouldn't let me see them. By now my son was born but I was still working. Even at my job, he would call and if I didn't answer the phone it would be like, where were you and that kind of thing. A couple of times I had to work overtime because he wasn't working, so I would leave the baby home with him and if I was late from work, I would get a beating. It was so hard, this never ends, it's the same thing. It was really bad, but I still wanted this marriage to work. I understood what he had gone through and I was going to help him.

When he started hitting me when I had my son in my arms, I started thinking that this was getting too bad to let it continue. I began to realize that I couldn't save him because he had grown up seeing his mom beat up and I don't think he really knew what else to do with his feelings. It was going to be a cycle and I could not watch my son go through this. It was so hard because I thought, "Where am I going to go? I am here all alone." Then I found out I was pregnant and so it made me stay longer with my husband. But I am so glad I was pregnant, because my daughter is the best thing that ever happened to me. One time I was ready to go to a shelter, but I didn't, and then something good happened. I had applied to a co-op housing project that was being built. When I applied to it they asked me if I wanted to be a board member and I told them I wouldn't know what to do, but they said, "Don't worry, we will teach you." So I went and I used to have big fights with my husband about going. They were so nice; I used to take my kids with me. Then one day while I was there, the president of the co-op board noticed that something was wrong with me. She did not come out directly and say she knew what was going on, but she said, "You know, if you are in an abusive relationship, you don't have to stay, we give priority to women in abusive relationships." So, I started to realize how bad the abuse had gotten and I thought either I would go to a shelter or I would go to the co-op. So I went to the co-op and that was the best thing that ever happened.

You have this person who is your partner and you don't want to break it apart—it's like you're going to be alone. And my kids are very young. My daughter was still nursing when I left. So it was really, really hard. But when my husband started hitting me when I had my son in my arms, I just thought, "Okay, this has got to stop." Partly, I stayed for a while because . . . first of all, I know he had gone through a very traumatizing childhood, my husband. And so, I was trying to be helpful and I didn't want to desert him like everybody else in his life had. But there came a time that I had to think, "Okay, this is going to . . . I'm continuing the cycle of having my child, my boy, watch his mom being hit and then how will he react to . . . ?" It was very, very hard. It's really the hardest thing I've ever had to do, yeah. And so, I left and, obviously, my daughter was breastfeeding. My son was very young, because they are very close in age.

It went against everything that I had known or I thought I knew, but again it was a choice. I did not have to stay in a violent marriage. So now when I look back I think it's awesome that women have that choice, you know, that they may not be in, like, the most ideal places but at least you can . . . you know you don't have to stay in a violent relationship. But luckily I was able to get housing, actually co-op housing with rent geared to my income.

And so getting that place was just a great thing because even though I had no furniture, I knew at least my daughter had her room, my son had his room, and I had my room. We were sleeping on the floor, but the fact that I knew this was my space and my husband didn't know where I had gone made me feel peaceful. I didn't have to worry constantly, because before I used to have to walk on eggshells to try to not provoke him. And sometimes, especially when somebody has their own issues, there's nothing you can do to make everything be okay all the time. I tried to talk to him. I wanted us to get counselling to deal with it. But it became obvious that he wasn't going to—he was not ready to change or to do anything about it. So luckily in this new place that I moved into, I didn't have to worry about being hit. At least, even though it was really kind of miserable—because we didn't have any furniture—it was a happier place.

My son was really traumatized by being exposed to the abuse. I remember he would just cling on to me. He would not let go of me at all. And I was breast-feeding his youngest sister. It was so hard for him especially because he had no speech. He didn't speak until he was five—but I'll get into that in a little bit. It was really tough, but one of the hardest things was the fact that I had to get social assistance. I needed to go on social assistance because how else was I going to feed my kids? How was I going to pay for my rent? And so, that was another thing. Because my plan was . . . okay, my husband and I had planned that I would go to school, go to a university, and he would work during the day. We were going to be a team. But here I was, now going on social assistance. Everything that I had heard about social assistance made me think it was just for the people who are lazy, who are not educated, who didn't want to work. And so that went against what I knew. It was really hard, but it was the only way I could manage. I had no other way.

So my son who was at this point about four years old started going to daycare and he had no speech. He was behind in a lot of things. But I thought, well, children, you know, develop differently and they're not all the same. So I thought he would take his own time . . . whenever he was ready. But it was concerning me. The daycare staff really helped show me, and especially seeing him alongside other kids, I was able to see there's something that's not right, and so I took him for a test. We had an appointment with this doctor and after a while, after many kinds of appointments, he was diagnosed as autistic with developmental delays.

That was, like, a huge shock. Everything you dreamed for your child . . . you have these dreams for them and you're going to be the best parent no matter what happens. Okay, I was going to be, like, the best single parent. And then, I find that he's autistic. So you're thinking, Is it something I did, maybe, or maybe something I didn't do? And that's very painful, even today. I'm dealing with accepting that right now. I'm getting counselling right now to just be able to . . . in some part of myself I know it's nothing I did, but still, I just could not accept this. I know now that when you don't accept, you keep wishing and hoping. Meanwhile, you're getting frustrated. When you've accepted it, you still expect the best for your child and you want to do things, well, you know, for them to get better. But once you accept that they have this condition, then you parent from a different point of view.

So, I was seeing a lot of specialists with my son. And my daughter was developing, actually, almost above her age, so it was quite hard, you know. But I'm really blessed to have both the children. But with my daughter, it's a little easier, you know. Some people I know have more than one child who has special needs. I can't imagine what they go through.

When my children started going to school, I started preparing myself to go to university, but because I had my schooling in another country, I had to do my Ontario Academic Credits (OAC). So I did them at an adult learning centre. It was very challenging, though, to get into a university. I remember one time when my kids got chicken pox, one of them got it and then the other one after that. I had to take, like, about a whole month of school off because nobody's going to babysit your kids when they have chicken pox. So, with these kinds of setbacks, it took me longer to get to university.

And then, I finally went to university and it was a different . . . I loved being there. It was a wonderful experience. When I was in class, I would actually forget about my kids, really. The workload was very, very challenging. The problem was for me was that I had to get off social assistance because I got student loans to go to university and for some reason you can't have both— which really creates another barrier for women who want to get off the system.

For me to go to get my student loan, I had to be a full-time student. And for me to be a full-time student, it meant I had to do so many courses. And so, it was very, very hard to try to balance being a single mom because my kids come first. So, there I was trying to parent and to be an engineering student. It was really hard. I remember a couple of times when I would get someone to babysit the kids while I did homework, because when you are in university, the work doesn't end when you're out of class.

In fact, you'll probably have to do more when you're out of class. And so, sometimes some of my classes would be at 8 a.m., and my children's school didn't start until 9 a.m. So that meant I had to get somebody to babysit or miss the lecture. So I had to make another huge decision again—to drop out of the university. I felt, and I know it's silly, but I felt like I was a failure . . . like a failure. How could I give it up after I had worked so hard? But, I just could not keep up. Either I had to take part-time classes or I could not manage. But if I did part-time classes, I couldn't have student loans and we would have no way to live. It's kind of like a very complicated trap and I was thoroughly caught in it.

It's very, very frustrating. I'm still upset by it—I don't really understand why these rules were set up like that. I hope things are different now with the policies and I hope with the student loan people too as I didn't find them very easy to deal with. Full-time classes might mean six courses per term—who takes six courses in university? Even if you're just a single person, it's hard to manage that kind of workload. Obviously, it's not a choice to neglect your kids. So, it was really tough and it still is. It is tough.

Right now I work part-time. I'm on social assistance again so I have to report my income all the time. Some of the frustrations that I face relate to trying to work and collect assistance. My worker did not get my income reporting statement last month and so she called and said I was late. No, I wasn't late but she did not get the statement. She was away on vacation. And even though I had sent it in on time, my cheque was held. So, I called and I said, "Okay, why is my cheque held?" She said, "Well, I didn't get your income reporting statement." I said, "I sent it." And then she said, "Maybe, it came when I wasn't here." I said, "You went on vacation and because of that, I was charged $25, on top of my rent because of being late." And then, there are so many other things . . . it's very frustrating. So, I talked to her and said, "Please, if you don't get my income reporting statement, call me please if you don't get it in time. Just call me, you know." So, that's one of the most frustrating things is being so dependent on people who don't actually seem to care—they have their rules and that is all they care about.

One of my hopes right now is still to take some courses. Now, I know I would not try to take such a heavy course load. But I want to get some kind of a diploma, because I really would like to be independent of social assistance completely, if it's possible. So, that's what I'm working toward right now. It's still very challenging because my son is now 16 years old. He is going through puberty issues, growing, but having a mind of a seven-year old. So, that's really challenging and he doesn't understand what is going on because of his special needs. And also, it's coming between him and his sister because she's feeling that I'm spending so much energy on him and not necessarily on her, or making a better life for us. So really, that's one of the toughest things.

My life is a continuing struggle but I'm still really, really hopeful. By the way, one thing that happened, the first time I went on social assistance is that I had a worker who was a male and he was so mean. He was just so mean. One time, I couldn't make it for the appointment because I had nobody to leave my kids with and I couldn't take them both because they were too young. And I remember calling him to ask him if I could just reschedule. And he was so nasty. You know, again, having just come from a violent marriage, and then having this man patronizing me and being so insensitive, that was a very, very . . . that's one of the things I'll never forget. However, now, I do have very good workers. I've had mainly good workers, except the last one. I'm talking to her about this, letting me know if my cheque is going to be held. But it was a very bad situation that first time, and I think . . . now, I know better, like, I could have asked for a different worker or I could have asked to speak to his manager about the bad experience that I had. But in those early days, you're so vulnerable especially when you're coming from violence, if you lived in violence. You get so intimidated too because, you know, here's this guy who is just . . . you look at him and you think maybe he's just like your husband, that kind of . . . you know, I was not in a good place.

My kids, if I had raised them in that environment . . . and even though there are financial struggles, at least I don't ever have to be worried about my kids being abused or me being abused. And maybe my house is sometimes messy, but I have made myself a happy home. You are always just living, but thinking about what you did, and I realize I did okay. I am really happy that it's me that went through that and not my children, and what I do now is make sure I don't put my kids in that situation. I am really, really close to my daughter and she knows she can come to me and she won't experience abuse. I will protect her and they will always have a safe home.

Christina's Story

My name is Christina, and I was born in Portugal in 1967. I came to Canada in 1974. I'm an only child. My parents are very traditional Portuguese, blue-collar, uneducated people who work very hard. Within a year of coming to this country they bought their own house. This was the mid-1970s and they had a lot to work through—a language barrier, a social barrier, and leaving all their family behind. I only had one aunt, one uncle, and a couple of cousins here.

My parents did the best they could in raising me. There was always a roof over my head, and there was always food in the house. But somehow I always felt like something was missing, especially after I came to Canada. I used to cry every day and I wanted to go back home. The kids at school would make fun of me. I was a chubby child because my mom didn't know how to show love so she would give me food. My mom was a chef and if I cried she would say, "Eat this. You'll feel better." I did feel better and it got rid of the pain.

At school I tried to be really friendly with everybody. If there was one kid who didn't like me, I'd be extra nice to them because I wanted to be liked. I was really affected by what people thought of me.

By grade 2 or 3 I could speak English and things were better. All through school I had trouble focusing. Now they call it ADD, but back when I was a kid, I just couldn't focus. For example, the teacher couldn't sit me by the window because I'd be, like, gone. I've always had a really creative imagination. I was an only child and my parents were very strict. I would stay in the house and watch my friends play outside. I was not allowed to go outside because I was a latchkey kid. From the time I was six years old I'd come home and babysit myself. We couldn't afford to pay a mortgage, pay the bills, and have a babysitter—back then it was pretty much acceptable.

My dad was a character. He was a very honest man and full of integrity. My dad was also the life of the party. My mom was more serious. She had no time for games. It was all about work for her. She had a full-time job at home. Our house was immaculate. We had plastic on the furniture. We would clean the house from 7 a.m. to 3 p.m. every Saturday. She'd get me out of bed one way or another, and corporal punishment was very much in order in my house. I remember as a kid being outside in winter, wearing my winter jacket, and cleaning the windows. I would spray the Windex on and it would freeze by the time it hit the window. I couldn't finish until my job was done, and when I went back in the house my mother would go and check it. At the same time, she tried her best. She tried to show me how to take care of the house, and she tried to show me how to take care of myself.

I started working when I was 14. I never had summer camps or anything like that. My mom worked in restaurants so every summer I'd work in good restaurants in tourist areas or in hotels and they paid really well. And by the end of the summer I would have $3,000 or $4,000 in the bank. So my mom taught me how to take care of my money. Basically her advice was not to spend it and leave it in the bank. I really respected money but I also knew the power it had.

Throughout high school I was really ashamed of my body. I remember when I was 15 my mom used to bug me about my weight. She was actually projecting her issues because she'd gained a lot of weight when she came to Canada. She took me to a doctor, who gave me diet pills. And I loved diet pills because I felt good. I really enjoy anything that makes me feel good. Food made me feel good but then there was the consequence of the weight. Now diet pills made me feel good and I thought there were no consequences. I could go to school, go through my classes, and I didn't have those hunger pains. I was up, up, up, up. There's speed for you.

By the time I was 15, I was very rebellious. When I was a kid all I ever wanted to do was to grow up. I used to sneak makeup and I'd keep it at my locker at school. I always did really well in school and I didn't have to show up to class. I remember my teachers used to say something like, "Christina has a lot of potential," but I didn't understand what that meant.

When I was a teenager my mom and I didn't get along. My mom was like a warden. It was like this: If you don't like it, then get the hell out and don't let the door hit you in the ass. It was her way or the highway, and she didn't believe in compromise. She thinks children should be seen and not heard. There was a lot of friction during this time, which was also when I met someone who was close to the family.

He was my first boyfriend and I was madly in love with him. He was everything that I would have liked to be. He was close to our family, his parents owned a store near where we lived, and he just did whatever he wanted. That's what I wanted to do, but I didn't have the courage to stand up to my mother.

My mother had often told me that I'd never finish high school because I was an idiot. In grade nine I went to a high school my friends didn't go to because I knew I had to finish. And I did. I ended up getting my high school diploma in large part because my mom thought I wouldn't. Once someone dared me to do something I would do whatever it took, just to prove them wrong. So that's what I did and when I was 18 I graduated from high school. I put my graduation diploma in my mom's face and said, "See, now I'm leaving." The next day I was gone.

I moved into my cousin's house who, to this day, my mom still doesn't talk to because she can hold a grudge like nobody's business. After I moved in with my cousin I started a relationship with someone who basically didn't really care about me and who didn't respect me. He was a kid; we were both kids. He was very immature and so was I. He was five years older than me and already a full-blown alcoholic. He was verbally and emotionally abusive, but I didn't know that's what it was. I just thought he did what he wanted to do and I was going to do what I wanted to do. Within a week of leaving home, I was introduced to drugs and alcohol and I was using everything. I didn't like drinking but I drank because of the effect it produced. Sometimes I'd hold my nose and drink it because I knew there was that feeling coming. I wanted whatever would give me that feeling, whether it was the guy or the job—whatever it was, that's what I would go after.

I believe alcoholism is a progressive disease. So is drug addiction. At the beginning it did what it was supposed to and kept me afloat for many years. At first I had really good jobs working in hospitals and I would only drink and use on weekends. Now, this was my problem—my whole life, I came out of the gate running, but I couldn't sustain it.

You see, I had no coping skills. I was in survival mode most of my life. For a long time if I came in late and you pointed a finger at me, I would have to defend myself. All I knew how to do was survive. I didn't know how to really talk to people. Oh, I knew how to talk—I knew how to tell you off and I knew how to talk about you behind your back. But I didn't have the courage and I didn't have the maturity to deal with life on life's terms. I didn't have any skills, and I wasn't I even willing to listen to anyone. Since I was a kid, if I was caught making a mistake I would lie myself out of it. I already felt bad about myself and if it was shown that I was wrong, to my mind, there would be nothing left.

I didn't know how to fix that. I knew that if I had a couple of drinks or I did a couple of lines, if I just put some stuff in me that would change my mood, it would all go away. The problem with that is that you're just prolonging it. You're putting it on the sideline and you're not growing. You're staying stuck, but I didn't know that.

Within a couple of years I wasn't able to hold a job anymore. I wasn't responsible and I was constantly lying. My grandmother must've died three times. By this time I started having very negative feelings. I used humour a lot to mask what I was really feeling because to me, feelings were no good, especially negative ones. My relationship was not working out, and I didn't care because I was just drinking and doing what I could to stay alive. This meant that if I was fired in the morning, I'd find another job by the afternoon. In the 90s it wasn't hard for me to get a job, but I failed to notice that the jobs were paying less and less.

After high school I apprenticed as a hairdresser. You have to take a test to get your licence and I scheduled it three times. All three times I didn't show up. The night before, I would pick up a drink or a drug and I wouldn't show up for the appointment the next day. I felt bad every time, and finally after the third time I decided, "That's it. Three strikes I'm out. I'm not doing this." I gave up on that career. I thought I must be missing that part in me that other women got. I thought that when you're born you're given a set of instructions. I wasn't given a set of instructions and I basically felt like a piece of crap. I would never let anyone know though. My mom always said, "You know, you always put your best foot out there. You never tell them how you're feeling, because they'll eat you up and it's a hard world." I believed that the world was going to eat me up and it was going to get me.

It was important that whatever I did I should bury things as deep as possible. But for me, doing that was killing me. I didn't know it though because the substances I was putting into my body were keeping me numb. It was like the substances were the buffer between me and the world.

By the time I was 25, I'd already had four abortions. I don't say that because I'm proud. I say that because I wasn't capable of taking care of myself, so, I thought I would do an injustice by having a kid. Basically I was scared shitless to have a kid. I knew I would be a single mother and that was my worst fear because I was always scared about what people thought about me. Today I'm not scared about what anyone thinks about me, but my whole life depends on how I think about others. I can't judge people anymore because it all comes back to me. I believe in cause and effect and that whatever karma I send out there I get back tenfold, whether it's now or whether it's when I'm 90.

When I was 25, I got rid of the ex. It was the most toxic relationship that I'd been in up to that point, but I wanted him so bad. I wanted him to change. I thought, "If you just do what I say, we'd be okay, damn it!" God bless him. He wasn't capable of change and he had the disease of addiction too. So we ended that relationship.

About six months later, I met my son's father. He was a cocaine dealer and he showed me how to make a lot of money. At the time I owed six months' rent. I didn't have the option of asking my ex-boyfriend because he'd moved back home. My parents had disowned me by now, and I was a disgrace to the family.

When I met my future husband it was all great. I do need to say that my son's dad had a good heart despite being lost in this world of addiction too. We had money, and I thought, "I know what to do now." But it was blood money—the kind of money you pay a very big price for. I didn't get that. I thought people would see all the virtues and all the morals that I used to have even now they'd totally been compromised. We had cars and a lot of this and that, but it was all material stuff. I hated what I was doing, and I hated myself. I hated everyone, but I hated myself most because I knew that if I wasn't part of the solution I was part of the problem. I knew that part of what I was doing was hurting other people including myself. It was sucking me in, and my addiction was growing like nobody's business.

I had gone back to school for hotel management. I started the first semester off with a bang—a 90% average. In the second semester, I quit. When I look at my whole life I see I've started so many things and not finished them. It's not because I can't but because I think it'll be impossible and I get scared and I don't know how to ask for help. I don't know how to say that I've made a mistake because my ego won't let me. My own worst enemy is me. I know that today without a shadow of a doubt. These are the things I've come to learn.

So, in the second semester, I got pregnant, and I was scared shitless. In the past I hadn't told the men I was with when I got pregnant. I just went and had the abortion. This time I told my husband. We were married by now because we wanted him to stay in the country. When I told him he said to me, "You know what, if you have an abortion, I will never, ever, ever want to see you or speak to you. We won't have a relationship." And I was like, "Okay, that really sucks." I was so scared to have this child but I had him and it was my saving grace. I was 29 when I had my son.

It was funny how I found out I was pregnant. I was going to the pub one Friday afternoon with the people from school. When I got there I ordered two beers. I'd always get two beers. Just before I'd sit down with my friends I'd have to drink one beer because I was so tense. I put back the first beer and immediately had to run to the washroom. I projected the beer out of me and thought, "Well, there's something wrong with that beer. Must be skunk." When I drank the second one the same thing happened, except this time I didn't make it to the washroom. I went home and I told my husband, who was on the phone to his mother in Puerto Rico. She said to him over the phone, "She's pregnant." I said she was crazy. In my mind I couldn't get pregnant because I'd had a cervical procedure four years before. The doctor hadn't said that I couldn't get pregnant but that it would be hard for me to carry a baby full term. I thought God was punishing me for giving up those babies and I was just damned. My view today is that God doesn't punish anyone.

When I was pregnant, by God's miracle, I couldn't smoke. I couldn't smell cigarettes without feeling sick, and I couldn't smoke a cigarette. I also couldn't drink beer and I couldn't use drugs. So, the only thing I could do was eat. I gained 75 pounds in my pregnancy and I got gestational diabetes. Again, I needed a buffer. I remember praying the whole of my pregnancy because my worst fear was to be a single mom. I even made my husband sign a paper that when the baby was born he would stop dealing drugs. We would buy a house in the suburbs and everything was going to be fine.

The night the contractions came my husband drove me to the hospital and left me there because he had to go do a deal. I was in the labour ward for 36 hours because I was so scared to go back home. I had a very intensive labour and my husband came in once in a while. When I had my baby and they put him on my chest, I knew at that point there was a God. There was something. My child was the most perfect thing I'd ever seen in my life. I knew my life had to change because I was responsible for another human being. Until that point, I couldn't even take care of a healthy plant—they'd all die. So I knew something had to change. I knew . . . but how? How was it going to change?

I was so scared to go home with the baby. I made excuses as to why I couldn't go home. They wanted me to leave the hospital in two days. I stayed for seven. I can really grind in my heels. They would have had to bring in cops to physically take me out of there. Think about it—I had a husband who had drugs in the house and I had this baby who needed me. What the hell do you do with a baby? I didn't know how to bathe him. The first time I changed his diaper I took too long and he peed in my mouth.

I was blown away by how much I loved this child. I loved him more than I loved myself. I knew I would do anything for him. When I finally went home, I made some definite decisions. My husband moved to his cousin's house because I told him, "I don't care what you do to me but this child is not going to be affected by all this."

We were separated within six months. I moved to the north end of the city because I thought that if I just got far away from him it would be fine. But he wasn't willing to stop. He'd tell me, "Things weren't as bad as that, Christina, you're just being a little over the top." I probably was, but I knew if I didn't do something, I was going to get sucked back into that world. I knew I was going to lose my baby. My biggest fear became Children's Aid. I didn't want to start anything. It's amazing that the obsession to use cocaine was gone after my son was born, but I still thought I could drink.

Six months later my first ex-boyfriend who had been a full-blown alcoholic, called me up and said, "I want to meet you at the church." The last time we had spoken was eight years before and I tried to run him over with my car. That's how we broke up. So I was kind of wary to meet him because I didn't know what he had planned. You know, payback's a bitch. Still, I was very curious about what he was up to and in the end I went.

When we met he made an amend to me. An amend is step nine in the 12-step fellowship. We met outside his AA meeting. I wish I'd had a tape recorder to record him because I was so in awe of what he was saying. Everything that he had denied in our relationship, he now admitted to. There was also something different about his eyes. I knew, without a shadow of a doubt, that God had come into his life, and I couldn't believe it. This was the man who used to tell me that God didn't exist. He used to tell everyone that God didn't exist. He stood in front of me, telling me everything he ever did wrong in our relationship, completely owning his part. This was not the same guy who, if you found him with his hand in your wallet, would explain how it was an accident and he was actually trying to help you. As he told me everything that went wrong all I could think of was, "How long have you been sober?" "A year," he said, "And I'm doing this because I need to continue to stay sober." I said to him, "You need to help me get sober." And he said, "Okay. I'll take you to meetings. I'll do whatever I can." And he did.

I started going to meetings when my baby was six months old. I actually went to as many meetings as I could because my mind was so strong, the voices were so strong, but, I'd relapse every once in a while because I still wasn't ready.

There was a lot of damage that had been done. There was a lot of stuff that I hadn't dealt with and I still wasn't ready to accept that I couldn't drink at all. I still wanted to drink on my birthday. I still wanted to drink at New Year's. I figured the drugs were bad but the drinking was social. I'd go out for a night and relapse and all hell would break loose. The feelings that I had the next day—the guilt, the shame, the loneliness—were unbearable.

About seven years ago, when I had been in the program 18 months, I went to the States to be with my husband. He'd been deported, had got into trouble down there, and was coming out of the penitentiary. We'd been writing back and forth and he wanted to see his son. I thought writing to him was a good idea. I really believed that when we married we made a commitment to each other, and at the time I still hadn't divorced him. Like I said, I hated being a single mom and I just kept thinking of all the good times we had together. Once I was down there and we were together it went from bad to worse.

I never thought of myself as a physically abused woman because I hit back. I believed that if you're going to hit me, I'm going to finish it. I believed that anybody who said they were physically abused was lying, because I thought they would hit back. If I didn't have sympathy for myself, I couldn't have it for anyone else.

Compassion is one of the things I've been learning. I've also been learning honesty, love, tolerance, perseverance, patience, courage, gratitude, forgiveness, acceptance, trust, and surrender. These are my spiritual principles that I practise on a daily basis. It didn't work out with my ex-husband, but I pray for him every single day. I know that deep down he's a good man. He just has a lot of hurt that he covers up and he doesn't know how to express it. I never saw him cry. He's a grown man, but inside he's such a child.

So, I tried with my husband but he just couldn't connect with his son. That was the saddest thing in the world because the greatest connection I have is with my son. For his father to miss that in his life is so sad. It's not something you can replace and if you don't have it, you just don't have it. One time my son said, "You know what, Mom? Daddy's not a bad man. He's just a sick man." My son is like my little angel because the stuff he says to me comes right from God. If he sees me going crazy at home, like if I'm getting a little OCD because something wasn't put away, my son will ask, "Mom, isn't it time for a meeting? Shouldn't you phone your sponsor?"

Since coming back to Canada I've had to let my husband go. I had to go to treatment because I relapsed while in the States, mainly because of all the things I was trying to juggle. There was a treatment centre for women and children and I asked my son if he wanted to stay with his dad or come to treatment with me. He replied, "Mom, at least, you know what your problem is." So the disease of addiction took me to Alabama for treatment. I now know that I'm not just addicted to drugs and alcohol but also to relationships and wanting to save men who need to learn to save themselves.

The treatment centre was a Christian treatment centre. I'd judged Christians my whole life because I thought they were fanatics. But thank God for the family who owned the centre. They took us into their arms and they loved us both. We were allowed to go to their house every weekend and this really opened up God to me and showed me who God was.

I'm not a Christian. I believe there is a God but I don't believe one religion is better than another. I believe all religion was created by God and all things that are good are created by God. Now I try to find out about Buddha. I try to find out about Allah. I try to find out about all religions, because I believe, just like in life, if you take a plane, train, or automobile, it all gets there.

And I know the obsession to drink has been removed. I now help other people because I can identify with them because I've been there. When I would walk into treatment centres and talk to counsellors, the first question I'd ask was, "Did you ever take a drink? Did you ever do a drug?" They'd say, "No, but I went to university." It was great they had the book knowledge but they didn't know what I felt. Now I don't want to drink and I don't want to put anything inside me. Before I didn't really have a choice. While I'd be great in the treatment centre, once I left, I couldn't keep it up, except for this time.

This is the longest I've ever been sober and I'm just a baby. I'm just under two and a half years sober. I'm now learning how to be a grown-up. I'm learning it's okay to have feelings. I'm learning it's okay to make choices. I'm learning it's okay to say no.

I also know I can't do it alone. As women, I believe we take a lot of crap. We're made to feel ashamed by the media and everything that's out there. Since I've been in recovery this time I've really tried to stay active for women on the move. When I came back to Canada I stayed in a women's shelter because I had nowhere to go. I used to think other women were just competition. I now know that one voice is just one voice, but united we are so many voices. It's not a competition, and it's not a race. I also know that I can do a lot more than I used to think I could do. And that's awesome because, as a woman who believed all she was good for was getting married and having a guy support her, I've now taken a bridging course to go back to university. I participate with other women at meetings and in other functions and things to support shelters. I know that wherever we are from, we go through the same things. It's a living and learning situation, and there aren't any instructions.

Susan's Story

I was born in the UK. I am the second oldest of eight children. I came to Canada in the early 1980s as a runaway. The thing that has made my life extremely difficult is that for as long as I can remember my mother was never around for us. My stepfather sexually abused my siblings and me when we were growing up. He made my siblings do a lot of unspeakable things together. The abuse I suffered as a child has really fucked up my head. I am so not happy about it and hope that he is forever burning in hell.

I now have two children. My twin girls were born three months premature. My daughter Tina is deaf-mute and has cerebral palsy and autism spectrum disorder. The list goes on. I thank God that my other daughter, Julie, is okay. She only has epilepsy. I will never marry. I cannot allow anybody to act as a father to my children because I live in fear of what could happen to my girls.

Many of my childhood memories are of being trapped in a room. One of my siblings would pee on the floor and the rest of us would jump through it. That's what we did for fun. The house was always filthy, cluttered, and junky. My mother went to jumble sales, which are called garage sales here in Canada, and would bring home clothes for us. There is nothing wrong with having second-hand clothes. We also had second-hand toys, which were often broken. A bunch of us would sleep in the same bed. It would be freezing cold, and we would huddle together using coats as blankets and listen to the mice running around. God knows how many cats we had. In the morning we would find parts of the mice on the floor. I remember the smell of the paraffin heaters in the room where we slept. Smell is one of my big triggers of memories, and the smell of paraffin is so gross. When I was growing up we were never clean. We all had lice and we got bed bugs. My siblings and I used to squish them on the wall and think of them as marzipan.

I remember going to school in wet clothes. We only had one or two pairs of underwear each. I had to wash out my own underwear, socks, and skirt. I would hang them up and hope that they would be dry the next day. I wore jeans and skirts with ice on them many times. I would put them on and wear them proudly. One time, when I was a little older, I was walking through an empty house and found one brown shoe. I searched through the rest of that broken down house, looking for the other shoe. I finally found it on top of the roof in the eaves trough. I climbed out the bedroom window and slid down the roof to get that shoe. When I got it I tried it on and it was my size! I liked them very, very much. The pins inside the shoe were coming up so I took them home, wiped them down and cut out a piece of cardboard for the inside.

Actually, I probably ripped the cardboard because there weren't any scissors to be found in our messy house. I wore those shoes for the longest time.

I didn't see much of my mother growing up. We used to have aunties that came over. I do recall that my mother never had any money. She used to take coins from my stepfather's pocket. They were the equivalent to pennies and dimes. She used to put the money in plastic and then put it in her shoe. When we did go to the park she bought us popsicles, which we called lollies.

One vivid memory I have of my mother is being five years old and watching her bathe my three-year-old sister Mary in a metal bathtub. At the time Mary was my only sister. Neither Mary nor I were feeling well. I said to my mother, "Mother, Mary is going to die." My mother told me, "Don't be so silly." My stepfather came in, smacked me, and sent me to my room. I cried underneath my sheets because I felt so sorry for what I had said. In the middle of the night my stepfather came into the bedroom and shook Mary, trying to wake her. She had died. She had bronchial pneumonia, probably caused by part of the ceiling falling down on her—our house was extremely mouldy. At three Mary had never walked, and she barely ever talked. I also recall that she had never had a bed.

It forever bothers me that, at five, I knew what was going to happen to my sister. Mary's death was really, really difficult for me. After she died I remember walking down the stairs screaming, "My sister's dead, my sister's dead. Oh, my sister's dead. What am I going to do? I have no sister." The loss of my sister will be a memory that is always with me. My mother and stepfather didn't want me carrying on. I guess that they thought that was too shameful. They didn't think that the abuse and the extreme poverty were shameful, but Mary's death was.

The biggest fear I had growing up was to be alone with my stepfather. I knew what would happen—the buggering. I remember my stepfather coming into our room, listening so our mother wouldn't hear him, and getting us ready for his adventure. This happened pretty much every night. My oldest brother, Bill, told my stepfather that he didn't want to do this anymore and was beaten for saying anything. I remember there was an auntie who used to come over. My stepfather was having sex with her too. He made it quite obvious by standing in the door with his hand in her privates. Where was our mother through this? Where?

One time my stepfather said to me, "If you ever become pregnant don't let anybody know that it was me. If you ever tell anybody you will be put down in the floor boards." I was still a child and extremely naive when he said these things. I said to Bill, "How am I going to eat if I am down in the floor boards?" Bill was four years older and explained, "Susan, he means that you're going to be dead." My God, it was a complete, complete nightmare.

I feel very, very close to Bill and I guess I always will. He was able to make me laugh. Bill was born a blue baby, which meant he had a hole in his heart and needed many heart operations. Bill was in and out of the hospital a lot but when he did come home he tried so hard to study. If he sat up to read with a little light my stepfather came in and smacked him. Bill would cry, "Oh, leave me alone. Leave me alone." Again, my mother was never, never there to protect us.

When I was in my late 20s I found out that Joseph, who is a year younger than me, is my only real brother. I had an auntie, Auntie Mary, who I really liked. When I was about nine or ten she said, "Don't worry. One day you'll be okay. Did your mother ever tell you that you were adopted?" When I was 27 and back in England for a vacation I said to Bill, "I have some doubts in my mind. I have a feeling that we were adopted." He said, "What the hell are you talking about? I have no doubt in my mind that that pervert is our dad." I said, "No, I don't believe that he is."

I went on a mission to find my real dad. Joseph and I got in touch with a place called Beachwood House. We gave them our names and our birthdates. I found out that my real name is Jane Keith. Keith is my mother's maiden name. My stepfather adopted me when I was seven. Apparently that's what gave him the right to behave in such an ugly, inhumane manner!

Joseph and I made arrangements to meet our real father. Joseph was really, really nervous when he made the call. He said, "Is this Paul?" And an old man's voice said, "Yes it is." "I'm your son," said Joseph, to which my biological father replied, "Oh, oh, oh bloody hell." I guess he never thought that he would meet his real kids. We made a date to meet and I went to his house and met his wife and his other children. I have a sister who is only a few months older than me. Instead of trying to become friends, she was in shock and was jealous of me. I tried to make some connection but have now lost all ties with my father's other family, which is quite sad. At the time it was too overwhelming and I had other things to focus on.

Finding my real dad was quite nerve-racking but I was excited at the same time. The whole process was hard on me. I grew to like him. I can't say I grew to love him because I only knew him for a short period of time before he passed away. Given that I was in Canada and he was in the UK, we didn't meet more than six times. I regret that I didn't know more of him because he sounded like a fun kind of a guy. Maybe that's where I get my sense of humour.

Through the search at Beachwood House we learned that Bill had been adopted too. His father was Irish and also called Bill. Paul was Joseph's and my father. Mary is a question mark. She had blond hair and blue eyes whereas Joseph and I are both a little bit darker skinned than the average British person. Another brother, Peter, is named after my stepfather. Peter is an alcoholic. He knows his father used to yell and scream but refuses to believe that his father did anything else to us. My younger brother Ken is 41. He lives with my mother. He has no life, no girlfriend, he drinks, and he's unemployed.

Our brother Josh was the victim of horrible abuse. When Josh was five or six months old Joseph and I were in the room with him and we remember him crying, crying. Our mother was nowhere to be seen. My stepfather came into the room and picked Josh up by his feet. Josh was a tiny, tiny baby when this happened. My stepfather started to smack him. The screaming that went through that room haunts me to this day. I still find the sound of kids screaming unbearably painful. My stepfather threw Josh against the wall and his head split. My stepfather then threw Josh back in his crib and left the room. I, shaking in my footsteps, went to the crib and put my hand on his bum, feeling how hot it was. Joseph and I both said, "Oh my God" and ran back to our beds in fear that the same thing would happen to us. The intensity of the abuse was so unbelievable I don't know how we all made it through!

Josh had to have an operation on his head. He still has a scar all the way down his head. He was placed in foster care when he was three. I remember him leaving, wearing his little checkered jacket and little checkered pants, and thinking, "Poor little guy." We cried for him, but it turned out that he was the lucky one. He had an amazing guy looking after him.

I have often wondered why we didn't all go into care. We should have been removed. I guess that sometimes in life we just need to go through this kind of pain. Josh used to come home every now and again. He would come home with games and colouring books. They were just books from the dollar store but I remember being so jealous and angry that I would snap his crayons. I felt so sorry for breaking his things that I apologized to him as an adult one time I was visiting the UK, just to clear my mind.

I'm not in touch with Josh. I barely speak to Peter. The last time I saw or spoke with Joseph was when we went to Beachwood House. Because the abuse was so severe, Joseph's therapist has told him to cut ties with all of us. As my only real brother it would have been nice to speak to Joseph again. Of course, I love Bill like a real brother and we remain close.

When I was growing up I always had it in my mind that I should just run away from home. We were not loved. We grew up being told the worst things: you're going to be nothing, you're good for nobody, you're nothing but a black-headed bastard, you're just a lesbian. Even though I tried to do good things, I never got any appreciation. I do not believe that I was a bad child. I never disrespected anybody unless they disrespected me. When you experience such abuse as a child, you do retaliate. Even now as an adult I don't take a lot of shit from people. If I think you're full of shit, I will probably tell you so. I don't like that about myself but I have had so much torment in life that it's hard for me to tolerate it.

When I was 15 years old and finishing school I remember thinking, "What the hell am I going to do with myself?" I didn't really know how to read or write. I didn't know how to do anything because I was always home looking after all my other siblings. I felt like the real-life Cinderella, doing dishes, peeling potatoes, and cleaning up. Once I was out of school I found a job doing a paper route. It was okay to do the paper route. I tried to save up a little bit of money, but my mother and stepfather took whatever I could save. I was always the one trying to make money and my family always took it away from me. I really wanted to open a bank account. I was never allowed anything of my own. For example I had a bike for the paper route and I was paying back money that I had borrowed to buy it. I really loved that bike. I don't know if I completely paid it off, but when I was trying to come to Canada my mother and stepfather sold it.

New neighbours moved in when I was about 16. I used to babysit their kids, who were six and seven years old. I cleaned Dan's car. He gave me £10, which is about $20 now. After a little while his wife started to get sick. She died of lung cancer when the kids were nine and ten.

She was sick for about a year and a half, maybe two years. At some point I had essentially moved in with the family. The kids were in a boarding school so I was helping Dan. I washed clothes by hand, dried them, and packed them up in a bag to take up to the hospital. I walked to the hospital every day during that period.

My family moved while I was staying with this family but I didn't go with them. My stepfather constantly came and yelled at me that I needed to go back home. Often the police were called and I begged them not to send me home. I never did tell the police why I didn't want to go home. They probably thought I was just a runaway who didn't want to be with her family. That couldn't have been further from the truth. I just wanted to have a family that gave a shit about me.

After his wife died Dan sold his house. He is Canadian and wanted to move back to Canada. Dan and I had also become intimate, despite the fact I was in my late teens and he was in his mid-forties. I cried and begged him not to leave me in the UK by myself. I had nobody and didn't know what I was going to do. I was so worried that I might bump into my stepfather that I started to take Valium to calm my nerves.

Dan made arrangements for me to stay with friends of his. He left with his kids in January and I was to follow him in April. I was on welfare during this time. I didn't want to be on welfare but I couldn't read or write and just didn't know what else to do. I had no self-esteem and no confidence in myself. Often I didn't even want to be living. I had to pay this couple room and board from my welfare payments even though I was also helping them cook and clean. I even spent a lot of time sitting with their aging father, which was pretty boring for a teenager. I smoked a lot during this time to help calm my nerves. I didn't want to see my friends because I was afraid that they might tell my family that I was planning to run away to Canada.

The woman I was staying with helped me get my passport. Her husband wanted to touch and fondle me. It was the same thing again. But I got through that and I never told his wife. I just wanted to get to Canada.

I tried to phone Dan, but he had given me the wrong phone number. He obviously didn't really want me to come. I went to pieces. I was completely stranded in the UK. The woman I was staying with helped me to call directory assistance and get a correct phone number. I was able to reach him and we started to talk.

I came to Canada in the early 1980s. I didn't like Canada. It was totally different for me. The only good thing about it was that, somehow, I felt free. I was young, I made some friends, and I wanted to be with them and to party like I had never partied before. Before coming here I had never been to a bar. I never even drank. It was like I had been robbed of my entire life. However, when I arrived, I lived with Dan and he expected me to look after his kids. I looked after them the best that I could. I am only seven years older than his son. I didn't really have any idea how to be a good parent, and I was too young. But I am thinking now as an adult.

Dan and I were together for many years before I decided that I wanted to have children. When I was 36, I became pregnant with twin girls. It seemed that I received bad news at every appointment I went to. One baby was growing fine, but the other wasn't. I was sent to the hospital, where I was bedridden. I woke up to find a doctor looking at me. He told me that I needed to deliver the babies that day. It was three months before my due date. I told him that I had been told the day before that everything was fine. He gave me the choice to deliver now or to continue with the pregnancy. If I kept the pregnancy going the small baby would die. If I delivered that day it wasn't clear how things would go because the babies were very premature. I asked the doctor what I should do, but he said that he could not tell me. I started to cry. I was absolutely beside myself. I decided to deliver both babies that day. My girls came into the world together. The first one weighed one pound six ounces and the second one weighed two pounds six ounces.

The twins were incubated and taken care of at the hospital. The larger baby, Julie, came home three months later. She was later diagnosed with epilepsy. The smaller baby, Tina, came home three months after Julie. She was deaf-mute and had cerebral palsy. She also vomited and had diarrhea a lot. I was always going back and forth to the pediatrician. Dan was no help at all. The big age difference between us drove us apart. By the time the twins were born Dan was on his pension and there was very little money. With Tina being as sick as she was and my running back and forth to the hospital, there was no money for anybody.

Tina has survived. She is now 12 years old but still has a lot of difficulties. A year ago she was diagnosed with leg discrepancy and is extremely underweight. She weighs 70 pounds while her twin sister weighs about 112. So, my journey still continues. For example, I tried to get Tina a cochlear implant but was denied because she doesn't have a voice. She was on oxygen for so long at the hospital after she was born that her vocal cords were damaged.

I left their dad when the twins were five. I couldn't handle it anymore and ran away from the situation. I think the turning point happened one day when I was going for a walk with the girls and we wanted to go to McDonald's. I asked Dan for $20, but he said there was no money. Yet he had the money for him to do things like go to Euchre tournaments or to go bowling with his son. It seemed like there was just no money for us. Tina was getting disability benefits, but even that money was not going to the girls. Instead it was always spent on fixing the car. Tina wore braces on her legs and needed the extra-cushioned running shoes that were $100 a pair. I didn't want her to have to settle for Wal-Mart shoes. There's nothing wrong with Wal-Mart shoes, but that isn't what she needed. I decided that the girls needed to start benefiting from the money and that I would be better off as a single mom.

Things improved for me after we moved out. It was the first time in my life that I felt like I had some control over my situation. I never had any control as a child and even as an adult I had no control while I was living with Dan. Now I feel more independent. Because of my eye condition I always relied on other people to drive me around. I still don't drive, but now the girls and I take the bus. I never used to have any money in my pocket. I'm not flush now, but if I have $50 I can control it. If the girls ask me to buy them something, I say yes if I can afford it and I say no if I can't—but I am the one to decide. Dan is still involved in our lives—I will forever be grateful to him, even though it was hard at times. Without him I am unsure of where I would be today.

I still take the girls to Value Village. It's an amazing place. When they were small I could buy $20 worth of toys, bring them home and wash them, and the girls would sit and play. They used to be very grateful for that sort of stuff. It's more difficult now. The girls always want something and I have to tell them to wait until I have they money. We found an amazing website—Craigslist. I've bought lots of stuff off Craigslist. It's half the price that you would pay in the store.

I believe that I have survived all my abuse. It still bothers me at times. I'll have to live with it for the rest of my life. I haven't really spoken to my girls about it. Tina wouldn't fully understand. All I've said to Julie is that she is very, very lucky to have what she has. I try to make her think of where she is and where she isn't. I always praise her and tell her she is doing well at school.

I never had any encouragement whatsoever as a child. I want to be everything to my girls and to make sure they don't experience what I experienced. I keep a nice, clean house because, as kids, we never lived in a clean house. I always have food on the table because we rarely had food on the table. My experiences have made me a better person. I am more grateful to whoever can help us. Even if we are given something we don't need, I always make sure that the girls say thank you. I also help others. I never throw stuff out; I pass it on.

Life as a single mom has been a struggle. It's a lot for one person. Tina is not really a good sleeper. She often wakes me up in the middle of the night. I try not to complain as I want to be a good mother and to be there for my girls. It is not always easy to manage this given the combination of being poor and a single parent. My eyesight has really deteriorated and I have started to wear glasses. I used to make do with the sight that I had but at one point Tina was on oxygen and it was really important for me to be able to see properly. My eyes have gotten used to glasses, which caused my remaining eyesight to decline. As my eyes change I need new glasses which I can't always afford.

Money on ODSP isn't the be-all and end-all. The workers are not as friendly as Ontario Works. When I was with Ontario Works I had amazing workers who understood my situation and were very kind to us. My experience with my workers on Ontario Works was that they were happy for you to make an appointment to see them, whereas ODSP doesn't really want to see you. At Ontario Works my worker would ask me how I was doing and might give me extra bus tickets. ODSP says what they need to say to get you out of the office.

Things are still a struggle. For example, tomorrow I have to go to the hospital. The girls need to have neurological assessments to make sure their seizures are under control. The bus fare is very expensive—$3 there and $3 back. Sometimes we have quite a few appointments in one day. I have to pay for all the girls' expenses. Camp this summer was a stretch, even though it was subsidized. It was $400 for one kid and $600 for the other. I have a Visa card with a balance on it, and the interest is very high. I pay some back on it whenever I can. Although my life is not easy it is way better than when I was a kid and it's even better than when I was living with somebody.

Hanukkah and Christmas are always difficult. Kids expect more these days. When I was a child we got nothing like what kids get today. We might get a couple of presents each. Some of them were second-hand that had been wiped down and handed to us. I now have a few good friends who I buy presents for. I usually try and start a little bit early, find stuff on sale, and put it to the side.

When I first moved out with my daughters, I looked around in the garbage and thought, "How could I use that?" If I found a dresser my friend and I would go down, bring up it upstairs, wash it out, and I would use that dresser.

If someone had thrown out an end table, and it was better than the table I had, I would take it. That's how I built up my apartment. If you walked into my place now you would say, "Oh my God, honey, you have done really, really well." Friends used to give me bags and bags of clothes for the girls. I sorted through them, took out the best, and passed the rest on. So, we've learned ways to survive. I knew I wasn't one to fail. I'll do whatever I need to do.

As a parent it's sometimes hard to make sure you take care of yourself too. Right now I'm at the stage where, as a mom, I want to give my kids all that I can, but sometimes I sell myself short. I have a boyfriend who has a disability. He has asked me to move in together and to marry him. My answer is always "NO." I say no because I fear that something could happen to my kids. I know it wouldn't but I don't want to take a chance. Ever since I was a child I have told myself that I would never live with anybody and that I would never marry anybody. I will not allow anybody to touch my kids in the way I was touched. I am going to firmly stand by that decision, even if one day I will be a lonely old lady. At least I know that my kids will never have to tell a story like this because abuse will never happen to them.

My hope for Tina is that she will continue on with whatever she needs to do and will not live with me forever. I hope that she will be able to take care of herself and live a half-decent life. Even though she has disabilities she is nobody's fool. I think community living would be good for her. I would like to see someone available to help her with things like taking a shower, cooking a meal, and doing her own banking.

For Julie I expect nothing but university. I want to give her everything I never had. When I left school at 15, I was unable to read, write, or spell. I had no options. I've bought books for my daughters since they were tiny. We would read together a lot and even now I assign Tina two or three small stories before she goes to bed. Julie is a fluent reader and an amazing writer. She even helps me with my writing.

Although I still don't have all of the confidence that I should, I am way better and much more independent than the majority of people who have experienced the type of abuse I suffered. I just try to be a way, way better mother than the one I grew up with. I have met a lot of wonderful people along my journey who have been there for me and really cared about me. I get my strength from myself because nobody ever had the strength for me. One thing I have realized in life is that you have two choices: you either sink or you swim. I choose to swim.

Miriam's Story

I was born in Africa, and we had a really poor family—really, really poor, with six sisters and my mom and dad. I don't know what happened with them but they fought, and my dad managed to keep two of us, and my mom ran with the rest.

And so I stayed with my dad and I don't really remember too much about it, except that we were in a slum, a really bad slum and that he was really abusive and made us sell drugs and illegal alcohol. I was maybe two, my sister was three at the time—and his abuse was so bad, apparently, that the neighbours called the police. He was taken to court and my mom also got the elder from the tribe to come down and petition that she would be our guardian, but she couldn't afford us, she couldn't keep us. Anyway, the presiding magistrate—it was around Christmas time—put us in an orphanage, but kind of a high-class one. It ended up that the magistrate took us home for Christmas because she didn't want to leave two little kids in an orphanage; there was no one else. The orphanage was kind of like a nursery school. She said she just fell in love with my sister and me and she ended up being my mom. She and my real mom made an agreement that she would be my foster mom and she'd bring us up.

She was British. So all my life I've been through like . . . in the holidays we'd go back to the village, you know, no shoes, poor, and yet most of the time we were very, very rich, well off. They were a very well-off family. So we had both kind of things but we kept our language and culture. But it was kind of really strange. To this day, I always feel that just because of that I don't know exactly where I belong, where I fit in, but I fit in with anybody and everybody. My real father died a few years later, and by about 12 I just stopped going back to the village. It was really hard on us, you know, every three months going back, but it was also very difficult being two black kids, living in a black country, with white people, going to elite schools.

By the time I was 15, because I have never felt placed anywhere, I wanted to be out—just out of the country, out of—away from everybody. So I applied for a scholarship to college and I got it, a full scholarship to Canada, so I came here. I was 15 or 16 at the time. But it was okay. The scholarship included airfare and everything and I did the International Baccalaureate. I was always travelling even at that time and I never wanted any roots or anything with anybody. I was lucky to get another scholarship, and I went to university. I completed a B.A. and a year of a master's program, but I was tired of school, so I decided to move to Toronto. My best friend had finished college at the same time, so we drove across the US and we came to Toronto together to look for jobs and to live here.

I had a good time in my 20s. I just travelled the world. I went to Egypt, Germany, everywhere. I worked, I travelled, worked and travelled, that was really all. I was working at a publishing company but I got laid off and unbeknown to me, because I had never really resigned from my college job at the department store, when I applied for unemployment they said, "No you're still employed at the department store." So I kind of reluctantly went back there. I had been an auditor in another province and here the only job they offered me was in makeup, but I never wore any makeup, but anyway I took it. I did well. I moved up in the department store. I went into management, and I made good money, travelled, but I really didn't like it. I wanted to do another degree. I had a degree in archaeology and communications because I thought I was going back to Africa, but I ended up applying to stay here.

So I sort of had a useless degree in a way, but I lost confidence from being laid off from that first job at the publishing company. So I stayed with the department store and did this, what I called demeaning work. It wasn't demeaning; it taught me a lot. At that time I met a guy and I really liked him and he liked travelling and he seemed, well, more settled, a bit different from everybody else. He was from Europe and we used to travel on the bus together, then he got a car and he'd give me a ride home. So, we got to know each other and eventually we married. It was a whirlwind romance, really. He was really nice to me and we went for dinners, and we travelled, and, you know, everything was fine.

He was working at the department store too, but he was on commission and he was a superintendent and I decided I was still very discontented with what I was doing so I applied to do my social work degree, my master's. I didn't have too many credits left to do and I found out I was pregnant just the same day I decided to go back. I was torn—do I leave my maternity benefits after working for so long or should I take my maternity benefits? So I decided I would just stick at the department store for the remaining seven or eight months of the pregnancy.

Things weren't going really well with my husband and me. We were just not seeing eye-to-eye. He was very controlling and there were some things that I should've picked up on. When I first met him, he was going through a divorce from his first wife. I asked him, "Why did she leave you?" and he goes, "Oh, she's stupid" and blah-blah-blah, and there was this little hint when he said: "Oh yeah, she said I abused her." It was like, "Oh, really?" but you know, I'll never forget how it was . . . that he said it was all you know, all her fault and all that stuff. He never did it to me at first, but when I got pregnant that's when the verbal abuse and the, you know, "Why didn't you do this right?" started. But he was a little bit cautious because I was the type of person that could just go, leave him.

His ex-wife, she'd come straight from Europe, she didn't speak English, she didn't graduate from school, so she was more or less stuck with him until she saw the light. Meanwhile, my adopted father had died and he'd left me a bit of money so I was feeling pretty confident to have a child at that time and maybe buy a little condominium or something like that. But when I was about four months pregnant, he said he didn't want the baby. But I felt, "Whatever, I don't care. I'll have the baby." He didn't like that, and that's when he started to hit me and I just hit back and then finally once I called the police and they asked me if I wanted to charge him. I said no. I didn't, because I didn't feel like having a family by myself. I wanted a proper family, I'd waited so long, you know. I was 31 and I wanted everything just so perfect. I thought that at that time, but we were just not seeing eye-to-eye and I just felt so miserable all the time and like nervous, you know, but I could never really figure it out.

Then he started an online business and I gave him money. Well, supposedly I invested money with him; first $10,000 and then another $5,000, and I never saw this money again. He said he lost it. We had also bought a small cottage. We liked to go up north and stuff and he said that once I was on maternity he would assume the cost of it, but meanwhile I was paying the interest, the mortgage. Money wasn't the real issue with us and at that time; he was a superintendent so I wasn't paying rent, and neither was he, so I didn't really mind one way or the other. But once the child came, it really got stressful for me. I don't have any parents or anybody here. I had no idea on parenting or even how to do a diaper or anything. And he supposedly took time off to help me, but then broke his leg, so I had to take care of him as well. I had a newborn and him in bed. I was just exhausted and every second of the day we were irritated with each other. When my son was two months old, we had a fight of some kind and I threw a cup at him and he hit me. My best friend happened to be there and she said, "I'm taking you away from him. I'm taking you out of this." So she took me to her place and I cried all the time, was just feeling so miserable. My friend took me to the doctor, who said I had postpartum depression—really bad postpartum depression.

I have a sister in the US, and when I told her she called me and said, "I'll come and get you and the baby and you can come stay with us." So I stayed in Seattle with my sister for three months and that really helped me. Meanwhile, he wasn't feeling too proud of himself with his wife and two-month-old child gone, so he started trying to reconcile and be nice and all that stuff. He called and he was just trying to be nice and, you know, he said let's try again. My sister told me, "I don't think it's a good idea but, hey, it's your life." So I came back and we got together. It was okay but not really. So we decided that, by this time, that we were going to part, but it was financially difficult.

It really was not a good relationship and about a year later, I was still off work. I went back to the US to stay with my sister, and I was thinking that I would stay there with her. She's well off and I was looking for jobs. He had actually said something that really hurt me at that time. He said, "You can go and live there, I don't mind." And he really didn't want to see his child. But I decided not to stay and I came back. That was a big mistake. Soon after, in July, we had the biggest fight and at this point I was still really, really depressed. The doctor had given me pills for six months postpartum and then I thought, "Okay, that's fine." I didn't know anything about depression at that point, so I thought after six months I would be cured, that's it. One night when I got mad, I blew up. I went and I pulled all the books out of the shelf, and I threw the plants on the carpet. He hit me—he gave me a knockout punch and I fell on the floor unconscious.

When I came to, I went to call the police, but he got on the phone, too, telling them, "Oh, she's crazy, she's mad, she's cuckoo." And, meanwhile, while I was unconscious he had taken my son upstairs to the neighbour's place. It was four police officers that came, four big, big, big white men. When the police came they saw the mess and the weird part is, I was trying to explain to them and tell them what happened and they didn't listen to me—they just arrested me and took me to jail. I was so shocked. I didn't even have shoes on, you know, no shoes, no socks, no sweater, nothing. I didn't even know what was happening at that time, otherwise, I'd have said I have a child or whatever. So I thought, I'd go to the police station and get out. I had no clue what was happening, and it turned out that he told them that I was psychotic and crazy so they arrested me under the Mental Health Act or something like that. I went to jail, and that night I was so shocked I couldn't even speak, because I was thinking this is not me that this is happening to. I was thinking, Okay, tomorrow something's going to happen, and the next day I was wondering, "How come I'm not getting arraigned or anything?" and, you know, I was so shocked! I mean, I stayed in that jail for four days!

He didn't go to jail, nothing, even though he hit me. And then when I came out—a friend bailed me out and she called my sister—I was just devastated, totally devastated. I pressed charges against him but he still didn't go to jail although he got these charges. Then the first thing I did was I hired a lawyer, a criminal lawyer because I couldn't see my child, a family lawyer. That was one of the bail conditions and we had never been separated even one-half or one day in 18 months.

I paid for the criminal lawyer and the family lawyer with all the money that I had left. The lawyer said it was going to take a long time, but not to worry. I could only see my son under supervised visits through the Children's Aid. I was so devastated, that I felt like the only way out was to kill myself. So,

I took all the pills that I had. I don't know why I'm not dead yet. I had 28 sleeping pills. I didn't even want to tell anybody anything. I was just so ashamed. I stayed in the hospital for two months and got psychiatric help. The Children's Aid investigated and said that I shouldn't have my son at all, and because my husband was the building superintendent I had to move from where we lived. I had to find a place to live. I was overwhelmed, but I still got through that. I had not filed for custody because my husband said, "We won't file for custody," because he'd been through all this with his ex-wife and I was so stupid and naive as to believe him. He said, "Oh, we won't use lawyers and pay money, you know. You have Michael, he's still a baby, he's still young, so don't worry about it." Then about three months later he went and filed custody and he got it, but I got court-mandated access.

So meanwhile, I got a place to live. I went to the hospital for two months and they finally got me on the right drugs. They tried all different drugs, even the, I don't know, the electricity through the head. I got on the right dosage of medication because I got a really good doctor to help treat the postpartum depression. There were things that were helping me—the counselling, and I had some decent friends. So I got a place. I got a nice two-bedroom out in the west end because I was working out in there by that time. And everything was okay, but he kept blocking me from seeing my son. I remember, there was one period I saw my son two times in six months. It just was making me crazy! He'd say, "Go. You can't see him." He was just totally blocking me. Finally, I went to court and the judge was really horrified. She said, "I can't believe this," and she ordered him to give me my son right away that day and for us to have 50/50 custody.

Meanwhile, his mother had come from Europe for a year and the two of them just continued to conspire to get my son. My son was tiny at that time; he was about three. And finally, he just stalled the whole process. We went to court 16 times. I still don't know how the justice system works here when they say a speedy trial, but 16 times he adjourned Family Court. So meanwhile, Michael had been with him for two years, so there was supposedly no way I would get him because the judge wouldn't want to change his residence. I guess he knew this so he kept adjourning. It was ridiculous things: "I've got a bladder infection." "My lawyer is sick." "My mother's sick." "Michael's sick." And the judge still let it happen. It was 16 times I would go to court, get all revved up, plead, nothing, plead, nothing. Then finally I couldn't even afford where I was living anymore. I wasn't on welfare all this time, I was still trying to manage.

And then finally, I applied for legal aid and welfare. I had to pay over $69,000 for lawyers and moving. I paid $69,000 before I could get any help of any kind. So of the money my dad left me, which was $89,000, I gave my husband $20,000 for his businesses and paid $69,000 for legal fees. I ended up just being really persistent, really persistent until my son was five and I finally got joint custody.

While I was fighting for custody, broke, and homeless, I moved in with a friend of mine, because I needed to have a decent place for them to consider me for custody of Michael. But that did not work, and I ended up going to a shelter and I stayed there for two months. I was told continually by my therapist and my doctor, "Go to a shelter. They'll help you. They'll help you get a place to live, they'll help you with lots of different things." But I was stubborn. I always thought shelters were for hobos, but I finally went. It was the best move I ever made, really.

I still remember very clearly how my lawyer just shouted at me on the phone: "You fucking idiot! You won't get custody now. Why the fuck have you gone to a shelter?" But he didn't know it was on speaker phone in the office and everybody, all the counsellors and social workers heard. He was reprimanded and I got a new lawyer. I had the most wonderful worker at the shelter. If it wasn't for her I wouldn't be where I am now because I wanted to leave that night, and she said, "No, I'm not letting you leave. You're going to stay here, apply for housing and you're going to get it, and we're going to get your son back for you, and you're going to get a job or you're going to get what you want." I didn't believe her. I left the shelter after two months when I got a place. I got a place in the east end. I was so lonely and depressed there but I was still able to keep my son in the same school he was attending. All this time I kept him in the same daycare and the same school even though we were travelling from the east end to central Toronto. We'd get up at 6:30 in the morning. But it was just one piece of stability for him.

By luck, I had still kept in touch with my shelter housing worker and she told me that affordable housing that was associated with the shelter was available for me, if I wanted it. It wasn't through Metro Housing, it was through a different organization called Affordable Housing East. It was nice, it was okay, and I was happy by then, at least getting happier. I had joint custody, but it was a real bad situation because he thought that he could still make all the decisions and even if I would comb Michael's hair one way, he didn't want it that way. It was just really stressful every time I had to deal with him. Unfortunately, the joint custody wasn't one week here, one week there. It was this day here, then the next day he's back at the dad's. So I'd have to deal with this man like four or five times a week, which just wasn't working for us. But we still continued and then I got another place. I got a call maybe two weeks after I had moved into my townhouse that said I was approved for Metro Housing. At first, I felt like I didn't care because I had a place, and then I realized it was central and right next to my son's school. It was also a beautiful apartment— I couldn't refuse it. Even though moving two times in a month was hard, I did it.

Social services were so awful to me at that time. They were giving me only the single supplement because I had joint custody. So I was receiving $495 for Michael and me for those two years, and we . . . we literally couldn't manage. Luckily, at that time, they had the special diet supplement. My doctor was good. She signed the form and I got the additional $250. But, you know, a transit pass was $100 and rent for me at that time was $450. Finally I went back to my worker and she was so angry for me. She said, "Oh my goodness." Her actions are the reason why I am such an advocate of advocates. I didn't know better, but she picked up the phone and in maybe 10 minutes I got all the back pay for a single mom and a part-time job because I still had to provide exactly what a mom with a child had. Even though my son was not with me full-time, I still had to provide clothes, food, shelter. So I got enough money to cover all that and my worker said, "Who was your social assistance worker?" I said it was a man, and he wasn't nice, and she said: "I'm going to sort him out." And so she started a big inquiry; however, nothing happened. Nothing ever happens to those workers because they deny it. They always deny culpability for the things that they said.

I owed the movers so much money that by the time I moved, I couldn't even pay my rent for the new place so I ended up already in arrears with the new place, but luckily my new spirit was, "I don't care," and something will have to happen. They took me to the rental tribunal and again the rental tribunal worker said, "No, we'll help you pay it." She told me that I should have been given a startup. My response was, "What's a startup?" She explained that it was for moving expenses and that everybody is entitled to it every so often. Nobody had told me.

After we moved to our new apartment, everything was going okay, but I noticed my son wasn't very responsive. He was really frightened every time he had to go back to his dad—he was crying. Then one day while I was bathing him I looked at his body and I saw all these bruises on him and I asked: "Where did those come from, Michael?" and he said, "Oh, my dad did it." I was stunned. I asked how he did it and my son responded that he used a belt. I asked if it was the first time, but as it turned out he had been consistently beating him. He was in grade 1 at the time.

At the time I was working as a child care provider to supplement my money, and the lady I worked for was a nurse, a nurse at SickKids Hospital. I told her what happened and she said, "Don't say anything, I'm coming right now." She took us straight to SickKids and they called the police and had Michael's dad arrested.

But you know, the story was the same—I experienced the same issues with the system. Children's Aid got involved and the police arrested him and he got convicted. They took pictures of Michael's body and I was furious with the system for letting this go on even though I had told them that he was abusive toward me. Up to this time I had been sad and cried a lot, but this time I became furious with the system. I had reported the abuse toward me and nothing happened. I had said he was abusive, nothing happened, and then I had to report my child's abuse. He was found guilty of child abuse; he was put on the Child Abuse Register for three years, but, the funny part is, they still let him have access to Michael. At first it was supervised. He kept campaigning for unsupervised, but they wouldn't give it to him, but eventually he got it. He had to go through counselling, which he was so opposed to, but he had no choice but to go through it. Every time we went to court he was abusive to the judges, he was abusive to my lawyer, and after all that, he still has access. It's very limited. It's every other weekend, but he still has access. I don't think he has changed, but maybe he has realized he can't get away with it. He realizes Michael tells me everything and so I feel confident that if I leave Michael with him now he's not going to do what he did.

I think he's very careful right now. For the past year, he's been extremely careful in how he approaches Michael or me. This has put me in a more powerful position. It's not a power struggle, but at least now I don't feel afraid or tentative of him or how to approach him. That part of my life has really changed. I still feel very upset and angry at the system quite often. In many ways it failed Michael and me but we got through and we got what we needed. Then my doctor, in the meanwhile—she's a most amazing woman—and she said, "Miriam, you don't have postpartum depression, but you do have clinical depression." Which means it has more to do with the circumstances of my life, but she said I do have to get it addressed, so she told me to apply for disability. She made me do it. I got it right away and that's where I am. It's enough money for us to live on. It's not enough to have luxuries, but those things I can work for on my own.

I also have a new set of friends, amazing friends. I'm just more open, I guess, and my relationship with my son is amazing, I love him and he's come through all this so unscathed, almost. We went through a lot of counselling, me and him, and he's just a really bouncy little kid. He's a good kid and I feel blessed to have him.

Where I'm going I don't know. But I do feel I want to do something that helps other women or kids that were in my position, because I didn't know anything and the system does not care to tell you anything. From the first moment, when I should have applied for custody of Michael right away and nobody told me about this—everything fell apart just because of that. If I'd applied for Michael the first time when we had the fight, much of this would not have happened: a lot of situations with welfare and stuff, and the social worker not telling me what I was entitled to, what I wasn't entitled to. What I dislike the most is the variance. If it's one way in one place with one worker, it should be the same way in another place with another worker. They shouldn't need someone saying, "Well, you need to give her more money" and only then it is given to me. It should be provided because I am entitled to it. I also feel with single moms, the work situation is outrageous. I'm on ODSP. I'd love to go back to university. I have one year left to do. They don't support any programs for college, nothing. So either you have to take a menial job, rely on your old experience, or you just don't bother. And at the point I am right now, I don't want to bother. I've given up on them so I'm going my own way looking for what I want to do and when I want to do it. I feel more in control of my life and look forward to moving forward in a positive and happy way.

Victoria's Story

I was born in Central America, and I lived there with my birth mom until I was five. I later learned from my adoptive parents that I may be half American, so I think maybe my father was American. My brother is two years younger than me, and he also lived with my mom at that time. I don't remember much about living with our mom, but I remember her long hair. I don't remember her personality, just that she was a kind lady. When I was five, government soldiers came to our home and took us away from our mom and put me in an orphanage. I was told years later that my mother did not have a suitable job, and that she was not taking care of us well, so that is why we were taken away from her.

I remember the orphanage. The orphanage was fun for me; there were lots of kids. There were lots of beds in each room, and the boys and girls were mixed together. I remember my attorney; she was a very nice woman. I remember my foster mom, and I remember the two other ladies who took care of me in the orphanage. My foster mom wanted to adopt me, but she had health issues. My brother came to the orphanage later, when he was five. I don't remember much about him before he came to the orphanage, and I don't know who he stayed with—if he was allowed to stay with my mother or not—after they took me away. My brother and I took care of each other; we hung out together. I only stayed at the orphanage until I was seven, when my brother and I were adopted. Most people wanted to adopt me separately, but the people at the orphanage refused to separate us; we were to be together, no matter what.

The woman and man who adopted us were Canadian volunteers who had been working in the orphanage for weeks, painting and doing things. They had not thought about adopting a child until they got there to help. When we left, I remember looking at my foster mom and crying a lot. I loved my country very much. I had everything there. I could run around with no shoes and have fun. It was very secure, very safe. I loved my school. I wasn't sure what was going to happen, but I trusted people and thought, "Maybe this is better than staying here." I think if I had known they would listen to me, I would have told them I did not want to go. I had good instincts, but I trusted people too much.

We came to Canada in November. When we arrived, I noticed that there was snow on the ground. I didn't know it was snow. In my country, the clouds come down, so that is what I thought the snow was—clouds. I went outside in my bare feet and I yelled out, "Mucho frio!" (This means "very cold" in my language). We lived in a pretty nice house. My brother and I spoke no English, and my adopted parents spoke to us mostly in English, with just a little bit of

Spanish. The only way we could communicate was through facial expressions or by pointing. My brother and I learned English really fast—in one or two years—and we adapted very well to school.

At first it was okay, and then my mom became quite unstable. She would do really weird things to insult us and degrade us. She would use punishments even though we didn't do things to deserve those punishments. As one punishment, she would have my brother sit at the top of the stairs outside and tell me to stand on the sidewalk or the road in front of our house. She would have my brother point fingers, laugh, and make mean remarks to me. Then she would do the same thing to him. If my brother was to be punished, I was to sit beside my mother and degrade him. This is how it all started, and it was very weird for me. It was just like out of the blue, my mom would snap or hit.

My brother was beaten up more than me. I was the tough one—I fought back. I don't know what was in her mind; if we did the slightest little thing or silliness that children do, she would go off. At this time—when I was around nine—my mom was extremely abusive. My dad never liked to hit us, even though he did what he did to me. Although he didn't like to hit us, my mom would get my dad to spank us, and she would tell him to spank us hard. It came to the point where every time they spanked us, we ended up bleeding. It was that bad! They would spank us with wooden spoons and belts, but it was my mom's hand most of the time. I remember her hand being very red because she spanked us so hard. I remember the pain—a lot of pain.

For another punishment, my mom would beat my brother—who was naked—on the floor. She would just beat him up, and I would watch this. He would be crying and screaming. My mom had really weird ways of doing things.

My father was a very selfish man, and he sexually abused me. He started when I was nine, and it went on until I was about 15, after I had told my mom. She did not take it well. She says she didn't know, but I think she did. My father would come into my room while my mom was teaching—my mom was self-employed and had a job teaching a musical instrument in our home. Because the only times my mother would say goodnight to me was when I was sick, my dad had a lot of opportunities to come into my room and do whatever he pleased to me. I pretended to be sleeping at the time because I just— I didn't know how to take it.

Because of my mom's rules, every pantry and every bathroom had a lock. At first we couldn't reach the locks, but as we grew we were able to reach them. The locks on the bathrooms were used when my mom put us there overnight to punish us. She would get my brother to sleep overnight in the bathroom with no food. Of course, there is water in there, but he would literally sleep on the floor, sometimes with just underwear on. No pyjamas. No clothing. No blankets. No nothing. She did the same thing to me as well. This happened during the same period of time that I was being abused by my dad.

And then we moved to another house. This time, the punishments became even worse, and because of that it was really, really hard for me to concentrate in school. When I came to Canada I was put immediately into grade two, although I was supposed to be put into grade one because I didn't know English. Because I was put into grade two, I was told I would be given ESL help. I know that I speak English well now, but I was diagnosed with a disability as an audio learner and I find I have trouble writing essays and all that. I needed more concentration in English and ESL, but it wasn't given to me. At school I just tried to keep up with my friends. My friends had amazing grades, but they would complain about them. When my assignments were handed back, I would get C's—really low marks—and this wasn't good enough for me. I had to pretend to my friends that I got good marks. I told them I got A's, but it wasn't enough. I just wanted to have friends and to be part of a group. I pretended to be balanced, like everything was okay at home. In grade 6, I was looked at and touched inappropriately by my teacher but did not tell anybody because how my father was treating me made me think that any man had the right to me. If I had ever told my friends what was going on at home, they would never have believed me—*never*!

It was really hard to concentrate in school because my mom would call the school, and the school would tell me that I needed to talk to her on the phone. She would tell me that I needed to come home right away, because I hadn't finished the laundry, or I hadn't finished this or that. I had to clean up a lot at home, and it wasn't normal, because it had an impact on my educational development. I could accept this in my country, but not in Canada because in order to keep up with educational expectations I had to focus on my education. I had to clean up everybody's stuff, and I had to take care of my brothers and sisters. I have my birth brother, an adopted brother, and my sister, who was also adopted. When they were first adopted, I had to take care of a lot of things. My mom didn't even know how to change diapers. I had to show her how to change diapers. I cooked a lot. I put them to sleep. She got me to do this. They were not abused; I told my mom and dad that if they touched my siblings I would not be okay with this. I told my mom once not to lay a hand on them. I was very protective of them. But she was envious of my close relationship and the maternal instincts I had for my siblings.

When I was around nine or ten, my mom, for punishment, used to put me in a diaper and get me to sit in my room on the floor all by myself. It was very degrading and insulting. I have no idea why she did it. She just wanted to make me feel really bad about by myself. And I think she, to this day, really accomplished that, because I don't have much self-esteem. I present myself like—you know, like I'm okay. But I feel tortured inside, like I'm fighting it. I have been in therapy for the past 15 years and oh lord I'm so glad I continued this voluntarily! I know I would be in a worse place if I did not receive the support that I have been getting, but at the same time I would have preferred a psychiatrist or psychologist a long time ago and consistently for my unresolved issues, deep level of pain, and negative habits that endure.

My mom got me into piano, ballet, and swimming lessons. I was thankful for swimming lessons and I am thankful now for piano lessons. Ballet was not my thing. I was playing high grades on the piano for my age—memorized and eight pages long. When I got the wrong key on the piano, my mom would pinch my neck or pull my hair so that I fell back off the bench. I was really scared to make mistakes on the piano, so piano became torturous to play, not fun. Everything was torturous—not fun—at that age, from about age 8 to 12, I believe.

If my birth brother or I got hungry and took something without asking and my mom found out, she would force us to eat double the amount of the thing that we took. Even if we were throwing up, she didn't care—we still had to eat. One time, we really wanted some icing—you know how kids are, they just want to eat junk. We weren't really thinking about the consequences, we were just thinking that we wanted something sweet. My mom found out and forced us both to eat two buckets full of icing. My brother started to throw up, and my mom said if he threw up, we would have to eat it too. My brother was also forced to stand outside naked in the winter on our outside patio, standing in the snow freezing! I remembered crying quietly, so my mom would not hear. My brother hates my mother; he has some awful words just for her . . . I don't blame him.

My brother began stealing things. He was going through a lot. I don't blame him because of how he was treated by my mom, who insulted him and beat him up. Anytime my brother got in trouble, I would try to take the punishment. I always said that I did it, I broke it, or I stole it, so that he wouldn't be punished, because he was punished even more than I was. My brother did not take the abuse very well. He was taken out of our home when he was 13 years old. My mom put him in an institution, a treatment centre; that showed me how much she did not love him. I kept in touch with him as much as I could. That's when I saw clearly that he was gay, but I didn't care—I was confused but loved him so much still. My brother disappeared three years ago and I have not seen him since. I miss him so much!

I missed my brother very much when he was taken away at 13. I really hated my mom, and the rage and violence between us became intolerable. We couldn't stand each other. I couldn't stand her. I literally thought of doing something to her. When I was 14, I told my mother that my dad had been sexually abusing me, touching me. My mother gave me mixed signals. I didn't understand at all if she believed me; she heard me, but she wanted to hear his side first before making a decision. I was scared that she wasn't going to believe me, but I felt that she sort of believed me because she confronted him and he didn't deny it. My dad looked at me in shock that I knew that he was doing that to me. Because he didn't deny it, though, my mother let him stay, and he tried to sexually abuse me over again and again. He kept trying to do more things and I got even more scared because I did not want him to have sex with me. So, I told my mom again, and this time the cops escorted him out of our home. It was great for me, but very confusing. I thought I had destroyed the family.

I was 15 when my dad left. We went to court. Well, we didn't actually go to court—we were scheduled to go court, but supposedly he didn't deny any-thing, so I don't know what happened—but basically, he didn't get in trouble. He didn't go to jail, and he didn't serve time. After that, my mom and I got into worse fights. One day, she came up the stairs. I was sick and tired of her hitting me. She came up the stairs to punish me and hit me again, and I told her if she touched me I would seriously kill her. She touched me and tried to beat me up, so I pushed her down the stairs. I thought something bad had happened to her, but she literally just came back up, ready to hit me again.

When I was 17, on the week of my birthday I put a lot of thought into leaving and how I would, then I threatened to leave. My mom said, "If you leave, you will never be able to come back." I said, "That's what I planned; that's why I'm leaving." She tried to force the door closed and put herself in front of it. I told her to move and she said, "Are you sure you want to leave? Because you will never be able to come back." She would say this over and over! Of course, I was really scared. I was 17. I was like, "What am I doing?" But I'd rather have been anywhere else but there. So at 17, I ran away and dropped out of grade 10. I ran all the way downtown to my brother's treatment centre, which was far from where we lived. They said I couldn't stay with him. They said I had to go to a shelter. From 17 until 20, I stayed in shelters. I stayed with friends here or there, but mostly I stayed in shelters. I am a very quiet person and some people at the shelters didn't like that—they found it intimidating. The years in the shelters were horrible, and a lot of things happened. I dated men who were not so good for me, who treated me like garbage, and who did things that really hurt me in a lot of ways. At one point, I was sexually assaulted by an 18-year-old—he attempted to rape me. He was disrespectful to women. After I came forward, a lot of girls stated that he did this to them too, and when they heard that he was sentenced for two years. Because of me, they all came forward and talked about this more freely. Through the court process, I had an amazing officer. After everything was over, she still kept in touch with me.

I was young; I didn't really have anybody to protect me, so I did things in order to protect myself and to survive and to make money. It was very hard because, if there was no room in a shelter and you had nobody to turn to, you were alone and you got into trouble. If you had nothing to do, obviously you turned to drugs or smoking or hanging out with people who are also on the streets. I did not get caught up in drugs. I tried marijuana and drinking, but they were not for me. The only thing I did was smoke, and I quit a couple of years ago but started again recently. Being in a room with a bunch of girls, having your stuff stolen, having to defend and prove yourself all the time, and hanging out in places you don't want to be was scary, and I didn't like it at all. I knew I had to survive no matter what, and even if the other street people were not great, I had to depend on them to survive, and they depended on me too.

At one point, I dated a guy who took me to a house that he told me was his friend's place. After we got there, he said that he had to go to the store. I asked him, "Why do you have to go to the store now? What is so important that you have to go to the store?" But he just told me he wanted me to stay there. After he left, his friends came into the room and I was gang-raped by three or four men. Given what happened with my father I just pretended in my mind like it wasn't happening. These men kept coming into the room to play games and manipulate me. I felt like if I did anything to stop them, something would happen to me—like I would get beaten up or something, so I just went along with what they were doing and they all had sex with me. Of course I blamed myself and told myself I deserved it. My boyfriend came back, and I freaked out on him. I asked, "Where did you go? What were you doing?" He said, "What do you mean? What's wrong?" I said, "Well, your friends, you know, they did whatever they wanted to me." He freaked out, but I feel like it was all a set-up. I honestly feel like he was in it for a game. He pretended to be really mad at them and said he would deal with them. But I was done with him. It's still hard to get over and let it go, even now.

It seemed like people were coming at me from every direction, even though I was minding my own business. I had girls coming to me who wanted to fight with me for no reason. I was shocked. I was confused. The people who accepted me were boys and men, even though they treated me badly. I didn't get much money when I was living in the shelter—I got an allowance of 26 dollars a week—and it wasn't enough for me. Because I didn't have enough money I unfortunately did some things I'm not proud of. I had sex with men for money. I was treated like garbage, and I didn't even care about the money afterwards. I didn't have anything left of me, and I was upset. I was like, "What am I doing to myself? This is not me."

Although a lot of the shelter staff were helpful, I had to do it on my own—move out of the shelter. I did this by moving in with a man. I used to go online to talk to people; again, it was about not being alone; I hated being alone. So when I was around 18, I moved in with this man who was 30 years old. I knew it was not going to last—it was just about getting out of the shelter. This man had met me in the shelter and knew I was going through a lot of rough stuff there. He always protected me. He was a nice man and treated me like a princess. He would never hurt me. So I lived with him, and during that time I met my son's father. We met through a telephone service and we got to know each other even though I was still living with the other man. I thought I was in love and I wanted to have a baby. I thought the baby's father would take care of me. I got pregnant, and I was so excited and proud. I wanted to be a mom—I guess I knew I was meant to be a mom. I wanted to be a mom so badly, to have a baby and to take care of a baby, so I moved in with him and his mom. I lived there until I had the baby, and it was hell. His mom was cold and called me Nothing. That was my name, Nothing. She would call me by this name and I told my son's father, "'Nada' [nothing]. I think you know she's disrespecting me." Of course, he just let her do whatever she wanted. She was rude and insulting, but I knew that this was her way of dealing with people who were in her son's life. She could have been a lot nicer, but it was always like that. To this day it has never changed.

When I went to the hospital to have the baby, things started to become very clear to me. This was supposed to be the most amazing day of my life, but of course my son's father was controlling it, although I didn't see it that way then. I just thought he was protecting me. But anyway, I wanted to take the epidural, and he didn't want me to. He told the doctors and the nurses that it was his right to refuse the epidural on my behalf in case I had side effects later. He swore at them and was hostile. He said to me, "If you take this, I am leaving." I told him he could leave. I was in labour. I was in pain. He whispered in my ear and said, "If you take the epidural, I will leave right now." I was crying. I said to him, "What are you talking about? My body is in pain. You're not going through what I am going through." The nurses and the doctors were worried for my health and about jeopardizing my life and my baby's! My mom was there; she was holding my hand in the labour room. (I had called my mom before I got pregnant. I was trying to reconnect. We didn't get along very well, so here and there I made calls, but she never knew where I was. Then when I got pregnant, I asked for support.) The doctor said that if I didn't take the epidural, I wouldn't be able to relax and my son would be in jeopardy. I couldn't feel my body, so how could I push? The baby and I could both die. I took this very seriously and said, "Yes, I want the epidural." My baby's father began swearing at the doctors and the nurses and causing this terrible scene. His mother, who was there, said: "Oh, I didn't do it with an epidural. I did it normally; I didn't have to use that." I was like, "How is this helping me?" So security escorted them all out. They kicked them out of the hospital while I had the baby. This was all going on, and I couldn't even believe it. I remembered thinking, "How can they be so selfish? I do not deserve this kind of treatment from her let alone him!" He didn't have a mind of his own and his mom was a controlling manipulative woman.

I had my son in the late 90s. He had the umbilical cord wrapped around his neck, so when he was born he couldn't breathe. My mom was concerned, but I said, "Mom, God wouldn't let me go through all of these things only to take away my child." I was the most patient, calm person. She said it was like I knew it was going to be okay. As soon as they took him away I heard him crying and he was breathing. He came back to me, and I was so happy. I didn't care what else was happening. Because of all the drama that his father created, I had to stay in the hospital for about a week. Children's Aid was involved; they came to the hospital and were there for me. They didn't want any problems from the father. They also wanted to take me to a secured shelter. I didn't want to go. I wanted to go to my mother's house, but my mom said I couldn't go there. While I was in the hospital, the baby's father came once, even though there was security. I don't know how it happened, but he and his brother came around midnight. He wanted to see his son, and I could tell that he and his brother were high. They were very disrespectful. I talked to him, but I was pretty weak. I remember telling him not to touch the baby, and asking him how he could come there high. I was really mad. I tried to call the nurse. Finally he left, and his brother left too.

I begged my mom not to take me to the shelter. I did not want to go to a shelter with a week-old baby, but she drove me there anyway. I didn't fight it because I was too distressed. At the shelter, I couldn't even do the paperwork because I was so upset. Every time they asked me a question, I would cry. I was so angry with her, but I did not tell her. I was not surprised by her selfish behaviour, though. Considering all she had done to me, why couldn't she just let me stay with her? If I was stronger I would have told her not to bother to see me again! I was not a good judge of character in my life then, but now believe me, it's way different.

When I went into the shelter with my week-old baby, I was scared for my child because I was put in the upper bunk bed and I was told to put my son in a bassinet in the middle of all the bunk beds, where people could easily step on him. I guess because I was a new mom, I was very paranoid that he'd get stepped on, so every night when the staff and everyone else went to bed I took him up to bed with me. Of course in the morning staff would tell me, "You know that you can't have a baby on the top bunk." And I would go, "Are you kidding me? He's two weeks old. You know, leave me alone." So every night I did that, until they actually gave me a bottom bunk to stay with him.

I said to myself, "I'm not going to stay here more than four months." I wasn't going to stay there with my child because already women were trying to approach me and fight me. One time I was shocked when a woman wanted to have a fight with me for no apparent reason, just because of a TV show. I was holding my son at the time and I told her not to do anything to me. I was very protective of my son. I was having a lot of trouble in that shelter. When my son wouldn't sleep, I had to pretty much snuggle him, and I would have to sleep sitting up. Every time I put him in the crib, he would scream. I was told he was colicky. When we were in the hospital I had to walk him back and forth, back and forth every night. It was hard, but I would do it even to the death of me.

I was going through a lot then; I wanted to sleep so badly. I wanted to feel what it was to sleep, but all I could think at that time was, "I just have to take care of him. I have to be here." Nobody else was going to do it for me. When I wanted to take a shower, my friends in the shelter would offer to take care of my son for me, but I was like, "No, he's coming to the bathroom with me." They would tell me that I couldn't take him to the bathroom in case something happened to him. So I would go, "Okay," but then I would go get my stuff and take him in the bathroom anyway. The same happened when I had to do my chores. People would say, "You can't take him with you when you do your chores," and I'd go, "Okay." But then I would go do my chores with him anyway. I wouldn't let him out of my sight.

And then one day—even though I told the shelter that my son's father was abusive and that I did not want him or his family near me—one day, the staff told me there was someone there to see me, and my baby's father was waiting outside. He was waiting right upstairs, standing in the part where you can see through the door. I don't know how he found out where I was—he said he checked around and asked people, but I believe his mom helped him, for she worked in a child protection agency. I was so mad at the shelter staff. I said, "What is wrong with you? I didn't want him to know where I was that is why I'm here." I couldn't believe it when he found me. I just couldn't believe it. He said he wanted to see my son. I didn't want him to cause any trouble, so I just let him see the baby. At this same particular time I received a phone call that another girl was pregnant with his child—of course at the time he denied it. This should have been a huge sign for me to get out, but I was stupid in love or so I thought.

Four months later, I was really determined to get out of there, so even though it was winter, I took my son and I went from place to place to look for a place to live. I found one for $650 a month—it was in a basement but it was our own little home. I was very proud of myself. It had green carpet and blue walls, a fan, and even though it was, like, way deep in the basement, it was pretty colourful inside. I was really pleased with myself. I had an amazing public health nurse who brought me all sorts of stuff and then helped me settle into my new place. After that, I think I was getting depressed. It was really hard to be on my own. I literally didn't have anybody. I had my mom occasionally, but I was still mad at her and never had her come to my home, unless it was my son's birthday or something special.

Of course, I called my baby's father up and started building a relationship with him again. Mistake—in thinking of it now—after all the things he did. He sold drugs and had drugs there mostly every night. He was disrespectful, disloyal, came home so late and threatened to throw away kittens in the garbage that I found for my son. I then found a picture in his wallet of a baby boy. I questioned him with disgust and anger. He of course denied it again, telling me that someone put it in there as a joke. I was catching on but too slowly, of course. He pressured me in getting this other place for $1500 dollars a month. It was a very bad mistake but it was a beautiful house . . . I imagined the kind of life I would have . . . he had a good job, so of course I trusted him. He told me he was paying the rent, but he wasn't. I didn't know this then, but I know it now. I depended on him because I wanted a family so bad, and a husband in the future. I was working as an assistant in a daycare. I volunteered first because my son was there. I wanted to see how he was doing in a daycare, so because I wanted to keep an eye on him, I decided to work there. It did not pay enough, so I went on welfare.

In early 2000, I was on the phone with a friend, and my baby's father assumed that I was on the phone with a man and went crazy on me. He accused me of cheating and doing all these things and became very abusive. He ripped up a shirt of mine, put some bruises on my arms, threw brushes— threw anything on my dresser—my way, and a neighbour called the police. My son was sleeping at the time. The police asked me if I wanted to charge him and I said no, and they said, "Okay, we're going to charge him anyway." So they charged him; they took him away. He was in jail for maybe one day and he was told to go in for anger management. The police took a statement. They told me to get away from him. What you call this, I don't know, but I guess I was dumb because I let him come back maybe a week or two weeks later. Thinking about it now, I'm like, "What on earth?" But I was alone. I wanted a family. I wanted to be in a family. And it just wasn't going to happen with this guy—now I get it, but then, oh boy!

After that I stayed in my home. We couldn't pay rent anymore. I was told I was going to be evicted . . . it was 2003, August of 2003. I remember when I was in the shelter, they always told me to come up with a Plan B, and that always stuck with me. Thank God I called housing. I had applied for public housing when I was at the shelter. They said they had been trying to reach me since I was in the shelter with my newborn, and they tried to speed up the process of trying to get me a place. During that time I tried really hard to have a plan to get out of the relationship ASAP after getting housing. I wanted to ease myself away from the relationship but I was just waiting for the perfect time to do so! I knew the relationship was done and I would not have a chance for a better life if I did not get out soon. Housing showed me a lot of places, some quite far away—some were awful and some were what I had asked for but not good enough. I was like, "What on earth?" But they were in a rush for me to get somewhere because I was getting evicted. The second-to-last place I was offered was in a basement, and I knew I did not want to be in a basement again. So I asked them for one more try, and then they offered me a place in a great neighbourhood on the fourth floor of a nice building. They said, "Do you want to take it?" I said, "Yeah, I don't even care; I don't want to see it. I just want to go. I just want to take it." And I was so thankful, because I knew that they guaranteed a subsidized rent I could pay. It was a big difference not having to worry about the rent—a big difference from $1500 to $234. I was so thankful, and I knew that I would be able to provide my son with a secure place and not have to feel like I had to go to a shelter. I never want to put him through that again. His father didn't care at any point that what he was doing could put us at risk—he did not mind us being at risk of being homeless—but I knew better because of what I went through. My mind was thinking more rationally for the sake and well-being of my son. I learned the hard way that it's not my responsibility to change people, it's up to them, even family members, especially if they want to be in my life or my son's life. I no longer put up with anyone who is an abuser or who has a negative impact on my son or me.

At this point, I did go back to high school and finished as a mature student. Then I went to college for five years. I took a certificate and two other diplomas. I was very proud of myself for that, because my mother had predicted that college would be hard and that most likely I would not make it. My learning disability (audio learner), made me feel stupid, and having her say that did not help at all! I went off welfare and took out student loans to do it and now I owe $40,000. I just wish I could get a job that pays enough, but I feel like the programs I took at college are not noticed as much as the title "social worker" is. Because of that, I might go back to school. I recently fractured my ankle, so it's delayed some things, and I'm also going through a lot—as you can imagine. I am still presently working on all the things that happened in my childhood, especially regarding the childhood sexual abuse that I endured. I consider myself as a survivor but continue to receive help. I saw a psychologist, but because he was a man I said, "Sorry," he could not help me with this particular matter. I've been seeing therapists since I was 15 years old.

Now I feel like I'm taking care of myself, like I'm paying attention to me and to my son and what I truly want. It's just—it's really hard because I feel, you know, that having a solid career would make such a difference, financially, for us and for the future of my son. At the same time, it's really hard getting a job because I applied to a lot of places and I find that I just don't get the calls—it's been like this for maybe two years. I like to work. I'm the kind of person who wouldn't even care about being paid; I just want to help people. I want to offer a hand. I want to be there. I want to tell them that, you know, they can do it too—to motivate them and help them through tough times. I know I'm good at these things. I'm very intuitive, reliable, understanding, and a hard worker at what I put my mind to. I am now working at a public school over lunch hour. I love it there, but the hours are not great and the pay is not great. I have recently been asked for an interview with the school board and hope very much that this leads me to a better place! I love my son, and I believe in God tremendously, and without him I know I would not be here, for he stuck with me through it all.

I still connect with my father to get questions answered about my past; with regard to my mother, I don't connect with her at all because she never wants to talk about how she treated me. So I forgive and move on to a better life. I learned that forgiving is not about forgetting and certainly does not have to do with keeping that person in your life; it's about finding peace and joy within yourself, and this is how I live my life now. I take care of my health now and have lost 50 pounds. I now jog and love it, and I participate in marathons.

On another note, welfare is ridiculous—people on it are just barely able to get by on a monthly basis, especially if you are a single mother with no child support. I am glad I am working now, but that cheque is not much and it goes really fast. I am glad that I am in Canada because otherwise I don't know how I would be living, but still it is hard. When you work they deduct half your cheque; instead they should be crediting you for work and providing transportation, especially for youth who have to use transportation to get to school. This would help people in this situation not to stay on welfare and provide a better life for themselves. Welfare should—with no hesitations—provide assistance to those that need a psychologist/psychiatrist, especially those who seek help. In my experience there is a huge difference in quality between them and therapists/counsellors/social workers who are free in a lot of places. Those people are great but those with severe need of help need more. I am surprised that this is not noticed and put into action, for if you have people with a great state of mind, they do better. In my opinion it makes sense and those who are on social assistance, especially the single moms, are there because of trauma. They can't do a good job of being independent and raising their kids if there are no skilled supports.

My son is 13 now and he is doing well. I am raising him to be a productive and successful member of society. He is a really good student, and he wants to be a doctor. I am very proud of him. I love him so much. I don't have much in terms of family to provide for him, but I have a great, supportive group of friends. I only hope that things improve in today's systems, welfare being one of them and access to jobs. That could make a huge difference toward improving individual lives. There are a lot of people, especially mothers, who try very hard to make a better life for their children. They deserve the best for their children, and the children deserve to have a fulfilled lifestyle to be successful for the future.

Izabela's Story

I was born in Eastern Europe and I was the only child. I had the most amazing grandparents, and from probably six months or so I grew up at my grandmother's. This was a big blessing, because my mother had some health issues. I was able to get to see farm life and I absolutely got to see nature and to love animals—back home that was the norm. Whoever went to daycare was not considered lucky. People thought I was lucky that I had grandparents and I could spend wonderful summers with them and didn't have to go to some summer camp.

When I was growing up my mother was quite mean. I don't remember one time that was heartwarming, or any moment in my life that I felt close to my mother, unfortunately. That is why I said I was so blessed growing up with my grandparents, my grandmother in particular. She was very sweet and she was like a mother to me. My mother would swear a lot at me, and she would call me names. It was difficult, and I grew up thinking that I was not good enough. My mother's sister also played a role in my growing up. She was very nice and kind to me and taught me a lot of things. So I struggled with my mother and yet I had a lot of good support and guidance and role models like my grandma and my other aunts. It helped me to become who I am—a fighter.

My parents divorced when I was about three, and of course I don't remember that time. Shortly afterwards my mom met my stepfather. When I was about 12 or so he molested me, but I didn't know that that was wrong and I didn't know what he was really doing. That kept on going until I was about 14 or so, when he left to go to Canada. My mother had a very difficult time when he left because he left us unexpectedly. After that, my mother slowly but surely became an alcoholic. That was when I was 15 or 16, and I experienced a lot of shame and embarrassment because I could not have any friends over because I didn't know what condition my mother would come home in. It was very difficult for me.

My stepfather came back and sort of got back in touch with us and invited us to come back to Canada with him. It was very difficult for me, leaving everybody behind. Now that I know more about alcohol and addictions, I think, "How could anybody let me leave with this woman who is such an alcoholic to go to some strange country?" I was a child, 16; how could they let me go? But they did, and I have been in Canada now for 18 years. After arriving in Canada, I struggled a lot. The abuse continued with my stepfather. When I reflect back on that time, I think that a big, big important piece was that my mother actually knew what he was doing. That is what hurt me the most. I don't think that what he did to me affected me as much as the fact that my mother knew about it and she didn't protect me. Although I should have been used to her behaviour because she was not really there for me much, some choices that she made really hurt me and that was one of them. I couldn't understand why. I knew she loved me and that she sacrificed a lot.

I was about 18 when I confronted my stepfather at a time when neither he nor my mom were drunk. He owned up and said he was just teaching me sexuality. My mother, however, started screaming at me like crazy and said that I was making it up. That hurt me a lot because I was certain that she would stand up for me, and she didn't, and that really, really hurt me. I moved out of their house just before I turned 18. I had lived in Canada for half a year. I didn't know much English, but I was studying English on my own. I was in a specialized school and I was very linguistically inclined. I knew German, Russian, and my own language, and then in Canada I had to learn English, which I had no problem doing because I had a good grip on languages. That was quite easy, and I think in about seven or eight months I was fairly fluent in English.

I worked at different jobs, babysitting, and then ended up working in a bar. I was not working legally because I did not have my papers yet. People tried to take advantage of me because I was not legal. There was no mother for support and nobody to turn to, and I knew I had to grow up all on my own. At the bar I met a boyfriend. I didn't know it at the time, but he was very controlling and turned out to be very abusive. He was 10 years older than me. He took me under complete control and brainwashed me; some of that still haunts me. I started getting jobs that were not really acceptable but were bringing me a lot of income. Then and only then, when I was financially independent, did I get rid of the abusive boyfriend. I actually took him to court for abusing me and he ended up in jail for six months. I still think to this day that I did a good thing.

That same abusive boyfriend kept telling me I was fat and that was detrimental to me; I started to starve myself and developed anorexia. I also developed bulimia. Back home, one of my aunts made a remark to me that I was getting kind of bubbly or a little roundish. I was really far from fat but that's what she told me, and I got concerned. I also had a very slim girlfriend— naturally slim—who was a dancer. She was an example to me, so looking at her I felt like I was fat. Due to these things I developed eating disorders.

When I came to Canada I continued high school and at 18 I was in grade 11. Because of these eating disorders I was seeing a counsellor at school who noticed bruises under my eyes and that I was missing school. I opened up right away to her because of course I didn't have anybody to talk to. I was grateful for anybody that would talk to me. She recommended a counsellor who specialized in body image at Women's College Hospital. From there I got some guidance and I was getting a little bit better, and I was also talking to the counsellor about my abusive boyfriend and my struggle against his brainwashing. Obviously the brainwashing was far more painful than the physical abuse. He crushed me. I was this beautiful young girl and he just crushed me and made me feel like I was a nobody. People would look at me on the bus, and I thought they looked because I was ugly or something was wrong with me, not because I looked beautiful. So both the counselling and becoming financially independent helped me. I never regretted that I went into the wrong line of work, so to speak, because actually that made me stronger— that didn't crush me or make me into a bad person, and I didn't get addicted to all kinds of things. It was the opposite. It made me stronger. I called the police and they came and they finally documented everything. I got a lawyer and I went to court, and it was a good ending.

After that, I was beginning to live a good life and I was becoming more and more confident. The eating disorder was still there, but not as much. I was still very needy and clingy, however, because I didn't have any family with me. I didn't have anybody to be there for me. So whenever I would meet a boyfriend or fall in love with someone I would look for a father figure, someone that would take care of me. Almost all of my boyfriends were like that.

In the end, I was with the abusive boyfriend for about three and a half years. It was on and off, but still, three years at 18 is a big thing. As soon as I opened my eyes, I had no respect for him. Then I met somebody else who was the very opposite, who was very mature and had good sense, and he was even older—16 years older. He really taught me a lot of good things. He really made me feel more confident. However, he didn't really support the idea of my going to school and I just thought that was the way things were done, so I just never went to school. I finished high school and that was the end of that. I thought I was going to be a housewife and I was going to be happy with that, because I was afraid to try new things and school was one of them. It's the insecurity that was haunting me combined with thinking that maybe I was not smart enough to go any further.

I started to drink at this point, but not very much. I was in touch with my mother on and off. She would call me when she was drinking and she would call me names. Then after a while I started to recognize when she would call me drunk, so then I wouldn't even talk to her. Sometimes I wanted to have a drink too, but never too much and not every day. There were times, however, when I would get really drunk and I would black out and I would not remember what I did. I knew that we have addictions and alcoholism in the family and I thought that it would not touch me—it would not be me because I already knew so much about it. But I didn't really know much at all; I just thought I did.

I was 25 when I broke up with the second man who had actually been very good to me. There was one problem that I couldn't handle—his children.

If I loved someone, the children seemed like a competition to me. I would always ask him, "If there was an accident, who would you run to rescue—your children, or me?" Obviously he couldn't answer that and I was just never satisfied. I was actually obsessed with that, and I really suffered a lot because of that, and I know it sounds very sick but they were very true feelings. I just couldn't take it. The children were a competition to me and I was threatened that he loved them more than me, and that he saw his ex-wife in them. I was very insecure, and so we broke up.

Unfortunately, after that I met someone who introduced me to drugs and even more alcohol. The drugs never stuck to me even though we were partying from Monday to Sunday. I had never had a chance to party before because my first abusive boyfriend prohibited me from going out anywhere. We wouldn't go anywhere because he was actually insecure too, and that's why he had to control me. He wouldn't want to go anywhere with me because men would look at me, and that would be a threat to him so, I didn't go out myself and we didn't go anywhere together.

When I met this third man I was 25, and a whole new world opened up to me. I felt pretty good about myself. I had stopped working when I was 22 or so and the second boyfriend was supporting me and paying for my car and everything. Then the third took over. Now I almost want to smile or laugh at how ridiculous that sounds, but really it was that way—somehow men would just take care of me. I was living in a nice apartment and dressing very well. The third boyfriend was not a father figure; he was only five years older than me. He was just really a lover and I really cared for him a lot. It was a lot of partying and I had a lot of friends, something that I had never had before. I grew up as a single child and I was somehow different, so I never had a big circle of friends. This new life was all very cool for me because I had always been dreaming of it. We would party, and everyone was drinking from morning until night. Very shortly after that I realized that I had become an alcoholic. I knew I should go and get help because my boyfriend was telling me it was becoming an issue. I was also a binge drinker from the get-go: once I started drinking, I would just continue.

I decided I would try to do something about the drinking, so I went to the hospital, but I was too embarrassed to take any classes on addiction or anything like that because I thought I was so popular that everybody would recognize me. So I just got some pills to take that would help me maybe to stop drinking, and I took them for a month or so. I thought I was cured, so I stopped taking them. Afterwards, everybody that I had in my life was taking care of me and I was still not secure and not happy with myself even though I tried to put on a façade that I am very confident.

I separated from my boyfriend. My drinking had progressed a lot. That's all I did, basically: drink. Then I met my son's father. He was much younger, and I was very needy. It was the first time in my life since I was 16 that I didn't have a boyfriend. I was desperate, and I needed someone. I couldn't live without someone because I was not used to it. I was 27, and all this time my big desire was to have a family and a lot of children—I know what I said previously about children and being competitive about them—maybe I thought it would be different if they were my own! I was a very good cook and I always took wonderful care around the house. I was reading a lot of books, and I was still trying to keep up and make my brain work—somewhat, at least. I was also very interested in computers; my big passions were computers and books. My hobby is music. I have tons and tons of CDs.

So I had always wanted to have children but I was very responsible with regard to that. I knew that this was not the right time and that's why I was not getting pregnant and having children just like that. The young boyfriend was very insecure because he was very young and he suddenly wanted to have children—that was the very first time in my life that somebody said, "I want to have children with you." I was like: "Wow, that sounds good. I want that too." I tried to look at the pros and cons, but of course the pros seemed way stronger even though they were actually practically non-existent. But it seemed like there were some pros; he was from a good family and even though he was not educated—he'd only finished grade nine—I thought he had a good head on his shoulders! So I thought, "My child is going to be smart and he's good-looking." That's what I was thinking, and we started trying to get pregnant, but we were not successful.

We had started living together right away and because of his insecurity and my drinking, which had really progressed; we were drinking together and sometimes using drugs. He became abusive and I fell into the same abusive cycle. I started to blame myself because this time I was drinking—so I explained his abuse that way. Before, I knew it was no fault of mine, but now, again, it was the same ridiculous thing. It was the same cycle of abuse and I would just convince myself that the abuse was my fault and forgive him. It was not all the time—he would have a big few outbursts and then it would end. One time he threatened me really badly and that was the worst experience of my life. I was afraid of losing my life, actually. The only funny part of this story is that the police and the wine delivery guy arrived at the same time. I ended up going to the station with the police and did a video recording of my bruises and what he did to me, and they took the knife that he threatened me with. It was really the worst experience because it had never escalated to this point in my life. There was abuse, there were slaps, but it had never escalated to the point of choking and having my head bashed to the floor and almost losing consciousness.

The police arrested him and he was in jail for a little while; however, I didn't go through with the court proceedings and I was never even called to court for that. I don't know how it ended, but after a few years it did. He ended up living with me again. His parents were very much against me, even though before his jail time his parents and I had the best relationship. We would talk every day and his mother would thank God and thank me for taking care of their son. We were all very good friends and we would have family dinners at least once a week. But after all this business with the police and jail, they turned against me and they didn't want to have anything to do with me.

Then Boris started to come home extremely late from work and a few times he didn't even come home. I would tell him to leave and he would just not leave, so I asked my mother one time when she was over to ask him for the keys and tell him to get out of my place. I felt that I didn't need to stay with someone who was not coming home—that was the last straw. So she did that, and he started crying, but he packed his little bag and he left.

I was very miserable, and he called me again and I was very sad about it. I started calling him because of that longing, the loneliness that had kicked in (and of course, the drinking didn't help). But he had decided that he didn't want anything more to do with me. I felt something was different with me health-wise, but I didn't know what. So I went to the walk-in clinic, they did a blood test, and in January 2006 I found out I was pregnant. I was the happiest girl on the block. I jumped up and down and I started crying and I kissed the doctor. I remember how he wanted children and how much we talked about it and how much he kept on wanting to have a child and how much we dreamt about having a child. He had written a letter to me once—a very long letter, about four pages—about how he was going to be a good father, but that was about the time he was arrested, so his feelings were all messed up too! Later, when I did get pregnant, he was nowhere to be found. I went to his sister because I knew where she worked, and all she said was that he had somebody else already. The whole family didn't want anything to do with me—absolutely nothing.

He did contact me when I was five or six months pregnant, on my birthday, and he was high, I could tell. He told me some love words and whatever, and I think he spent the night with me, but his new girlfriend was already calling and stuff like that, so there was a lot of heartbreak. My pregnancy, however, was the most amazing experience. I was very happy. I was never sick; it was just amazing. Now when I see my friends going through pregnancies and how much they suffer I cannot believe that God spared me that because He saw that I was alone and I needed at least some little help. At least He never made me sick.

My mother never really accepted my pregnancy. I had been seeing my mom on and off and at that point I was already seeing her regularly. When I was 18 there was one time I didn't see her for six months; I just cut off everything because I was very, very hurt. But I still kept in touch with her and we were seeing each other quite a lot—at least a few times a month or even a week sometimes. As my drinking escalated it was like a common thing between us. I had moved back with her for a little while, but not a long time, and I would drink either by myself or together with her. But my dream was that I could have a mother to rely on—all I wanted was that she wouldn't drink. Of course she wasn't hitting me anymore like when I was a baby or child. She didn't call me names any more because I was a big girl and she knew that I wouldn't take her nonsense.

I had a few good friends, and I had this one very important person in my life—Frank. He was always beside me. He was 20 years older. There was never romance between us—he did love me, but I never felt the same way. He was always there for me no matter what and had supported me financially at times. Even through all my drunkenness, I always had these people in my life that helped me to avoid being on the street and for that I am grateful. I always had my own place. I also had a big dog and he actually kept me alive. There were many times when I was drinking that I wanted to die and I wanted to commit suicide and I was really thinking about that and I would look at him and think, "He needs me." That was before the pregnancy. Then when I was pregnant, everything was going well and this man Frank was always beside me if I needed helping. He was really hurt because of my drinking, and because of that I definitely took advantage of him. His health was not very good and maybe I had a little bit to do with that—I don't know.

I gave birth to a beautiful healthy boy in August. I was just very happy, really, and I had some friends beside me and they took me home from the hospital. My girlfriends chipped in and they set everything up. Everything was going fairly well. Boris was never really interested in the child. One week after I gave birth I met his sister in the mall. We passed by each other and didn't even stop, didn't even say hello. The father never attempted to contact me. Half a year passed and when my son was about five months or so the father did make an attempt to see the child for about one hour. He was high and drunk. That was the last time I saw him.

At the end of January 2007, when my son was six months old, something really horrible happened. I continued drinking and, as I mentioned, I was a binge drinker, so I would drink to the point of passing out. Apparently I had put something on the stove to cook before I blacked out. There was smoke in the apartment, and the fire department came—we could have burned, you know. Then I woke up in the hospital and of course I was asking where my son was, and I was told that he was safe. I found out they were asking for my mother because they wanted to give the child to my mother, but I told them not to. I probably did the right thing, because she couldn't take care of him either because she was drinking all the time too. So my son ended up going to Children's Aid and that was the most devastating thing in my entire life. I put everything aside, all the shame, all the embarrassment, what the neighbours would think, what the people on the street would think. I went to the hospital and started a day program treatment. I was really trying not to drink, and it was only then that I realized I actually couldn't stop. I didn't know that I couldn't stop because I had never tried. I knew I had to stop drinking, but I couldn't stop. I would not drink for a month and then I would relapse again.

I eventually got my son back under my mother's care because I was not doing that well. It was a condition that she would live with me and it seemed liked a fine idea to me at the time—we were doing quite well, and that was the only time that we were actually close. We actually talked, and we spent the most time we have ever spent together. I am very grateful for that time with my mother, and I think God had a plan at that time too.

My son was home, but my mother, after not drinking, wanted to drink again. So she left my house and she started to drink again. When my worker would visit my mother had to be present, but she was practically never there, so I lived in the biggest fear because my mother, who was supposed to be there 24/7, was not there. I was afraid to go outside—what if my worker drove by? Which was not really like me, but I was very scared. I was paranoid. It was very scary, and of course that drove me to drinking and I tried not to drink for four or five months, which seemed liked four or five years to me at the time. I relapsed several times. Frank would go and bring my mother back to my house just before the appointment for the worker from the Children's Aid. After several times doing that I guess everybody just gave up, and I realized that it was not going to work because I was already drinking again too. I felt like it was not going anywhere; my son was suffering, and everybody was suffering. So one time Frank just didn't bring my mother home back to my house and my worker came. I actually called her and I told her what was happening.

I actually had a hangover myself (which she didn't suspect at the time) and I said, "This is what is going on," and they took him away again. I knew I had to do something different. My worker suggested I go to an in-patient treatment program, like rehab. I was getting a lot of counselling and a lot of everything with regard to the alcoholism, but it was not really successful. So when my son was taken away again, I realized that I had to do something, and that is when I went to a live-in treatment program. They did a good job, but then again I think I had suppressed so many things for so many years because I had developed a way with dealing with these things by supposedly throwing them out of my mind. I thought I had figured it out. I had it under control. The treatment centre people called that self-brainwashing. If I have learned anything from my very first abusive boyfriend, it is that if you tell me something enough, I will start believing it. And so I turned that around, and I told myself something positive and I thought that I would be okay. So after having this coping strategy for so many years I guess everything was so deeply hidden that one treatment place could not unlock that key where everything was hidden. It was too deep. So that didn't help me. The live-in treatment didn't help me, and I kept on relapsing, and then after that I knew I had to do something because I knew I was about to lose my son forever. It was dragging on and he had been in the system already for more than half of his life.

He was two and a half at the time, and I was lucky that I had a lot of access to him. I was seeing him five days a week, a few hours a day. Sometimes I was seeing him up to six days a week. This was very lucky for me because a lot people get to see their kids once or twice a week. I was becoming a better and better mother. I started to feel the bond with him that was never quite there. I knew I loved him, because I knew that was the right thing to do, and I never questioned myself about that, but really I was not responding to his needs. When he would cry I would think that's normal, but I would not necessarily pick him up. There was just something missing, but through all this painful experience I developed a strong bond with him and I really got to love him. I learned to listen to him, and I went to some parenting classes with him as well, where I would spend three days a week from morning to evening with him. I was getting a lot of in-depth parenting information that I didn't have before. My mother's example of parenting had not been the best, to say the least. I knew that, and I really didn't want to be the parent that she was.

Eventually, I went to a program run by the Salvation Army—it was a three-month treatment program. It was actually two and a half months, but because I had to leave a few times a week to see my son and miss some classes, I voluntarily asked for an extension. That is how committed I was, and I knew that I had to do something that I had never done before. I had heard about AA, but it seemed too exposed, too open for me, maybe even too religious on some level. I thought that it was just not going to work for me. Then I sat down and thought it through, and I realized that it has worked for millions so maybe would work for me too. I started to go to AA.

I was also introduced to AA at the treatment program, and somehow I got in touch with God as well. I realized this and I started asking HIM to do something for me that I could not do for myself: to lift the desire of drinking. And slowly, slowly, I became very involved in AA and I completed the program. I did it and I actually learned a lot because I wanted to. I realized without a doubt in my mind that I had to do it without reservations in order to permanently stop drinking. Otherwise I would always go back to my old ways of thinking that I just don't have the will when it's really not the case. That's what AA taught me.

The desire to drink for me was lifted. I have never wanted to drink again, and I have been sober for over two years.

There was one particular moment at the very beginning of my treatment, when I came to visit my son, and I was being observed because all the visits were supervised, and one of the workers came in. After observing me with my son, he came in and he said, "You know, I never usually do this, but I just wanted to let you know that I know your case and I don't want you to give up. You are an amazing mother. You have a talent for being a mother." I told him that I had no hopes of getting my son back, because at the time I had really lost hope in my own mind. He said he knew my case and he reassured me that no matter how hopeless it seemed, he had seen worse and it might be possible. And that's all it took. From that day on I never gave up on a hope and I thought, "As long as I don't drink, I will get him back." Getting my son back was next to hopeless, but with my hard work, dedication, and some self-advocacy, I did get him back. I was able to convince everybody there, even the general manager of Children's Aid. I asked them to just give me a chance, and told them I was different and I had so many supports. They had never seen so much support; I had almost 10 people backing me up! I think there are only a few cases in Children's Aid history of people getting their children back when they had relapsed so many times and whose child had been in the system for so long. It took me a very long time, a good year, but I was able to prove to everybody that I had changed.

I have learned a lot about myself, and I have learned that I have to take care of myself in order to take care of my son. This is what helps me not to burn out, because I am a perfectionist. Throughout all those three years or so that I was trying to recover, I was learning more and more about myself. I was getting real confidence back, and I knew my struggles, and I knew my defects, and I knew what to work on and what to watch out for. I knew if I didn't pay close attention, I would fall again, and I just could not afford that, because I really, really love my son and he's very attached to me. Even though he was in care, we still had a really strong bond. While in care, after spending the full day on Saturday with me, he would cry. It was strange because usually after such a long time in care, children don't cry when a visit ends. But with us it was different, we were actually building a bond, and the Children's Aid workers were impressed with that and they saw what a natural mother I was becoming. I was taking care of my son. I would come with a container of different fruits and vegetables. Everything I would bring was of my own making. I would never buy anything in a store because I wanted the best for him. I think the workers saw that I really loved my son and they saw that I wanted this really badly, wanted this relationship and to be a good mother, so they decided to give me a chance. I got him back last year in December and he has been with me ever since.

My son and I have an amazing relationship. He is really very loving. He is now in daycare and in daycare everybody says that he is the best. He is the most polite child. He is the most educated. He is just a wonderful child.

I have been living on social assistance since 2006, since I got pregnant. Right now, I am getting the child tax benefit and it has increased significantly since two years ago, by almost $200. So I am almost living comfortably and, yes, I could go to work, but that would mean that I could not go to meetings. Actually my worker would not allow me at this point to go to work. That is not even an option right now because my worker from Children's Aid wants me to take care of myself. I get that that is more important sometimes than money or a job. The most important thing right now is to take care of my son, and in order for me to do that, I have to take care of myself. My Children's Aid worker is encouraging and is not pressuring me, because it is clear that I am not going to lose my son again. The process of recovery and AA have given me confidence that I have rights and that my son does come first. First of all, I would not even be able to support both of us unless I got a $30,000-a-year job, which is not too realistic because I basically don't have any skills. With daycare and paying an apartment, how would I survive? That's already $2,000. It almost begs the question, "Why? Why bother?" And it's sad but it's almost true. "Why bother?"

I don't want to get stuck—not bothering—so my plan is to go to college when my son gets a little bit older and once I feel more secure with managing my addiction—when I am not as afraid as I am right now. Right now I am still very afraid, and that is a very good sign actually. I really take very good care of myself. Before I used to think that taking care of myself was selfish. Now I view that as the only option in order for me to be a good mother for my son. And so I go to meetings and I take care of myself and I get plenty of rest so that I can be a good mother to my son.

Right now my son calls Frank daddy. And of course I don't object to that, I always encourage it. This is another little scheme that I made up. But I think that there is not much harm in that because Frank is extremely dedicated. He has no family—all he has is us. We live together as roommates and we want to give my son the best life possible.

He still helps us a lot. There were times when the money was so tight I was relying on him buying us food. Even when I got my son back, it took us three or four months to get the child tax benefit. Meanwhile, how do you live on the $50 that is left after paying the rent and the phone? How do you do that? I still go to food banks. I was going then and I am now. I stock up on food because I have fear of not having enough. I still live wondering what is going to happen tomorrow. I always have this fear, and this is my biggest fear at the moment. Finances are a big struggle. I want to give so much to my son. I have had it worse, and I still did not end up living on the street, and still I had food. So I think I will be okay, and I am blessed with a few good friends.

I really enjoy cooking, and I have progressed in my abilities and started my own blog about cooking and recipes. I always invite somebody to test my food. Otherwise, you know, who am I going to make it for? So Frank is really lucky in this department. I even started making my own bread—rye without yeast. It rises on its own. It is a very special process. And I pride myself on those things. I want to raise my son on homemade food only. I make every-thing from scratch.

I go to meetings. I go to a lot of meetings. I go to see my counsellor. When I look back and when I see my friends who live with partners and are fighting every single day, I feel blessed that I have a peaceful life. I think because I had such a difficult life and I went through so much that now I am fighting for what I believe in. Because the one thing that I'm going to fight for till I die is my son—and being sure that he is well taken care of and loved. If it was not for my son, I would never be where I am right now. I would be dead in an alley somewhere or maybe on drugs or something.

When I was going through the treatment program at the beginning, I kept a little bit in touch with my mom. One time I called and she was drunk again. Being in a treatment program and hearing a drunk woman—it just didn't go together. I could not expose myself to that, so I never her called again. When I got my one-year medallion from AA, I was very proud of myself. A year was huge, a huge thing. Because the longest sobriety I had ever had was a period of four or five months, a year was a miracle for me. I really wanted my mother to see that, that was my dream, but she never did.

Then when my son was home and Christmas came, I started longing for her again. I called and she was drunk again and I was just about to ask her to come and spend Christmas and New Years with us. But I talk to my family back home on Skype almost every day, and my aunt kept telling me to be care-ful and not to go visit her. So I didn't see her. Then this spring I was feeling good and I wanted to contact her, so I wrote a letter and I carried that letter in my purse for three or four weeks. Then I finally did send it, and the letter was returned and I got worried. I went to her old apartment, but it was no longer an apartment building and she was not there and my stepfather was not there either. I even got family tracing services at the Salvation Army to help me, and I called the police. The only thing that they saw in their computer was that she had been taken to the hospital in January—it was already June. I had called her family doctor but thought I would hit a brick wall because of confidential-ity. Finally the family doctor called me back and started telling me she had been sick a lot. I was surprised at first that he was telling me this because of confidentiality, but then he went on and told me that she had passed away.

I thought about not having been there to visit her. She was all by herself. For me, the most devastating and sad part was that when she was being asked by social workers at the hospital if she had any children, she said no. This really hurt me, and I will never understand why. Maybe she was trying to protect me. I hope that she knew that I was doing well. I try not to regret and keep on reminding myself that I did what I did for my well-being and for my son's welfare. I really couldn't have done differently because there was a huge chance of me falling down again, and I couldn't take that chance. And I had no reserve left—there was none.

In spite of all the tragedy and hardship in this story, we have a fairly good life right now. I live for my son. I try to give him a good life. Sobriety has been great. God is guiding me every day. I can't wait in the mornings to wake up and start a new day! Life is very exciting, and we are blessed to have each other. I have made peace with my mother's passing. I am not angry anymore. I cherish the good times we had. My son is excelling in school. He is at the top of his class. He attends professional dance classes, swimming, and soccer practices. Next fall I am starting university.

Jenna's Story

My name is Jenna, and I am from the Philippines. I have nine brothers and sisters and I am the eldest. My parents are very loving parents. My father is a farmer, and they also do buy and sell. He grows rice, corn, and vegetables. Being the eldest you get all the attention at first, but then you have to be independent and do your best. I have happy memories of my childhood. Our family is very united—we have 100 on my grandmother's side. When my grandmother died, they said we were 100 grandchildren. We were a happy family; we struggled, but we were happy. There were some financial struggles, but there was enough food.

Being the eldest, I had to work really hard to get an education. I went to the city when I finished elementary school at 13 and stayed with my aunt. I went there to help them with their restaurant for two years. Then I went back to study to become a medical secretary. I did well in school. I had all A-pluses when I was in high school. My parents wanted me to have an education, so I went to study with my aunt's help. I supported myself by working in a factory on the weekends.

My brothers and sisters are all back home still. We are all close. I was the one that supported them. Even now, if I have extra money I help them, especially mom, who is really sick. My parents are still alive, but I haven't seen them for about 15 years now.

I have worked so hard all my life. I started to work when I was 13. In 1980, I went abroad to work as a caregiver. I was 21. I had one year of medical secretary school, but I went to Hong King to help support my family. My family was still young, so I was the one that supported them. The couple I worked for treated me like a daughter. I worked for them for eight years. They even took me to their home country—they introduced me as a daughter when somebody came over. They were so nice to me and I was happy.

Canada, they said, was a good opportunity. I was told that it was a good place to live as long as you worked hard, so I decided at the age of 30 to come to Canada for a better life and more opportunity. The couple I worked for was so sad when I told them I was leaving.

When I came over, I had just arrived at the airport, and as I got out of the car I fell down on the ice. My new employer picked me up and said, "Don't break a leg." They were nice. I worked for them for eight years and even to this day, they are still helping me in many ways, including financially. They are good with my son. They take him to Raptors games. I was lucky to a have a good employer when I arrived in Canada—they really treated me like family.

While I was working for this family I studied part-time at night, and through hardship and perseverance I earned certification in hospitality management. That's why I left my country—to have a better place and a better job as well. I worked with the family for eight years, and then with my newly earned certification I got work in a nursing home as a cook. I worked there for eight years. I love cooking. My employer loved my pasta. I love to cook anything, but I am not good at baking. When I was in high school I took two years in home economics and I always won first place in cooking. It is a hard job but if you love it, it is fun. Life was good at first, working in the nursing home. However, I had to wake up at 5 a.m. and by the time I got home to my son I was really tired.

I am a very hard-working person, and I worked very hard until 2006—the day that changed my life. There was a gas leak in my workplace. Since I was standing in front of the stove, I was the one who was most affected by it. I collapsed and was unconscious for seven hours in the hospital. That was the day my life changed. I came home from the hospital very weak and I could not walk.

You can't imagine how scared and frustrated I was. I was a very active person, and then suddenly I couldn't walk. I had a seven-year-old son to look after. I wondered what would happen to me and how I would do all the things I used to do.

For six months I underwent therapy and I began to use a walker. The doctor couldn't figure out what wrong with me, and this added to my mental, physical, and emotional frustration. The pain I suffered during that time was unbearable. On a scale of 1 to 10 my pain was much higher than 10. I used to cry and I could not sleep—the thought of being paralyzed really scared me. For this reason, I really tried my very best, even though I had to drag my feet. I had to do it. I remember that there were times that my legs just stopped moving while I was trying to walk. I cried, but I didn't stop. I wanted to get well again and to be back to my normal life.

During that time I did not have any money, because the company I worked for didn't pay me. They were waiting for the doctor's diagnosis, as the pain was chronic. My doctors couldn't see what was really wrong with me—if they only knew how much pain I was going through! I couldn't sit and I couldn't sleep. It was unbearable. I borrowed money from friends and family for my therapy and withdrew all of my RRSPs. At first, I didn't know about OW and ODSP. Then, after I used up all my money, I applied. It was a struggle for those three years. Now it is a little bit better, I have an income and I can buy what my son needs and wants. I remember telling the woman at the ODSP office that the money I was getting was only enough for my rent. I didn't have enough money for food. She said, "Why don't you go to the food bank?" I was crying when she said that to me. Food has always been abundant in my life. I cried—I couldn't even walk to get to the food bank.

It took more than one year before they found out what was really wrong with me. I was persistent, despite the fact that my family doctor told me that there was nothing wrong. I asked her, "How can you say there's nothing wrong with me when I can't even walk?" I begged her to send me to a pain specialist. She agreed, but said it would be the last time she would send me.

I went to see the pain specialist. From there, he sent me to be X-rayed and for the other procedures that needed to be done. I had therapy to alleviate the pain. I told him to send me for an MRI, which he did, and they found that I had slight multiple sclerosis and that my spine had a dislocated disk. These findings were related to the weakness on my left side, arms, legs, and entire body. Despite this, my family doctor did not agree with the pain specialist, and this is why it took more time to process my insurance claim. In the end, the pain specialist talked to my family doctor and explained to her that I had inflammation. You can't even imagine how upset I was by this situation. I didn't want to be like this, disabled. I wanted to work. I'd rather go to work, but I couldn't because of the pain and because my mobility was limited. I isolated myself and I didn't want to talk to anybody anymore. Overall, it was a three-year struggle, physically, emotionally, mentally, and financially. I was very depressed because of everything I kept inside me I didn't open up and I didn't share, and I guess those things build up in your body.

And then one day a friend invited me to a group called Lone Mothers. This group is made up of mothers who are on ODSP or OW. At first I was very hesitant to join because of my disability. I was using a cane and it was winter at the time. A few months passed and I realized how glad I was that I joined the group. The person who facilitates the group is very understanding. She doesn't judge what or who you are. She listens to everybody. Everybody tells their stories and shares their struggles and the problems of their daily lives. The lone-mothers group helped me with my recovery because everybody in the group opened up and shared their stories without hesitation. Each and every one of us has a different story to tell and nobody judges us. I guess I realized through this group that although, I had been doing quite well until my accident at work, I was pretty isolated as a single mother.

In everyday life there are always trials to face, but in Lone Mothers we are there as a group to share our problems, to cope, and help each other, to realize that we are not alone. We are there to release all the pent-up emotions that build inside us. Through this group, we receive a little extra money as an honorarium for participating. Although it isn't much, it helps us buy food, because the money we receive on ODSP isn't enough to pay rent, buy food, and support kids. I salute these single moms because being a single mom is not an easy job. You have to be proud of yourself no matter what. You're still the heroes in those kids' lives because you're there when they need you.

I believe that there's a reason that things happen, and they happen for the best. Behind every cloud we face there is always a light.

Being single mom is a very demanding job, especially if you're alone to face all of the struggles, but being a mom is the best thing that ever happened to me! Though life is very hard, I am lucky to have my son because he is my life, and he is what kept me going through my recovery. Despite the pain, and even though it was very difficult for me to walk, I continued to take my son to his activities. I am glad I did. In the end, I recovered from my disability and at the same time my son accomplished something, too—he was awarded his black belt in karate last June after three years of practise. Now I am back at my old job. For the people out there who have a disability, don't lose hope! Just pray and have faith in the Lord that even with everything in life, there is always hope. I am an example of that.

While I am working now, it was very hard at first. I tried my best. When I went back, they gave me a job that is harder. They said it was modified, but it was not. I had to push a cart with all the trays. I had to clear the table. I did not say anything because I did not want to jeopardize my job. Sometimes I felt like I was going to collapse, so I would run to the washroom and take a breath. I did not show them that I was really not able to do the work, because if I did not do that modified job, I knew that I would be out of a job. I did the modified job for two months.

Through God's grace, through faith, and through friends and family, I am back to a normal life. My life is back on track now. My pain is still there, but I don't think about it. I just do my best and don't think about the pain. I feel like a new person. I feel that those trials that were in my life for three years helped me think more positively. I am very thankful for my son because he was there when I needed him. I am also thankful to the lone-mothers group and to our facilitator, Judit. You are a part of my recovery. I hope the lone-mothers group will continue to help people like me in the near future.

Making Meaning

Lea Caragata and Judit Alcalde

This following section of the book is a departure in style and form from Part I. We felt it important to let the stories of Part I speak for themselves and to not engage in any direct analysis of the very personal narratives of our co-authors, the women who have chosen to tell their stories. Yet their motive, and ours as the volume's editors, is to bring to light some of the broader structural issues, to tell "the whole story" that explains so much of the life experiences of so many single mothers. This whole story requires an adding up of the personal life experiences related here to make apparent their relation to contemporary values and ideologies as well as the policy frameworks and initiatives that have been shaped by them. In order to engage in such analysis, we have summarized the stories with the intention of working analytically with these summaries rather than directly with the lone-mother narratives. We realize that this is an uncomfortable compromise, and we do so only because we think it serves a larger end congruent with lone-mothers' interests. The stories themselves must be told, but as well there should be no ambiguity about their meaning and their being grounded in the structures and systems of western neo-liberal ideology.

Summaries of the stories follow and from these we draw and then discuss the political, economic, and social issues that underlie them.

Story Summaries

Sara

A single mother for 35 years, Sara is the fourth of 16 children from a working-class, rural Newfoundland family. From the age of 11, Sara was made to take on domestic duties, such as cooking and cleaning, because her mother was often unable, due to severe obesity, and unwilling to do the work herself. By age 12, Sara was taken out of school and forced to carry out all the household chores as well as work outside the home, along with her siblings, to help support the large family. Her father was an alcoholic and authoritarian who was often absent from the home, and he and Sara's mother were both physically and verbally abusive to all of their children. In one particularly harrowing incident, Sara's father shot at her as she fled the house after a violent altercation with him.

Sara's father hunted and used bribes in the form of prime cuts of meat and wild game he had shot to convince local authority figures, like judges, to turn a blind eye to his abuse. As a result, there were few if any community supports or resources available to Sara. Although he also abused his wife, Sara's mother refused to leave her husband because she claimed they were in love. Sara soon learned that love and physical violence are compatible and even interchangeable.

In her late teens, Sara married her late husband, a university-educated school teacher and principal who died in a car accident five years after they married. A widow at age 23, Sara soon moved to Toronto, met a man, and had a daughter with him. When he became verbally abusive and threatening, Sara left him and, because she had difficulty supporting herself, applied for social assistance. Her experience negotiating the system was frustrating because she found many of the case workers to be condescending and unhelpful.

Sara finally found her own voice while working in a long-term position in a flower shop. Participation in various women's groups also helped her to find the confidence to begin speaking up for herself. She eventually started writing children's poetry, which she continues to do. Sara enjoys a close relationship with her daughter and grandchildren.

Martha

The youngest child and only girl in a family of four children, Martha had a happy childhood in north Toronto with a stay-at-home mother and a hard-working father who took their children to church on Sundays, took annual summer vacations in northern Ontario, and celebrated the holidays with family and friends. Despite the carefree appearance of her early years, Martha was sexually abused as a child and still suffers from the negative psychological and physical effects of that violation, including a lack of self-confidence and an eating disorder.

Martha became pregnant with her first child before she graduated from high school, at age 17. Pressured by her mother and another family friend,

Martha put the baby girl up for adoption but had a change of heart soon after and managed to regain custody two weeks after the birth. Martha had excluded the baby's father from the entire birth and adoption process because he disagreed with her decision. When the child was returned to the family, however, she and her boyfriend rekindled their relationship and within a few months, Martha was pregnant for the second time. Several months after her son was born, Martha, now 20 years old, married her boyfriend. About three years later, she had her third child, another boy, and stopped working so she could be a full-time mother. Her husband resented the burden this placed on him, and two years later they divorced after six years of marriage. When he left he emptied their shared bank accounts, leaving Martha almost destitute. His regular visits with the children soon dwindled to occasional visits until he all but disappeared from their lives. This absence caused behavioural problems in the youngest child, making it necessary for the family to participate in intensive therapy over a six-year period. Martha also advocated for him when the medical professionals and her ex-husband's family wanted her son to take the attention deficit disorder (ADHD) drug Ritalin to control his outbursts.

Even before her divorce, Martha was making ends meet with the help of the social assistance program. Because her ex-husband often visited the many relatives, including his mother, aunt, sister, and grandfather, who lived in the same apartment complex as Martha, she was informed that her cheques would be withheld. Social services assumed she was still being supported by the children's father, whose vehicle was spotted in the parking structure. Her monthly cheques were held up on many occasions by the agency when Martha was wrongly accused of some minor infraction. The drug card she depended on to purchase the asthma drug Ventolin, which both of her sons take, was also often late arriving. On the whole, however, her children were healthy, happy, carefree youngsters who excelled at sports, enjoyed school, and were doted on by their involved mother. Eventually Martha found part-time work at her children's school, and the extra income allowed the children to participate in extracurricular activities. She took her ex-husband to court to force him to pay child support, but the paltry sum he contributed made little difference in the end, since an equivalent amount was deducted from Martha's monthly social assistance cheque. With her children all in their twenties and doing well, Martha has begun to attend to her own needs.

After taking a course in Microsoft Office, Martha worked for more than a year in customer service. The stress of dealing with a supervisor she did not get along with and a heavy work load nearly led to a nervous break-down, and she was laid off. Now collecting employment insurance, Martha is looking for work in the volunteer sector, where she has more experience. She has become a savvy navigator of the social system she has depended on for assistance and has identified many counterintuitive and short-sighted policies that undermine parents' good intentions and put children's well-being at risk. These include the limits of the drug card, which does not always cover adequate or appropriate drugs, and the practice of retention by pharmacists of the original copy of the card, which makes it impossible for card holders to register for other necessary programs and services. Martha was also forced by the social assistance program to use, for daily living, monies she had inherited for educational purposes. Because those on social assistance cannot attend school simultaneously, Martha's plans to return to university when her children were young were thwarted by the very system that intends its beneficiaries to stop using it. Her experience with social assistance taught Martha much about the system's benefits and shortcomings, and she has applied these lessons to her life, using them to strengthen her resolve to be independent and socially involved in her community.

Mary

Now the 39-year-old mother of two children, Mary and two siblings were raised by a single father after their addict mother abandoned the family. Mary was saddled with adult domestic duties at a young age and learned quickly that her survival at home and in the wider world depended on being outwardly tough and intimidating.

A self-described tomboy, Mary became involved in street life at her downtown Toronto school and by age 13 she was using drugs and alcohol, which were often supplied by her mother, also a substance abuser. Mary dropped out of school and left home in grade nine, when she was 14 years old, and embarked on a life of drug and alcohol use, prostitution, and trafficking, for which she was later arrested and briefly incarcerated.

At 19, Mary began a relationship with an older, abusive man who, she later discovered, was also involved with a friend of hers, with whom he had children. Mary's second relationship, with a professional thief or "booster," was also dysfunctional. At 29, Mary was raped and decided to keep the baby even though she had already had several abortions. The man she was platonically involved with at the time of the rape, also a drug dealer, convinced her to keep the baby and offered to act as the child's surrogate father.

She went to and completed a stint at rehab, moved in with her friend, and gave birth to a son. Only a few months later, Mary was pregnant again, with her friend's—now boyfriend's—baby and, though he had become physically abusive, she decided to stay in the relationship and, at his insistence, have the child. Her boyfriend, who was in Canada illegally, was soon deported and the stress of raising two children alone led to a relapse into drug and alcohol use.

Although she applied to and received a scholarship to attend George Brown College, Mary instead used the money to move with her children to South America to join their father. Once there, the cycle of abuse resumed and the drug use worsened. The Canadian Embassy finally flew Mary back to Canada, but she was soon arrested, incarcerated, and forced to sign over responsibility for her two children to her mother, who was also still an addict. Upon release from prison and following a six-month stay in a rehab facility, Mary finally won back custody of her children and managed to stay sober for more than a year. On a construction site where she was employed, she had a work-related accident that resulted in both feet getting crushed. As a result, Mary had to rely on money she got from the Ontario Disability Support Program (ODSP) to support herself and her children. She felt that she was treated contemptuously by ODSP representatives and was humiliated by the experience. Over time, Mary learned that her foot injury was more complex than initially thought by doctors but an impending surgery will hopefully address some of the constant pain she has experienced since the injury.

Most recently, Mary passed a grade 12 equivalency test and hopes to upgrade other skills. Completely sober for eight months at the time of telling her story, she continues to attend and benefit from Alcoholics Anonymous (AA). She has a new appreciation for the peaceful, tranquil life she and her children lead.

Anne

Always shy and withdrawn, Anne learned in childhood that alcohol numbed the feelings of depression and anxiety she felt. Because her father made his own homemade wine, which was consumed regularly and abundantly in the home, Anne developed a taste for alcohol as a youngster and drinking on a quotidian basis was normalized by the time she was 12 or 13 years old.

Anne was raised in the west end of Toronto by her divorced single mother until the age of 15 when she and her fraternal twin sister began acting out. Anne and her sister were sent to live with their father and his considerably younger second wife. By age 17 and to her father's dismay, Anne began dating a man nine years her senior. When she refused her father's demands to end the relationship she was kicked out of the house and moved in with her older boyfriend. Securing a job at the insurance company where her older sister worked, Anne worked her way up in the organization and eventually got a Registered Insurance Broker of Ontario general licence. She and her boyfriend married and had their first son when Anne was 24. One year later, Anne divorced her husband because he was an alcoholic and, with her son, moved in with her mother until she was back on her feet and able to buy a townhouse with her twin sister, who was also divorced.

Throughout her twenties, Anne managed to restrict her drinking to weekends, but as time went on she found herself starting to drink before the weekend began. When both Anne and her sister became involved in new relationships, they parted ways and both remarried. By this time Anne was drinking heavily and her alcoholism was leading to increasingly serious consequences, including a first impaired driving charge. Although she had a second child with her new husband, who had already been charged with assaulting his ex-wife, the relationship was marked by drinking, violence, and abuse. Despite the chaotic home life and the fact that the nature of her husband's work kept him away from the home for long periods, Anne's career advanced. At 36, she had her third child, another son, and decided to stay at home given the exorbitant costs of daycare and after-school programs. When the abuse became intolerable, Anne had her husband arrested for the fourth time and had a restraining order brought against him. She then sold their house and she and her three children moved in with her mother, who had purchased a new home big enough to accommodate five people. Anne's alcoholism was a strain on the relationship, however, and her mother called both the police and the Children's Aid Society.

Anne completed a 21-day treatment program as a condition of keeping her children. Not yet ready to face or quit her addiction, however, Anne cycled in and out of various treatment facilities and Alcoholics Anonymous for five years. Finally, in mid-2007 and at the lowest point in her trajectory, Anne made a commitment to seek and succeed at treatment for her alcohol addiction. Unequal access to appropriate supports and gender stereotyping about alcoholics hampered and lengthened Anne's recovery time. As a single mother of three children, she had responsibilities for their welfare that the various alcohol recovery and social assistance services could not accommodate. As a result, her children were split up among relatives so that she could focus on treatment at a six-month residential facility in Toronto. Anne finally found success and peace while in treatment by following the 12-step AA program with her sponsor's support and help. For the following six months, Anne stayed at a sober living facility. There she applied for and received a disability benefit.

Anne now lives in an apartment with her children after having launched and won a court battle with her second husband to regain custody of her youngest child. One of her biggest battles has been with social services. Both the Ontario Disability Support Program and the Child Tax Benefit arm of Revenue Canada have been stumbling blocks for Anne because of their bureaucratic systems and frequently unhelpful or obtuse staff. Anne has had to supplement her meagre income with financial donations from friends and family members, and relies on a strong network of women in the various groups she attends for other kinds of support.

Having completed a program in addiction studies at Centennial College, Anne is now looking for work in her field while attending to her youngest child who, as a result of the chaos of his early upbringing, is now acting out in defiant ways. Armed with the clarity, energy, and resources necessary, Anne is seeking appropriate professional attention for her son in the hope that he and the rest of the family can deal with the pressures in their lives together and in healthy ways.

Madison

The only girl and second child of five siblings, Madison was raised in Toronto by very strict, traditional, Italian-descended, Catholic parents. Her mother stayed at home to raise the children and care for the home while her father started and managed a small construction company. Madison's early childhood was happy and uneventful, but her life changed when she was a teenager and began dating boys.

Madison's first boyfriend, also Italian and from a working-class Catholic family, was seven years Madison's senior. The first two years of their relationship were idyllic and Madison's parents assumed the two would marry. When she ended the relationship with plans to date other people, her parents became verbally abusive. They expected their daughter to be monogamous, marry her first boyfriend (from the community), and start a family. Thereafter, they attempted to control her interactions with boys and curtail her social life outside the home. Madison's second relationship followed a similar pattern. Because he was also older and established, her parents approved of the relationship and reacted in a similarly violent way when Madison ended it.

Although she was still living with her parents, Madison was studying full-time at university and working long hours to pay for her degree. The home environment became increasingly tense as Madison strained against her parents' unrealistic and deeply old-fashioned expectations of their daughter. Following one particularly heated and increasingly violent argument, Madison stormed out of the house and was followed by her brothers who tried to force the bus she was on to pull over to the side of the street. After the police were called and she told her side of the story she was taken to the local police station. There, with the help of police officers, she and her parents reached a tentative détente and Madison returned home temporarily. Within a week, however, the stress had become unbearable and Madison moved out with the help of her school friend. Overwhelmed by the discord in her family, the move, her onerous school and work schedules, Madison regretfully left university and began working full-time at one job and part-time at another in order to make ends meet. Although she was now a financially independent 21-year-old, her parents began harassing her when they found out where she lived. They went so far as to undermine her landlord's confidence in her as a tenant, and Madison had to move out of her apartment.

Madison's decline into drinking, drug use, and risky behaviour were precipitated by the stress she experienced in her teenage and early adult years. These issues were compounded by problems with self-confidence, independence, depression, and an inability to make commitments to and trust others. Before long, Madison was working as a stripper at a series of clubs. After several years in the industry she began helping her new boyfriend, a DJ and manager of a strip club, run his business by co-managing, waiting, and stripping. Eventually, she moved with him to the west coast, where they also managed a club together, and where Madison's boyfriend began stealing her money to support his increasingly serious drug habit. Although Madison also experimented with drugs, she never became addicted. When she became pregnant with her first child, Madison left her boyfriend, who had been charged with possession of drugs, and returned to Toronto to her parents' home prior to giving birth to her son. Because she was no longer working and had no support from her child's father, Madison ended up receiving social assistance and support for daycare while she first volunteered at a local food bank. She then got off assistance and worked in a paying position at the same food bank. Although she eventually quit that job and attempted to make a relationship work with a boyfriend whom she had known for a long time, Madison ended up alone again, raising her son as a single mother with help from a close friend from her past and occasional visits from her son's father.

Although they are not particularly close, Madison's mother also helps with child care. Madison is intent on building a better life for herself and her son and is currently enrolled in school.

Stacey

The youngest daughter of six children by three different fathers, 49-year-old Stacey is a second-generation Canadian of Caribbean descent whose mother was the victim of disfiguring domestic abuse by one of her partners, and whose father, while a gentle man, was a heroin addict who died from an accidental overdose just before Stacey was born.

Stacey's mother was separated from her own siblings when her grandmother died and her grandfather was unable to care for his children. As a result, Stacey's mother was temporarily placed in the care of the Children's Aid Society before striking out on her own. She developed alcohol, gambling, anger, and other problems as a result of this early disruption and abandonment. As a youngster, Stacey was often left to fend for herself while her mother was out drinking. These binges changed her mother's behaviour, and Stacey was often on the receiving end of her mother's violent rages. Although they existed on social assistance benefits, Stacey recalls never wanting for food or clothes and said her mother carefully managed the little money they had.

Stacey began working at a young age and never completed high school. She moved into her boyfriend's house when she was 23, and, although they planned to marry, the wedding was called off because of his parent's racist attitudes about interracial couples. Toward the end of the relationship, both began using crack cocaine and Stacey continued using drugs when the relationship ended. When she became pregnant by her second boyfriend, at age 32, Stacey still occasionally used drugs. She became a single mother when her boyfriend, unable to handle parental responsibilities because of his heavy drug use, left the relationship. Once she was established in her own home with the help of her family, however, the child's father returned.

Although they tried to make the relationship and parenthood work, both fell back into their old patterns of drug use. When Stacey became pregnant again, her boyfriend absconded again. During this time she supported herself primarily through social assistance programs, and odd jobs like babysitting provided extra money to pay for drugs. Stacey's lifestyle resulted in many violent altercations with drug dealers and necessitated a move to another neighbourhood, where she still resides. Stacey has gone through three drug treatment programs and with the help of social assistance and bursaries, she attends George Brown College as a mature student. She also got involved in the Voices from the Street program that encourages marginalized people to speak out on current issues as a way to affect change.

Stacey now enjoys a close relationship with her two daughters, who are well-adjusted, confident young women. She continues to attend recovery meetings to talk about and get help with her everyday struggles as a recovering addict. Stacey is learning coping techniques to control issues of anger and fear.

Robin

The younger child of a First Nations mother and a Scottish father whose divorce was precipitated by their mutually abusive relationship and alcoholism, Robin found herself performing the role of caretaker to her parents, who both relied on her for moral, physical, and emotional support from the time she was a youngster. Her early memories of her parents are of long sleepless nights waiting for or accompanying her inebriated mother home from the bars where she drank, and indulging her father when he would arrive, often intoxicated, hours late for their arranged occasional meetings. Fortunately, her maternal grandparents provided an early safe, secure, and loving environment for Robin and her older sister.

Robin identifies the origins of alcohol addiction in her family with her biological maternal grandmother, an Aboriginal woman who suffered the horrors of residential school and almost a decade in a sanatorium being treated for tuberculosis. She became addicted to alcohol as a young woman and often gave her young daughter—Robin's mother—alcohol when she was a baby to make her sleep at night. A kind-hearted woman, Robin's mother opened her home to all who needed lodging. One of these guests, a troubled woman and victim of sexual abuse, ended up sexually abusing Robin who kept the trauma she experienced from her mother until she was an adult. Life improved, however, for Robin and her sister when their mother and her new partner, whom Robin refers to as her other mother, moved in together and created a secure home and intellectually stimulating space for the girls. Encouraged by her other mother to explore the arts and other scholarly endeavours, Robin excelled when she attended an alternative First Nations School, where indigenous knowledge and Aboriginal world views were taught. During this time Robin's mother made valiant efforts to stop drinking. The newly constituted family's idyllic life was shattered by a frightening racist and homophobic encounter that had long-reaching, long-lasting, and unexpected effects.

Robin and her mother were sexually, physically, and verbally accosted by three plainclothes Toronto police officers whose fellow officers attempted to bury the charges brought against the officers by Robin's parents. Years later the charges resulted in the officers merely being demoted to desk jobs. This and the several other sexual assaults Robin experienced in childhood caused considerable emotional and psychological damage. That legacy of abuse and her inability to make sense of it led to drug use and other illegal and risky behaviours.

By age 17, Robin was a single mother, but she tried to improve her life by returning to school. At age 21, she had her second child, with an abusive man who shared her cocaine addiction. Her mother, who had returned to alcohol use and had ended her relationship with Robin's other mother, was no longer a part of her life, though Robin still had occasional contact with her second mother.

By now completely addicted to cocaine, Robin was caught in Miami, Florida, importing the drug from Jamaica and ended up spending six months in the Dade County Jail and three years in a maximum-security penitentiary in Broward County. During that time her children were in the custody of relatives. In prison, Robin experienced and witnessed a range of crimes perpetrated by guards against the female inmates, who were overwhelmingly un- or under-educated, poor, members of racial minority groups, and victims of sexual abuse. One of the most egregious abuses was the seemingly systematic, unwarranted, and surreptitious hysterectomies performed on inmates. Robin's complaints only led to warnings to keep quiet. While incarcerated, Robin managed to get her GED certificate (high school equivalency) and complete a drug rehabilitation program. When her sentence was completed, Robin returned to Canada, where she eventually reunited with her son's father. Their codependence led to Robin's recidivism, another pregnancy, and finally the loss of all of her children. After successful rehab and a long and bitter battle with the Children's Aid Society, Robin regained custody of her youngest child.

Following a decade of introspection, hard work, and drug-free living, Robin has managed to work toward repairing her relationship with her older children. She completed a bridging program through the University of Toronto and continues to take classes toward a major in Aboriginal Studies. She became involved in support groups, quit smoking, lost weight, and began working in the field of community support. Robin is transforming her life and believes she is finally becoming the person she was intended to be before violence, abuse, and addiction entered her life.

Emily

Emily spent her formative years, from age one and a half to six, in Eastern Europe in the care of her grandparents, who took charge of their granddaughter when her parents divorced and her mother threatened to put her up for adoption. Although she remembers her early childhood as happy and safe, her parents' abandonment created a void that Emily has spent a lifetime trying to fill. When she turned seven, Emily began school and starting living full-time with her mother, with whom she had difficulty bonding. Even though she generally excelled at school, her mother used corporal punishment when Emily made even minor errors on tests. It took her grandmother's intervention to make Emily's mother change her abusive behaviour toward her daughter and begin to forge a stronger relationship.

When Emily was almost 10, her mother remarried and had a second child. Her stepfather's psychologically abusive ways created an atmosphere of fear in the home which transformed Emily into an anxious, fearful child. Her unease and lack of self-confidence followed her into adulthood and, although she completed both high school and a post-secondary technical program, she remained plagued with self-doubt, anxiety, and low self-esteem. A year after graduating, Emily married and had two children with a man who also turned out to be abusive. Her now-ex-husband was controlling from the beginning of the relationship but became increasingly verbally, psychologically, and, eventually, physically abusive. After they moved to Canada to be closer to his family and relatives, Emily's isolation was exacerbated by her in-laws' vocal disapproval of her child-rearing abilities and open criticism of the two young boys. The negative environment within the extended family had the effect of intensifying Emily's husband's aggressive, controlling ways. He continued to isolate Emily from friends, colleagues and employers and restrict her access to social services in Canada which would have helped her deal with the language and other barriers she faced. Emily reached her limit of patience when she realized that her husband had embarked on a campaign to turn her children against her.

Finally, on the advice of a neighbour who informed her of her rights and pointed her to community services for victims of domestic abuse, Emily took her children to a shelter where they remained for the next three years. Although her husband showed up at the shelter and had to be removed by the police, Emily chose not to press charges again him but rather to forge ahead and create a safe environment for her children. After they moved into an apartment, Emily's husband once again began harassing her and threatened to take away her children. As a result of years of witnessing their father's abuse, Emily's children began acting out and she suffered from depression. Despite his demonstrated disregard for and neglect of his family, Emily's ex-husband waged a two-and-a-half-year battle for custody of the two boys. Unfortunately, the court-appointed children's lawyer was incompetent, consistently unprepared for court and provided misleading and inaccurate testimony on behalf of the children who decidedly did not wish to have contact with their father even though she insisted they did. Despite advising the Office of the Children of the potential danger of releasing the location of the children's school or the family's new address, the lawyer mentioned the name of the school in a meeting attended by both the children's father and his lawyer. The following day he showed up at the school with the intent of abducting one of his boys. As he was in violation of his bail conditions, he was promptly arrested and, in 2008, deported back to his country or origin.

Emily's dealings with both Family and Criminal Court and Immigration services were uneven and contributed to the stress and trauma the family experienced. The women's shelter and the police department, however, constituted valuable support systems throughout Emily's journey to safety and greater independence for herself and her children. All three continue to participate in counselling and recovery programs. Accorded the status of refugee claimants, for reasons of spousal abuse, Emily and her boys now enjoy a safe life in Canada although the scars left by the years of abuse they suffered have been slow to heal.

Catrina

A 28-year-old single mother of three children, Catrina and her first child immigrated to Canada from Central America to escape her abusive boyfriend and mistreatment at the hands of various immediate and extended family members.

Catrina is descended from a long line of violence, which she is determined to end. She was conceived in violence when her mother, who had married for the second time after her first husband's violent murder, was raped by her second husband. She grew up witnessing her mother's abuse and then, at the age of three or four, became a victim of incest by her father. Despite her own experience of violent sexual domestic abuse, Catrina's mother refused to believe her daughter was also being abused when Catrina told her mother what her father was doing to her. After emptying the bank accounts and cashing in the insurance policy, her father left the family when Catrina was seven years old. She and her mother were made destitute and had to move into an aunt's home where Catrina was mistreated by her cousins. Not long after that, Catrina's grandmother, with whom she had shared an especially close relationship, died. She had bequeathed her house to her granddaughter in her will. As Catrina was too young to take ownership of the house, her father sold it and pocketed the money from the sale. Her mother, now in her fifties, suffered a nervous breakdown and other physiological health problems and was hospitalized. Following a surgery, she lost part of her memory and could no longer remember her daughter Catrina who was now, for all practical purposes, parentless. Catrina spent the subsequent four or five years being moved from one relative's or friend's home to another until her mother had sufficiently recovered. During that period she lived with her stepsister who, much like Catrina's father, used physical abuse to communicate her dislike of and dissatisfaction with her younger sister.

Catrina began menstruating at age 11 and her body developed rapidly thereafter. When in public she was often sexually taunted by men and other strangers. As a strategy to escape the incessant focus on her body, Catrina developed friendships with gay men who had no sexual interest in her. Her only other close friendship was with her maternal uncle who was like a surrogate father, attending her school functions, looking after her when she was sick and, eventually, encouraging her to immigrate to Canada.

At age 16, Catrina became pregnant by her first boyfriend, who date-raped her. When her mother discovered the pregnancy she first beat her daughter and then tried to persuade her to have an abortion. Because she was ostracized by her extended family, Catrina decided to move to another city with her boyfriend. Too poor to rent an apartment, they stayed in a hotel before finding a small room. As there was only one room key, Catrina remained locked in the room all day and became increasingly isolated.

Because they had little money, Catrina did not eat properly or get the proper rest or health care a pregnant woman requires. Also, her boyfriend's paranoia meant that she never had the opportunity to visit a doctor alone or express her concerns to anyone. When her boyfriend discovered that a friend had contacted Catrina, he beat her for the first time, starting a pattern of abuse that continued throughout their relationship.

Partway through the pregnancy Catrina and her boyfriend returned to their home city and moved into her in-laws' house. When she witnessed her father-in-law beating her mother-in-law, she realized where her boyfriend's violent behaviour originated. Catrina fled to her mother's house and soon gave birth to a healthy daughter despite the incompetence and errors of the inexperienced medical staff. Her in-laws tracked her down at the hospital and tried to take the baby away from her. Although they failed in that attempt, they kept up a steady campaign of harassment and attempts to abduct the baby. Catrina spent the next several months at her aunt's house in hiding. When her boyfriend found them and threatened Catrina with a gun, she made a harrowing escape with the baby to a cousin's house where the two remained until enough money had been raised to send them both to Canada.

Once in Canada, Catrina was granted refugee status first, based on her history of abuse in her own country, and eventually got permanent residence status. The transition from Central America to Canada was made difficult by the language barrier, economic and social challenges, and inadequate legal services. Catrina moved into a shelter when she arrived in Canada, which is where she met the father of her second child. He neither wanted the child nor had permanent residency in Canada so was soon deported. Although his mother and Catrina maintain telephone contact, he has no contact with his own child. When she eventually moved out of the shelter, Catrina returned to high school to finish her diploma and also managed to work part-time.

Catrina met the father of her third child through a friendship with an older woman whom she met through her involvement in a community centre. Eighteen years her senior, suffering from diagnosed mental health issues and as a marijuana grower and smoker, he turned out to be ill-suited for fatherhood, despite initially appearing responsible. During the pregnancy they lived together, with Catrina's two children from her previous relationships, in a rented apartment that also housed his marijuana grow-op. After the baby's birth, Catrina had to be medicated for the postpartum depression she experienced. When her partner's previous charge for marijuana possession was discovered, a case worker from Children's Aid began monitoring the family which included weekly visits. Her baby's father became increasingly paranoid as a result of refusing to take the medication prescribed for his acute depression and not long after that, became first verbally and then physically violent and abusive toward both his mother and Catrina. She finally ended the relationship and took out a restraining order against him. Both his family and the police department have been supportive in Catrina's efforts to shield her family from abuse.

The deaths of Catrina's father and her former partner's father have left her children without grandparents. The absence of a family support system weighs heavily on Catrina's mind, but she is determined to support and protect her three children from the kinds of abuses she endured and be the kind of mother she wishes she had as a child.

Lucy

Despite the African cultural and social norms and expectations that kept Lucy in an abusive relationship for many years, her awareness that the domestic violence she experienced was affecting her children and the choice she had as an immigrant to Canada to leave her abusive husband helped her make the decision to end the marriage and begin a new life as a single mother.

The oldest of seven children, Lucy began working at her father's corner store when she was 10 years old and soon developed a sense of responsibility for her younger siblings and a love of numbers. From a very young age, when her mother was about to have another child, Lucy would be sent to stay with relatives. There, she was sexually abused by two cousins and, because they threatened to kill her mother if she ever told anyone about the abuse, Lucy kept the traumatic experience secret until she sought counselling as an adult. Part of her pain was the resentment she carried toward her mother for having sent her to stay with relatives—one of whom had a rape conviction against him—and not having protected her.

Lucy was close to her siblings, five of whom remained in Africa while she and her youngest sister immigrated to Canada and England, respectively, but geography has kept them apart. Although her parents were not educated people in the traditional sense, they recognized the importance of education and encouraged Lucy to excel at her studies at the government school she attended. (In fact, her father encouraged and supported all his daughters, in particular, in their educational endeavours.) At college Lucy studied Building Science (a course resembling engineering) and, as one of the top eight students in her college, won a place in a four-month exchange program with students at a college in Toronto from January to April 1986. Despite the Canadian cold, Lucy enjoyed her experience and began thinking about eventually making a life for herself in Toronto.

During the difficult economic period of 1987 when employment was difficult to find and educated, working women were perceived as taking much-needed jobs from men, Lucy, who had male employees, was verbally and even physically attacked by male colleagues and employees. Although she contemplated leaving her job to resume working at her father's store, Lucy was determined not to forfeit her hard-won education and career. She made two subsequent trips to Toronto: the first for one year, during which she worked and attended school on a part-time basis; the second as a business student at the same college she had attended during the exchange program in 1986. Making ends meet was challenging and Lucy's financial problems were exacerbated by the fact that, because of her status, she could not work in Canada to help pay for her college fees. As such, she eventually moved to Atlanta, Georgia, where she got landed immigrant status and did office work for a time.

Lucy's husband, a black Nova Scotian whom she met in Toronto, did not have the generally happy childhood Lucy had experienced in Africa and soon after they married, revealed himself to be a controlling man. Threatened by his wife's college education and her desire to go to university, he soon became abusive. He isolated her from friends and colleagues and used physical violence to undermine her self-confidence. When his violence progressed to the point where he would beat Lucy while she was holding their son in her arms, she resolved to begin the process of ending the marriage. Finding herself pregnant again, however, Lucy decided to stay in the family home until she had put in place an escape plan. A chance conversation with a woman at the building site of a co-operative housing project Lucy had volunteered to work on and who recognized the signs of domestic abuse led to Lucy being able to secure co-op housing with rent geared to income.

Though it was a difficult choice for her to make, Lucy applied for and secured social assistance so she could support herself and her children. Because her son's speech was delayed (at five years old he was still not talking), Lucy consulted a specialist who eventually diagnosed autism with developmental delays. The challenges of raising a child with autism are multiple but Lucy remains dedicated to making a good life for both of her children. Although she returned to university, the stipulation that students on social assistance cannot also receive student loans made it impossible for Lucy to meet her financial, child care and other basic needs so she eventually and regrettably forfeited the dream of a Canadian university degree.

Still collecting social assistance while working part-time, Lucy has to deal with the constant frustrations and humiliations of being dependent on a system that creates barriers to living independent of its own services. Despite these struggles, Lucy remains confident that she has made the right choices for herself and her children and is hopeful that their lives will continue to improve.

Christina

Christina, a 45-year-old single mother and only child from a deeply traditional, strict, working-class family, emigrated from Portugal with her parents in 1974, when she was seven years old. Her extended family, with the exception of an aunt, uncle and two cousins, remained in Portugal and the separation exacerbated the sense of isolation she and her immediate family felt as immigrants to Canada.

Within a year, Christina's hardworking parents managed to purchase a house. Despite a language barrier and many other social, cultural, and economic challenges, Christina completed her high school education and even excelled academically. However, she experienced bullying and taunting at school from peers and was made to feel both physically and intellectually inadequate at home by her authoritarian parents who often left her to fend for herself while they were working. Her mother used food as a way to express the affection she could not articulate. Christina's sense of inadequacy and her increasing lack of self-confidence, exacerbated by weight issues, made her vulnerable to prescription drugs (diet pills). Her relationship with her mother grew increasingly strained as Christina rebelled against authority. As soon as she got her high school diploma at 18, she left her family home and moved into a cousin's home. She later turned to other drugs and alcohol which she used as a way to artificially bolster her self-esteem and to escape from problems around family conflict, peer pressure, social isolation and weight.

An unhealthy first relationship led to an increased reliance on drugs and alcohol and soon Christina was unable to hold a job. At 25, she had already had four abortions and by 29 was married to a cocaine dealer with whom she had her first son. They soon separated because Christina refused to take her son into an unhealthy home environment and her immigrant husband moved back to his country, leaving Christina alone to raise her son. An ex-boyfriend, a former addict himself, introduced her to Alcoholics Anonymous, and although she relapsed occasionally the abstinence program helped her to begin turning her life around. A decision to move to the US to reunite with her husband so he could bond with their son, resulted in a return to drug and alcohol use. The realization that her husband could not establish a relationship with his son helped Christina resolve to use the strategies she had developed though AA to create a stable environment for her son back in Canada. A stay in an American addiction treatment facility strengthened her resolve to live substance free. That treatment also helped Christina realize that unhealthy relationships can be as toxic as drugs and alcohol.

Now back in Canada and more than two years substance free, Christina has a new sense of self-confidence and resolve. She is actively seeking help and support for herself and her son through participation in women's groups and events to support women's shelters. With her mind set on creating a brighter future, Christina has taken a bridging course in view of applying to university for post-secondary studies.

Susan

Susan, a UK-born single mother of twin girls with multiple health challenges, still lives with the unbidden, sensory-induced memories of a childhood marked by appalling squalor, extreme poverty, and horrifying abuse. At the age of five, Susan predicted the death of her little sister Mary, who died from bronchial pneumonia at age three. Of her remaining five siblings, only one shared a biological father, while the other four, like Mary and her full brother, had been adopted by their stepfather. Mary and her siblings were the target of her father's constant sexual and exceptionally violent physical abuse. One brother was placed in foster care following a particularly severe beating. Now adults, two brothers are alcoholics and another, with whom Mary was closest as a child, has severed contact with his family at the advice of a therapist. She is still in touch with and remains close to her oldest brother.

At age 16, Susan began working for a family in her neighbourhood and eventually moved in with them when the wife fell ill with cancer. When her family moved away, Susan moved in with these neighbours and took over most domestic duties. When the wife died and the father decided to move to Canada with his children, Susan convinced him to take her along as despite the fact that she was a teen and much younger, they had become sexually involved. Arrangements were made for Susan to stay with this man's friends until her paperwork was ready and she could join him in Canada. When she finally managed to reach her boyfriend, who had given her false contact information, plans for her move to Canada were finalized.

When Susan arrived in Canada in the early 1980s, she was expected to act as a maid and surrogate mother to her boyfriend's children. At age 36, with a husband already of retirement age, Susan became pregnant with her twins. The pregnancy was difficult and the babies were born prematurely and underweight. Her husband was uninvolved in the mundane and exceptional activities necessary to care for two disabled children and parsimonious with money for necessary clothing and health-related items. Eventually, when her girls were five year old, Susan separated from her husband and began her life as a single mother. Although he continues to be a presence in their lives, Susan feels she has more control over her own decisions and the lives of her children as a single mother. Though she faces financial and other struggles, she endeavours to provide for her girls the material comforts and emotional support that she did not get from her own parents.

Over the years, Susan has had uneven dealings with various social services representatives in her attempts to find financial support to meet her own and the medical needs of her children. While her encounters with representatives of the Ontario Disability Support Program (ODSP) have been almost uniformly unpleasant, she has had very positive encounters with Ontario Works. Her frugality and inventive ways of stretching a dollar have helped Susan to furnish her apartment, keep up with everyday expenses and sometimes indulge her two girls. Although she has a boyfriend who has proposed marriage to her, Susan prefers to retain her independence for her own peace of mind and as a way of ensuring the safety of her two girls.

Miriam

Born into a large, poor, slum-dwelling family of seven girls in Africa, Miriam and one sibling were separated from their five sisters and mother when their parents' marriage unravelled. She and her sister were systematically abused by their father who forced them into a life of selling drugs and illegal alcohol. When his abuse escalated to a point where neighbours noticed what was happening, the police were notified and he was arrested. Because their mother was too poor to support the girls, they were put into an orphanage temporarily and then taken in by the British magistrate who had presided over their case. With the biological mother's consent, the magistrate eventually became the girls' foster mother.

Miriam's father died when she was 12 years old and eventually she and her sister stopped travelling back to their natal village. Although she enjoyed a comfortable childhood, was schooled in elite private schools and lacked for nothing, Miriam felt out of place both in her new world and in the one in which she was born. The sense of being a stranger in both worlds fuelled Miriam's desire to distance herself from her home and her country; as a result, she applied for and won a scholarship to complete an international baccalaureate at a college in Canada. After completing a BA and one year of a master's degree, Miriam and a friend moved to Toronto. Miriam spent most of her twenties working in Toronto and travelling. Dissatisfied with her job at a department store, Miriam decided to return part-time to university to pursue a degree in social work. In the meantime, a friendship with a divorced work colleague developed into a romance that resulted in marriage. Discovering that she was pregnant, Miriam decided to keep working in order to take advantage of her maternity leave benefits. It was at this point that the marriage began to unravel.

Although she had noted her soon-to-be husband's dismissive and pejorative attitude toward his ex-wife, it was not until he began verbally abusing her that Miriam realized his behaviour toward her was part of a pattern. When Miriam declared that, despite his wish not to have the baby she intended to keep it, her husband's abusiveness escalated to physical violence. Although she fought back and even called the police on one occasion, she declined to press charges because she wanted to have a family. Not long after the baby arrived, Miriam's husband broke his leg, so she had to look after him as well as the baby. In the course of a heated argument in front of one of her friends, Miriam's husband punched her in the face. Her friend insisted on taking her and the baby out of the house. The doctor her friend insisted she consult diagnosed Miriam with a severe case of postpartum depression, and eventually, knowing she could not return to her husband, Miriam and her baby stayed with her sister in Seattle. Three months later she was enticed back to Toronto by her husband, who promised to change his behaviour. When that didn't happen, Miriam went back to Seattle for a short period before returning to try to make the marriage work again. Still suffering from depression related to childbirth, Miriam's sometimes erratic behaviour on one particular occasion elicited such a forceful punch from her husband that she was knocked unconscious. When she gained consciousness and called the police, her husband managed to convince them that she was the aggressor and they arrested her.

Miriam was detained in a jail cell for four days under the Mental Health Act while her husband went unpunished. When she was finally released, Miriam learned that her child had been taken away from her. She pressed charges against her husband, hired a lawyer, and 18 months later finally regained custody of her son. During that time, she had only supervised visits through Children's Aid. Traumatized by the situation, Miriam attempted suicide by swallowing pills. After she was discovered, she was hospitalized for two months, where she was given psychiatric treatment that included various medications and electric shock treatment. A Children's Aid investigation determined that Miriam was unfit to have custody of her son. To compound matters, she had to move from the family home, a building where her husband was superintendent, and into an apartment without her child. Her husband filed for and got custody of their son while Miriam had only court-mandated access. He made access so difficult that at one point Miriam saw her son only two times in a six-month period. Only after a long, protracted, acrimonious, and expensive legal battle did Miriam finally get joint custody of her son, who by this time was five years old. Because the legal process was so slow, Miriam had to apply for Legal Aid and Welfare benefits. Of necessity, she finally moved into a women's shelter because she could not afford to pay rent. There she got the help she needed to eventually move into subsidized housing.

During this time, Miriam was receiving social assistance, but because she had shared custody of her son, she initially received only half the standard payment. This was rectified when a new female social worker learned she was receiving only $450 monthly—an arrangement put in place by a male social worker. Her physician signed the special diet supplement form so that Miriam collected an additional $250 a month. When she had settled into the new, larger Metro Housing apartment, and her son was visiting, Miriam discovered that he had bruises on his body that were the result of being beaten with a belt by his father. With the help of a nurse for whom she was working, Miriam took her son to SickKids Hospital, where the police were called. Miriam's husband was arrested. Although he was found guilty of child abuse and placed on the Child Abuse Register, the courts allowed him continued unsupervised access to his son with the condition that he attend counselling.

Miriam was eventually diagnosed with clinical depression and was eligible for disability payments that help to support her and her son who continues to thrive. Although she considered returning to university once again, Miriam has decided to find fulfillment in other ways and, with the help of a new community of friends and advocates, is building a new more positive life for herself and her son.

Victoria

Born in Central America and traumatically separated from her biological mother at age five by government soldiers, Victoria and her younger brother spent several relatively carefree years at an orphanage in the care of staff and foster parents before being adopted by English-speaking Canadian volunteers when they were seven and five years old, respectively. Adjusting to a different culture, language, and climate was challenging, but both children excelled. Their lives changed for the worse, however, when their adoptive parents became physically, emotionally, and sexually abusive.

Victoria's mother instigated the abuse, which initially manifested as bullying, name-calling, and other humiliating and degrading behaviours. The abuse gradually escalated to include physical violence and, although the children's mother meted out most of the punishment, she soon enlisted her husband in her perverse program of abuse, which included starving the children, locking them in the bathroom overnight without blankets or pillows, and a range of verbal and physical assaults. Victoria's brother was the victim of severe beatings at their mother's hand and Victoria became the victim of her father's sexual abuse, which she endured for almost a decade. Although she was in grade school, Victoria, who by that time had two other adopted siblings, was often made to leave class and go home to do laundry and cleaning. Victoria's mother institutionalized her little brother when Victoria was 13; she eventually lost contact with him. Two years later, after Victoria confronted her father and told her mother he had been sexually abusing her, he was finally arrested though not charged or punished.

Physically and emotionally exhausted from the constant abuse, Victoria finally ran away from home and stayed in a series of shelters until she was 20. Although she felt more secure there, she was the victim of sexual abuse during this time. One perpetrator, who had raped several other young women at the shelter, was eventually charged and sentenced to a two-year jail term. During this time she had a boyfriend who Victoria suspected had set her up to be gang-raped by several of his acquaintances. He was never punished for his part in that incident. Because of this history of sexual abuse by men she knew and, for the most part, initially trusted, Victoria eventually turned to prostituting herself because she needed money to survive. During this period, Victoria temporarily moved out of the shelter she was in and into her boyfriend's mother's home. By this time she was pregnant with her first child, and even though her boyfriend's mother mistreated her she stayed until the baby was born. Following her son's birth, Victoria was taken by her mother, with whom she had renewed contact, to another shelter because she did not trust her boyfriend or his family, who had been escorted from the hospital by security because of their disruptive and abusive behaviour toward Victoria and the hospital staff and doctors during her son's birth. After four months in the shelter, Victoria moved into a tiny basement apartment with her son. Her loneliness drove her to reach out to the baby's father, with whom she rented an apartment that neither could afford. He slipped back into established patterns of selling and using drugs and abusing Victoria. Although she had him charged with abuse and he attended anger management classes, his behaviour did not change.

Determined to change her life and shelter her son from his father's abusive behaviour, Victoria applied for and got subsidized housing, completed her high school diploma, and earned two college-level diplomas and a certificate. Although she has a considerable school loan to pay off, Victoria is currently working and pursuing more fulfilling and higher-paying work while she cares for herself and her son. Victoria's experience with the social welfare system has been negative because the subsidy she receives is minimal and her monthly income is further reduced because she also works. Despite these challenges, Victoria is determinedly improving life for herself and her son.

Izabela

The only child of parents who divorced when she was three years old, Izabela was largely raised in Eastern Europe by her grandparents and aunts. Izabela's mother was an unhappy, verbally abusive, and eventually alcoholic woman, and her stepfather sexually abused her from the age of 12. The sexual abuse stopped, temporarily, only when he left for Canada; however, on a return trip to Eastern Europe he convinced Izabela's mother to join him in Canada with her now 16-year-old daughter. There, the sexual abuse resumed until Izabela was almost 18. When she finally confronted her parents about the abuse, Izabela's stepfather admitted his guilt, but her mother refused to acknowledge it or to recognize her complicity through silence. Her mother's betrayal helped Izabela decide to move out of the family home.

Although she did not yet have the documentation necessary to work legally in Canada, Izabela managed to support herself with odd jobs. When she eventually took a job at a bar, illegally, her precarious status made her easy prey to people wanting to take advantage of her. One of those was a man 10 years Izabela's senior who turned out to be abusive and controlling throughout their three-and-a-half-year relationship. He convinced her that she was fat and, over time, Izabela developed an eating disorder. A counsellor at her high school connected her with counselling services at Women's College Hospital, where she learned to understand and take control her behaviour. Her boyfriend also forced her to take high-paying jobs that he could benefit from. The only positive outcome of this situation was that Izabela eventually had financial security and felt strong enough to end the relationship, have him charged with abuse, and see him sentenced to a six-month jail term.

Izabela's second boyfriend was a divorced single father 16 years her senior, and though he was good to her he was not supportive of her desire to further her education; as a result, Izabela left school after getting her high school diploma. She began drinking during this time and this, coupled with her sense of competing with her stepchildren for her boyfriend's affections, led to the end of the relationship when Izabela was 25. Her third boyfriend introduced her to drugs and together they drank excessively on a daily basis. Like her other boyfriends had, he also supported her and she became dependent on him and his circle of friends. Although the relationship eventually ended, Izabela had become an alcoholic. The man who would become the father of her first child was considerably younger than her other partners and also very insecure. Together they used drugs recreationally and drank regularly and soon he became physically abusive. He was arrested and briefly jailed, but Izabela took him back in despite his violent behaviour. By the time she discovered she was pregnant, however, the relationship was over.

With support from some close friends and her mother, with whom she had a precarious but constant relationship, Izabela made a comfortable home for her son. She had resumed binge drinking, however, and inadvertently set her apartment on fire when she blacked out after a session of heavy drinking. Her son was placed in the care of the Children's Aid Society, and Izabela finally sought help for her addiction. One of the conditions of having her son back was also having her mother live with her full-time. Unfortunately, her mother's continued drinking and absence from the house caused enough stress to lead Izabela back into drinking as well. The constant pressure forced her to confide in her caseworker that the court conditions were being violated at home, meaning, inevitably, that she lost custody of her son again, temporarily. A live-in treatment program failed because Izabela was not yet ready to deal with the problems that led to her reliance on alcohol. Attending Alcoholics Anonymous changed Izabela's perceptions about herself and her relationship with and addiction to alcohol, and she was finally able to stop drinking and gain the skills she needed to take care of her son, with whom she was reunited.

Izabela supports herself and her son with help from social assistance programs. Although she has plans to go to college, Izabela is concentrating on developing coping skills and looking after her young son, who is doing well at daycare. An older friend, with whom she shares an apartment, helps out with daily expenses and tasks and has become a father figure to her son. Izabela enjoys cooking and baking and has even begun to blog about her passion for food. When Izabela attempted to make contact with her mother, who had continued drinking, she discovered that she had been hospitalized in the winter and had subsequently died. On her deathbed, she denied having a daughter. Despite this sad news, Izabela has managed to move on with her life and has plans to attend university.

Jenna

A single mother of one son and the eldest of nine siblings born into a loving, hard-working, but poor family in the Philippines, Jenna immigrated to Canada from Hong Kong, where she had worked as a caregiver for the same family for 10 years after studying to be a medical secretary in the Philippines. For her first eight years in Canada, Jenna continued working as a caregiver for a kind and generous family. That family continues to support her in many ways, including financially. While working for them, she earned a certificate in hospitality management that led to a job as a cook in a nursing home. During the eight-year period she worked for the nursing home, Jenna made many friends and won many fans through her skills as a cook. Although the work was difficult and the hours taxing, Jenna loved her job and would have continued in it if not for a workplace accident that changed her life irrevocably.

In 2006 Jenna was exposed to toxic fumes from a gas leak at work. When she regained consciousness in hospital, she was unable to walk. Dealing with debilitating pain, Jenna began a six-month regime of physiotherapy to relearn how to walk. As workplace compensation had not yet begun and because Jenna was not aware of either the Ontario Disability Support Program or the Ontario Works program, she drained her savings, liquidated her RRSPs, and borrowed money from friends and family to support herself and her young son before realizing she could apply for financial assistance. During this time doctors were unable to diagnose Jenna's health problem. Only after demanding to be sent to a specialist was Jenna finally able to get an accurate diagnosis: multiple sclerosis and a dislocated disk. Even with this definitive diagnosis, her general practitioner refused to take the necessary steps to file a clear diagnosis so that Jenna could file an insurance claim. After three years of intense pain, physiotherapy, and various medical appointments and interventions, Jenna discovered support with the lone-mothers group—especially the facilitator, Judit—through which she has gained valuable support, understanding, and friendship as well as an honorarium that helps to make ends meet financially.

Jenna acknowledges her son's role in helping her recover. He served as her motivation to literally get back on her feet, and Jenna delights in his many accomplishments, including a black belt in karate. Now back at her previous work place, Jenna has a different and more challenging position, but she perseveres despite the taxing demands of the job.

Pulling It Together

Our task now is to draw the reader back to what the stories represent: those structural and policy issues that have determined that hardship and abuse are too frequently a part of life for many poor, single mothers in our prosperous country. The following table provides a way to quickly identify some of the most commonly identified structural issues that shape the lives of these women. We discuss those enumerated in the table as well as other broader structural themes, including, perhaps most importantly, the formative issue of gender inequality.

Table One — A Summary of the Most Common Issues Faced

	Abuse[a]	Poverty	Family of Origin	Immigration[b]	Disability[c]	Service System[d]
Lucy	XXX	X	abuse by extended family	A	X	
Christina	XX	X	severe parenting	E		
Jenna		X		A	X	
Miriam	X	X	abuse, poverty, adoption	A		X
Emily	X	X	abuse	E	X	X
Catrina	XXX	X	abuse	LA	X	
Susan	X	X	abuse, poverty	E	X	
Victoria	XX	X	abuse by adoptive parents	LA	X	X
Izabela	XX	X	parental addictions	E	X	
Sara	X	X	abuse, parental addictions, poverty			
Robin	XX	X	parental addictions, residential school survivor, poverty			X
Mary	XX	X	parental addictions, abandonment		X	X
Anne	X	X	parental addictions			X
Madison	X	X	severe parenting			
Stacey	X	X	parental addictions			
Martha	X	X	abuse		X	X

[a]Abuse includes intimate-partner violence, childhood sexual abuse, and rape—each X references one of these types of abuse experiences.

[b]E—European, A—Africa and Asia, LA—Latin America

[c]Disability refers to either the mother or her children and includes physical or intellectual disability and mental health issues.

[d]We refer here to cases in which there appear to have been significant errors or failures in the structures and institutions of the state that should be available to every citizen.

Abuse and Trauma

Catrina's story is a challenging narrative, one that may be difficult to read, because the depths of abuse and distress are vividly and candidly described. That a child can be adopted into a Canadian home from the relatively benign space of a foreign orphanage only to endure humiliation, abuse, and childhood rape is a story that we prefer to imagine as an isolated circumstance. In addition, violence, despite its presence in movies and on TV and as part of our culture, is presumed not to affect the daily lives of most citizens. The very real and personal violence that the single moms describe here is therefore difficult to take in, and there may be a tendency to "other" those who have experienced these traumas—they cannot be like us. It is because of the possibility of such othering that we feel the need to emphasize—beyond the stories told here—the prevalence of the stories of rape and abuse in all of our longitudinal, qualitative research data. It is a theme in these women's lives that cannot be discounted, and it perhaps speaks volumes about women's sole parenting and what triggers their applications to social assistance.

In considering the place of abuse in these women's lives, it is important to reiterate that their involvement in this project stemmed only from their being single moms on social assistance. We did not recruit for experiences of abuse—they were simply there, part of the background (or foreground) critical to the shaping not only these women's lives but probably the lives of many more women in our society than we care to countenance.

It is clear, too, from these narratives, that incidences of abuse are rarely isolated. A girl is taught through childhood rape and abuse that her only worth is a sexual one, a view that is heavily reinforced through popular discourse. Abuse experiences and this early sexualisation are profoundly damaging to self-esteem such that a sexually abused girl or woman too often becomes a ready victim for the next perpetrator—of which there seems no shortage. In understanding abuse and its place in women's lives, we must also acknowledge shame and its pernicious effects. In story after story, women who were sexually abused and/or raped told no one; they felt that they were at fault and carried with them deep feelings of shame. Lucy says about her childhood abuse by her cousins: "You don't tell your parents about these things," and further comments that she thought that abuse was what happened to all girls. Abuse, particularly childhood sexual abuse, where the perpetrators are so often family members, remains an undiscussed and taboo social topic, leaving its victims, including the women in this book, with deep feelings of shame and self denigration. In the words of Caldwell (n.d.), "shame is so painful, so debilitating that persons develop a thousand coping strategies, conscious and unconscious, numbing and destructive, to avoid its tortures. Shame is the worst possible thing that can happen, because shame, in its profoundest meaning, conveys that one is not fit to live in one's own community." It is these feelings that leave victims of abuse so susceptible to subsequent abuse experiences, mental health issues, and self-annihilating behaviours, including addiction.

Understanding the place and prevalence of violence and abuse helps us to understand the stories of self-destructive behaviour, the stories of addiction. For all of the women whose stories are told here, finding and learning self-worth has been a long struggle against many social messages that negate their worth and social value, as women, parents, and citizens. In this psychic state, addiction thrives. Like single mothering, or welfare reliance, addiction is heavily stigmatized—even more so if the user is a woman and a mother. We tend not to see addictive behaviour as symptomatic, and yet in these stories and our broader research the tie between addictions and abuse experiences is very strong.

Abuse is present in most stories—some experienced it in childhood, some as adults, and for some it is constant in their lives. The experience of abuse, and the way legal and social systems respond, often serve to keep women stuck, never quite having the right package of services and supports that might enable freedom from abuse and oppression and economic self-sufficiency. The emotional trauma of leaving an abusive relationship is compounded by the need to interface with numerous systems related to housing, custody (family courts), immigration, and criminal courts (to pursue charges against their abuser). In each of these systems, which we will discuss further, women, especially single mothers, are often viewed as problematic, undeserving, system scammers, of dubious morality, and of uncertain mothering ability.

We often hear, "Why do they stay?" (referring to an abusive relationship) or "How can she be a good mother if she drinks?" or "Why isn't she working?" The views that these questions reflect suggest that blame lies with the woman/lone mother. The answers to such questions become clearer only as we understand the complexity of abuse: the terrifying power of the abuser as well as the cyclical nature of abuse—how each experience erodes the self-worth and personal agency necessary to choose healthy relationships. That six of the 16 women participating in this volume have had substance abuse issues suggests a very strong correlation with abuse experiences. This suggestion would probably not surprise anyone working in addictions treatment, but it goes unacknowledged when the service system engages with these women and their children.

The situation is similar for many single mothers who apply for social assistance. Lucy describes having to reschedule her first appointment with her male social assistance worker after having just left an abusive husband. She did not have child care and could not manage taking both her kids with her to her appointment. Her worker got verbally nasty, triggering many of the feelings that she had experienced with her abusive husband. This too is not an unusual story, often repeated in our longitudinal research with more than 120 single moms across the country.

The cyclical element to abuse and addiction makes it imperative that we intervene and address the issues to break the cycle. Most of the women who told us of parents with addictions themselves succumbed at some point to addiction, not because they were weak, didn't care about their children, or liked to "party," but rather a bad-choice/no-choice response to a self seen to be without worth. As Robin said to us:

> I'm at the point now where I believe that my mother did the best that she could with what she had. . . . And I then look at who I am angry at, because I thought at first I was angry at me, and then I thought I was angry at my mom, and then I thought I was angry at my grandmother who gave my mother alcohol in a bottle, in a baby bottle. But then I see that there are other factors outside of that that led to women making choices that they had to make and do the things that they did, which then helps take my anger off of me, off of my mother, and off of my grandmother. . . . Because there were so many outside issues, so much outside that was not helping in supporting women through, like, the last hundred years, let's even go back that far or further. . . . I really hope that people can see that with these stories, that they recognize that—because I don't want, for me personally, I don't want it to just be blaming, blaming, blaming mother, mother-blaming. Because if I jump into my mother's shoes, go back to the '40s or '50s, and then I jump into my grandmother's shoes and go back to the '30s, I can see it from a totally different light.

Robin's comment reflects her own reflective learning, but it also nicely illustrates Freire's (1970) idea of conscientization that we discussed in the introduction. As she sees herself against a bigger social backdrop, against the major structural and systemic factors that shaped the lives of her extended family, Robin is released from guilt, blame, and shame and can focus her energy on building her own well-being and working to change these corrosive systems.

Racism and Colonialism

In Robin's quote, above, she identifies the compound sources of pain and trauma for which alcohol is often a salve. She points to a web of complex issues, including the fundamental problems colonialism and the oppression of First Nations people, first through the occupation of their lands and then subsequently through the purposive and forceful destruction of their ways of life, traditions, and language. The imposition of residential schools, such as the one Robin's grandmother was forced to attend, exemplifies this systematic oppression. As the Canadian federal government now tries to redress these wrongs, the full scope of their horror is revealed by the spiralling number of abuse claimants (AANDC, 2013). How much of the abuse experienced by Robin and her mother at the hands of the police was related to their being native? As cases swirl across the country of police both perpetrating and failing to investigate crimes against First Nations women, Robin's experiences must also be viewed through this larger systemic lens.

The effects of colonialism can be seen in some of the other stories as well. The lack of scrutiny given to the adoptive white parents of Victoria and her brother, who, while orphaned, were safe and secure, speaks to a presumption of white goodness. In Miriam's narrative, her adoption by a white family of privilege afforded her an escape from abuse and slum dwelling but affected her being able to feel at home in either a black or a white world. Stacey ascribes her breakup with her first boyfriend to his family's racism, and one also wonders whether racism played a role in the problems of her family of origin, where there was ongoing—and seemingly inattentive and ineffective—involvement of social services.

Jenna's story is reflective of the ongoing story of colonialism. The Philippines is a country continually and successively occupied for hundreds of years, its traditional economy destroyed and now reliant on offshore remittances from citizens like Jenna. Her story was in a sense foretold by these structural circumstances. As Jenna eventually makes her way to Canada under the provisions of our much-critiqued live-in caregiver program (Alcuitas, Alcuitas-Imperial, Diocson, & Ordinario, 1997; Diocson & Sayo, 2001; Grandea & Kerr, 1998), she is one of many helping to fill a yawning gap in Canada's social welfare system, which continues to lack a national child care strategy. Instead, now that Canadian women constitute fully half of the labour market, we import poor women from the global south under restrictive immigration criteria and with few employment protections.

Immigration and Status Vulnerability

The stories told here are stories of vulnerability—of being unprotected and unable to protect oneself. An important dimension of this vulnerability is immigration status. Many of the women come from other countries and deeply appreciate the supports that they have received since they came to Canada. Lucy, for example, talks about how hard it is for a woman in her home country and says she always dreamt of coming to Canada. Although she ends up in an abusive relationship, she also acknowledges that in Canada she knew she had a right to leave the relationship, which she may not have felt in her home country. Some women came with abusive husbands and acutely felt their status dependence, knowing that they couldn't leave. For women who were in Canada illegally, such status meant being fearful of an interaction with any legal authority, deciding, therefore, that in some cases abuse was better than deportation. In Jenna's case, it was only a matter of luck that her Canadian employers were fair because the stories are legion of women in these circumstances who endure both abuse and exploitation because they are fearful of being deported.

Poverty

All of the women profiled in this book live below the poverty line. For most this is a function of living on social assistance, disability support, or a pension. Remarkable, however, is that almost half of the women grew up in poverty. The choices[1] they have made in their adult lives, the many horrendous and difficult situations they found themselves in, and the barriers they faced are not unrelated to their early life experiences, their early nurturing or lack thereof, and the impoverishment of their lives as children. Catrina makes a desperate plea to have her life understood as one deprived of choice, as set on course by her experiences in her early years.

While policy-makers and leaders talk blithely of the cycle of poverty, theorizing and formulating, we see in these stories that it continues without redress—at least from the formal service and judicial systems. Sustained levels of material and social deprivation have been well established as factors that affect adult outcomes (see Holzer, Schanzenbach, Duncan, & Ludwig, 2007, for a review of some studies). Children who experience persistent poverty are at higher risk of health problems, developmental delays,

---

[1] "Choice" is a word laden with subtext. This will be discussed in detail in the concluding chapter in order to acknowledge how few real choices exist in these women's lives.

and behaviour disorders. Their education attainment is lower, and they are more likely to live in poverty as adults (Fleury, 2008; Frenette, 2007). We see these effects in the lives of our narrators. Stacey describes a life on social assistance, with successive moves, with children in and out of care, and the context of severe and persistent poverty. Although she has done well with her recovery from addiction and reports that her siblings have moved from welfare reliance, her story of how difficult it is for her to access meaningful education exemplifies a too-frequent tale of initiatives that are insufficient and too short-sighted to facilitate an end to the cycle of poverty.

Extreme and enduring poverty is seldom experienced in isolation from other social issues. By its very nature it often shapes housing quality and neighbourhood, which in turn shape peers, real and perceived educational opportunity, and a host of other factors. Both Mary and Stacey, for example, may not have descended so quickly into addictions had they grown up in different external environments. As several of the stories illustrate and much research supports, taking children into care is often an inadequate solution to issues of family poverty and deprivation (Cameron & Freymond, 2006). We see too in the stories efforts by child welfare authorities to place children taken into care with other family members. In many of the stories told here, this solution was also fraught. A reality of intergenerational poverty is that the social networks of those who have experienced different and cumulative types of deprivation may not include family and friends with the social and economic capital to provide high-quality temporary families. Better options have been proposed, including providing a full range of intensive and targeted supports to the whole family (Wagmiller & Adelman, 2009).

Meanwhile, benefit levels in social assistance and disability support programs consign families to inadequate housing, to neighbourhoods with high concentrations of poverty, to insecure and sometimes unsafe child care arrangements, to inadequate nutrition, and to lives without the opportunities for social and recreational enrichment that are the norm for most children. Sen (2000) describes such deprivation as relational, affecting all spheres of life and having a deep impact on the self-esteem and personal worthiness that is critical to being a full citizen, which implies having a sense of entitlement to contribute to the public discourse, to *be* in the public realm. A criticism often directed to the poor and marginalized is that they lack drive, a sense of purpose; it is this sense of agency that Sen suggests to be diminished through experiences of relational deprivation and exclusion.

According to the Organization for Economic Co-operation and Development (OECD, 2010), one in seven Canadian children live in poverty and Canada fares 15th out of 17 comparator countries using their measure of relative poverty. For First Nations children the situation is much worse, with a new report identifying that 50% of Indigenous children live in poverty (MacDonald & Wilson, 2013). In addition to the already-mentioned long-term effects on adult outcomes, child poverty has been projected to negatively affect Canada's economic prospects in terms of our ability to sustain economic growth (Conference Board of Canada, 2013).

Other nations that have moved to improve child poverty in recent years have done so through a number of measures, the benefits of which can be seen directly in terms of the stories told here. These measures are in addition to the usual cash and tax-based transfers usually implemented to effect income redistribution. Each measure acknowledged in the OECD report as effective (OECD, 2010) is particularly relevant to addressing the issues most salient to lone mothers. First was the funding of job training. As we discuss in a subsequent section, the job-training programs offered through social assistance in most of Canada fail to help single mothers earn a family wage. They are oriented to "the shortest route to work" without regard for the complex needs of single-parent families, including their need for employment stability and an income that can sustain a family. Second on the OECD list is the provision of state-supported child care. We subsequently discuss this as a yawning gap in Canada's social welfare provisions. Third on the OECD list are tax incentives for lower-paid workers. In effect, these provide state support to help workers cope with low-paid employment.

Jane Millar (2008), a leading social welfare theorist, suggests that in policy terms the nature of the welfare state response has changed from its earlier role of supporting people when the labour market fails to do so. She suggests that, in our current employment-based welfare state, the state has two roles: supporting security in work and ensuring security of income from work. In a Canadian context both of these are policy issues that warrant more active consideration.

Gender Inequality

One can't really speak about the cycle of poverty without acknowledging its profoundly gendered form. In Canada, women are more likely to be poor than their male counterparts in almost every age group. Women still work in female-dominated professions—education, healthcare, retail—occupations that have lower rates of pay than their male-dominated comparators. Briefly in the 1970s and '80s there were federal initiatives to shift women from these gendered work roles, and we saw programs that supported women's entry into non-traditional trades. Such initiatives were short-lived, as too were programs at both federal and provincial levels that aimed to ensure equal pay for equal work across female- and male-dominated employment sectors. Women continue to earn about 80 cents on the male dollar and, unlike other OECD countries, Canada has failed to reduce its gender wage gap. Neo-liberalism's rise, the manufactured crisis about public debt, and the cost of social spending cut short these stabs at addressing gender inequality and, beyond just ending these types of policy approaches, they seem to have succeeded in taking such issues off the public radar. This has been an important discursive shift in Canada and has been the focus of much debate given the analysis by many social welfare scholars and journalists that it has been driven more by ideology than economic necessity (McQuaig, 1995, 1998; Bezanson, 2006).

Although we often think of Canada as much more advanced than many other countries when it comes to women's equality, it is clear that the issues women experience transcend culture and geography. When women come here from other countries, they can still experience abuse and poverty as a result of their status as women. While these issues are mitigated somewhat by some of the supports available to women in Canada, the stories in this book demonstrate that Canada still falls short of providing a social environment that protects vulnerable women and children from abuse, or supports them to escape abuse. Rape, childhood sexual abuse, and intimate-partner violence are very much a part of our society, and they shape the life experiences of women in profound ways that are not easily remedied. The issues of gender equality and the prevalence of sexualized violence appear to no longer be on our social maps. We suggest these to be the most critical and ignored elements affecting the security of Canadian women. The current "get tough on crime" focus largely deflects attention from issues of substantive social magnitude by focusing on our already falling crime rates.

Women and Single Parenting

The connection between abuse and women's single parenting also demands attention both broadly socially and from policy-makers. Women constitute 80–85% of all single parents, and such disproportionate levels of responsibility for parenting are accepted without much in-depth analysis because of two very different but compounding factors. First, it is seen as some kind of natural phenomenon, a kind of biological determinism that a mother will assume custody of the children at the end of a relationship. On the other hand, society casts doubt and moral blame on these mothers for having children in unstable relationships, for not better protecting themselves from unwanted pregnancy, and for having little regard for whether they can financially sustain themselves and their families. This latter lens is especially pernicious in its effects as it applies selectively to low-income women whose status frequently intersects with racialization and immigration and, as we have seen, relates directly to intimate-partner violence.

The stories told here reveal the lie behind these social constructions. These 16 stories are stories of abuse, and not even "just" stories of intimate-partner violence but stories of abuse in all of its hideous, insidious, and highly gendered forms. Rape—gang rape, date rape, rape of young girls by fathers and stepfathers and family members, other forms of childhood sexual abuse—along with physical, emotional, and psychological abuse; *in every single story* some, if not all, of these horrors appear. What are we inclined to make of this? The temptation may be to presume that these are isolated stories not reflective of the world most of us live in; however, while it is true that many of these women have lived lives without protection and that we can not generalize from this small sample, other research suggests that these experiences are less rare than we might wish to believe (Campbell et al., 2002; Heise & Garcia-Moreno, 2002; Leserman et al., 1996; Plichta, 2004; Tjaden & Thoennes, 2000). It is important to reiterate that the only criterion for the involvement of these narrators was that they were single mothers on social assistance. Furthermore, in our longitudinal qualitative research with more than 120 lone mothers across Canada, almost 70% of participants had disclosed abuse by the end of the five-year study. Thus, it does seem safe to suggest that abuse is a very significant factor in the lives of single mothers accessing social assistance, and that the moral censure applied to them serves to divert the desperately warranted attention from this more disturbing social picture and the scrutiny it requires.

Good Mothering

One of the things the stories clearly illustrate is that despite the barriers and hardship they have experienced, these women are good mothers. Some had to give up their children for a while in order to work on their own healing, but in the end with much hard work and perseverance they have all been reunited with their children. It is clear that for all the women, their children are the most important part of their lives. The mothers make huge sacrifices for them and put their interests ahead of their own. They are good mothers who are parenting with a lack of financial resources and many emotional scars. In many cases, it was the presence of children that helped the mother turn her life around—"saved" them, in Madison's words. Cristina, too, turned things around when she had a child, and many other women's stories echo this. Lucy ends her story by saying, "and I made myself a happy home." This is perhaps the main theme of this volume. Despite the adversity that they have faced, this is what all the women have done; they have regained control of their lives to create happy homes for their children.

Service Systems

If we regard this as a book of hope and hopefulness, as the women repeated over and over to us, we need to highlight the supports that are necessary and warranted to help lone moms overcome some of the significant adversity related here. Anne hopes that the book will help policy-makers identify what is needed. As she told us:

> I think the book would be really good for the government to study for doing social economic reform and improvement for women in society, because when they're making all these social policies with regard to the status of single mothers and welfare and ODSP and all those subsidies, they're not studying real case studies like this book is. This book reflects real case studies of women, how they've grown up, the barriers they face, the psychological problems they've had, that they're saddled with the kids and the burdens, and also, then, the scapegoat and the stereotyping of society blaming them for getting in trouble and for what happens with the kids and everything else while the men float away in Never Never Land.

The stories demonstrate that essential supports were missing in these women's lives, especially at critical points. In most cases we can see that the interventions that did occur were often limited, punitive, short-sighted, or all three. Many times there were no interventions at all. Amid a current and renewed interest in resilience and how and why it manifests, there is an increasing awareness that it does not derive simply from the psychological fortitude of particular individuals. It is supported through a broad range of protective factors that include social and familial affective supports but also a range of community and governmental instrumental supports that at their best are targeted, integrated, and planful (Caragata & Cumming, 2012). The final section of this chapter reiterates some of the service-system issues that were raised in the stories and analyzes both what was problematic in their response as well as what might produce more positive—and resilient—outcomes.

The system, or systems, that lone mothers cope with is fragmented, and women who must negotiate with different systems repeatedly feel, as Miriam says, that "the story was the same." They feel invisible, unheard, and like they have to fight and advocate continuously to get what they need. In Miriam's case, for example, neither the police nor the courts took seriously the abuse she had endured until she found herself back in the system, this time because her ex-husband, who had abused her, was now abusing her son. In both this and other research, women describe having conflicting court dates as they negotiate between criminal and family court and different and conflicting outcomes with abusing men found guilty in one system and given unrestricted access to their children in another. Stories of women having restraining orders against their abusive partners but no protection when they are breached are legion, both here and in other research (Logan, Shannon, & Walker, 2005; Moe, 2007).

The systems that are intended to support people are complex and bureaucratic, and women get caught in what Lucy calls a "complicated trap." After much perseverance and effort, Lucy completed her high school equivalency and got accepted into a university engineering program. Because she was going to university, she became ineligible for social assistance, so she had to apply for a student loan to cover her education costs and to support herself and her kids. However, this loan provision required her to take a full course load, which she could not do because of the workload coupled with her responsibilities as a single parent of two children, one with special needs. It was a "very complicated trap and I was caught in it" (Lucy's story). Martha describes how she had money saved for an education and had a plan, but social assistance did not allow her to keep this money or use it for education—she had to spend it before she could continue to receive assistance. Emily spent many years dealing with multiple systems with alarming instances of incompetence, ineptitude, or both. Her lawyer inadvertently mentioned her home address in front of an abusive ex-partner who showed up to threaten her the next day. Another lawyer thought her kids should see their dad in spite of the family having to flee abuse. Her immigration case was postponed six times. Another story tells of a father put on the child abuse registry and then given unsupervised access by the child protection authorities. As with the abuse experiences, it would be comforting, less disturbing, to see these as unusual, infrequent, or isolated cases, but they are not and to so consider them will enable systems to continue that repeatedly and structurally fail women and their children at every turn.

The social assistance system arises repeatedly and problematically in the stories, as all of the narrators turned to it at some point in their lives. Low benefit levels, the lack of clarity around entitlements and extras, and the moral scrutiny that women are continually subjected to cause real family hardship.

Many of the lone-mother narrators reported having a disability, and some had children with disabilities. For some lone moms the disability was depression—one suspects often situational, deriving directly from the highly stressful circumstances in which they were enmeshed. For others, it was postpartum or the effects of a work-related injury. For these women, the vagaries and blockages to a smooth transition to a disability benefit is revealed repeatedly in the stories. The relationships with workers, who are not likely to be trained in social work and are themselves under tremendous caseload pressure, cause additional stress and reflect lost opportunities for service planning, identification of other family issues, and appropriate referrals. After reading all of the stories in the volume, Martha comments:

> I think one of the things that ran through every story was that ODSP [Ontario Disability Support Program] and OW [Ontario Works] don't understand us and they don't make the effort to understand us. They don't really have enough training and enough patience, for lack of a better word, to try to understand us. I think they just make a blanket story out of each and every one of us and think we're lazy, we're stupid, and we need help. And all of us in this room, there's none of, none of us in this room can say that's [true]. We can't. We're all trying to better ourselves and better our children, and this story is proof of that.

Stacey tells us "you can't lump [us] all together, you have to find out who [each person needing assistance] is and work with them from where they are at."

While current workfare-oriented social assistance systems repeatedly tout the value of labour-market attachment, their approach to helping lone mothers achieve this is remarkably short-sighted. In Toronto, Canada's fourth-largest welfare-delivery body, the training program most frequently provided to women on assistance is the Personal Support Worker Program. This program yields its graduates minimum-wage jobs. Even more frequently, graduates work as independent contractors at minimum wage with extensive travel time as they move across the city providing an hour or two of support to as many clients as they can manage in a day. Such work is most often available in the evening and overnight, and even if the obvious child care problems can be overcome, earning a family wage as a single parent is almost impossible. So—given the apparent self-evidence of this as problematic training for a single mother—why does it continue? Its contrast with the fact that men are trained most often as truck drivers draws our attention back to the profound and gendered inequality that undergirds our social welfare state.

We turn again to Lucy's story to offer an example of the difference a system that worked could make. If Lucy had been supported to continue with her engineering program, through social assistance, student loans, and effective, affordable child care, she would have long since left the social assistance system. Even more importantly, she would have felt supported, felt herself worthy, and felt that the agency that she has demonstrated throughout her life was rewarded. In turn, we would have had a taxpayer, a contributor, and an engaged citizen, modelling her actions to her children and to others.

The prohibition in most provinces against receiving social assistance and student-loan funding makes taking the leap to post-secondary education a high-risk venture for most single mothers. As the OECD recommendation discussed earlier suggests, the most effective way to support these families and end the cycle of poverty would be to support these moms to access high-quality job training. This does not include being trained to work as a personal support worker. Post-secondary education also affects how we see and interact with the world around us and what we imagine for our children. As one lone mother in our broader research study said of her undergraduate degree: "It's true, I haven't yet found a job, but maybe it's even more important that now I know I want this for my kids; they're getting an education."

Amid much critique of systems that fail to support families, lack integration and coordination, and reflect inherent policy flaws, mention must be made of some systems and supports that work, and have helped to bring about some of the positive changes in our co-authors' lives.

Women's shelters quite simply have saved lives. They not only provide safe transitional housing for women and their children, but just as importantly, they employ shelter support workers who do what every social service worker should—actively engage with their clients. They help with planning and provide support to execute the plan; they demonstrate critical levels of caring, consistency, and advocacy.

Stacey and Lucy found secure housing in housing co-operatives and credit these with important changes in their lives. Co-ops offer rent geared to income but more broadly they offer a community with which to engage. This provides the ability to develop the much vaunted social capital that comes from having social networks that include people with different resources, experiences, and capabilities, networks from which the poor are increasingly isolated (Kaus, 1995; Ehrenreich, 2001; Portes, 1998; Putnam, 2000; Woolcock, 2001).

Grassroots community organizations too are consistently mentioned as important supports, especially those that perhaps, most simply, enable women to find their own voices and talk with other women to share experience, strategy, and strength.

As a society, we must acknowledge and end the abuse that is so prevalent. It underlies other issues in many women's lives including addiction, mental health issues, and poverty. Many of the women who have told their stories here had traumatic childhoods. They have experienced abuse, neglect, parental addiction and abandonment, and dealt with these traumatic events at a very young age. For some, talking about their childhoods— where they see clear links between childhood abuse and neglect experienced in childhood and their later challenges—was painful, in some cases a painful first.

While we struggle with acknowledging and acting on abuse as a systemic issue we must concurrently provide better support to its victims, many of whom are single mothers. Secure housing, real and valued educational opportunities, long-term counselling, supportive and gender-sensitized workers, liveable welfare benefits, and perhaps, as in some Scandinavian countries, transitional supports to single custodial parents can make meaningful differences in the lives of these women and their children. It is these critical supports that helped many of our co-authors move forward when they were fortunate enough to find them amid much unnecessary and often-damaging service-system interactions.

Conclusion

Lea Caragata

Lucy starts her story by telling us that she is a single mom not by choice but because she had to leave an abusive relationship. This notion of choice is a fundamental idea in capitalist western democracies. Lucy must declaim that she had no choice because the common presumption is that people, single mothers, have made sets of choices, freely undertaken, that have created their present circumstance. If this book seeks to refute just one element of the common public discourse—it is this idea of freedom of choice. Van Parijs (1995) suggests that there are three conditions that must be satisfied for freedom to exist. The first is the presence of a well-established structure that enables the rule of law, enables security. The second is that this structure enables each person to own herself (self-ownership), and the third is that the structure enables each person the greatest possible opportunity to do what they might want to do. Although this is but a small element of a much larger and more complex philosophical argument, it is important in concluding this volume to draw attention to this idea of freedom of choice.

Against the criteria set out above, none of our co-authors could reasonably be considered to have been able to act freely, to be agents in their lives. The rule of law that should have protected their basic personal security failed them, permitting often-repeated abuse. Furthermore, the very concept of self-ownership is inconsistent with any understanding of deep and enduring poverty, single parenting, and experience of abuse. The opportunity to do what they might have wanted to do has been constrained in most of these women's lives since childhood. Wendell (1990) suggests that "much of what women appear to do freely is chosen in very limiting circumstances, where there are few choices left to us," and this too accurately describes the life stories narrated here.

The feminist philosopher Marilyn Frye (1985) takes up this issue of choice:

> I am committed to the view that the oppression of women is something women do not choose. Those of our activities and attitudes which play into women's oppression are themselves strategies we are forced into by the circumstances of oppression we live with. A woman may continue to live with the man who batters her, but the choice to remain is not a free one; it is a choice among evils in a severely constrained situation, and she has not chosen that situation. The oppression of women is something consisting of and accomplished by a network of institutions and material and ideological forces which press women into the service of men. Women are not simply free to walk away from this servitude at will.
>
> But also, it is clear that there has always been resistance to female servitude, taking different shapes in different places and times. The question of responsibility, or rather, one important question, is this: Can we hold ourselves, and is it proper to hold each other, responsible for resistance? Or is it necessarily both stupid cruelty and a case of blaming the victim to add yet one more pressure in our lives, in each others' lives, by expecting, demanding, requiring, encouraging, inviting acts and patterns of resistance and reconstruction which are not spontaneously forthcoming? (pp. 215–216)

The stories of resistance and reconstruction told in this volume were offered spontaneously by women who see in such resistance and reconstruction the possibility that perhaps an entire system, but at least some of the individuals that act within it, will join them in this struggle for real freedom of choice. Such freedom is essential for women's lives, lone mothers' lives, to be celebrated—for their love and commitments to their children and for their contributions to their communities. Freedom for women can only exist if their rights, as both children and adults, to be safe from abuse and from the debilitating effects of profound deprivation are protected and safeguarded. Such protection—and the freedom of choice that derives from it—was absent from the lives of these 16 women and from the many others whose stories are similar.

Amartya Sen (2000) suggests that material deprivation in the contemporary era is sufficiently powerful that it affects both the social dimensions of citizenship and then, compoundingly, one's feelings of belonging, the construction of subjectivity. We see this in the narratives told: how poverty is tied, especially for girls and women, to a lack of protection and security, and how the resultant experiences of deprivation and abuse, and the shame of these experiences, which should be social shame but is instead internalized, shape subjectivities that feel, as Sen further suggests, "unworthy." The rest of the story unfolds from there, often into addictions, further abuse, single motherhood and welfare reliance, each such experience and its negative social scrutiny reinforcing unworthiness. We hope that this book provides an exception to this tale, or an antidote. We hope that in the lives of these narrators and the many other women who summon resistance with support from each other, the story turns, and worthiness and agency are reclaimed.

"I am not where I used to be. I'm not where I want to be, but I'm on my way. . . . We're all on our way" (Ruth).

References

Abelev, M. (2009). Advancing out of poverty: Social class worldview and its relation to resilience. *Journal of Adolescent Research 24*(1): 114–141.

Aboriginal Affairs and Northern Development Canada. (2013). *Statistics on the implementation of the Indian Residential Schools Settlement Agreement.* Aboriginal Affairs and Northern Development Canada. Retrieved from http://www.aadnc-aandc.gc.ca/eng/1315320539682/1315320692192

Alcuitas, H., Alcuitas-Imperial, L., Diocson, C., & Ordinario, O. (1997). *Trapped: "Holding on to the knife's edge." Economic violence against Filipino migrant/immigrant women.* Vancouver: Philippine Women's Centre of B.C.

Battle, K., Torjman, S., & Mendelson, M. (2006). *More than a name change: The Universal Child Care Benefit.* Caledon Institute of Social Policy.

Benoit, C., and L. Shumka. (2009). *Gendering the health determinants framework: Why girls' and women's health matters.* Vancouver: Women's Health Research Network.

Bezanson, K. (2006). *Gender, the state, and social reproduction: Household insecurity in neo-liberal times.* Toronto: University of Toronto Press.

Blau, F., and Kahn, L. (2000). Gender differences in pay. *Journal of Economic Perspectives, 14*(4): 75–99.

Caldwell, Robert D. (n.d.). Healing shame: Understanding how shame binds us and how to begin to free ourselves. Retrieved from http://www.psychsight.com/ar-shame.html

Cameron, G., and Freymond, N. (2006). *Towards positive systems of child and family welfare: International comparisons of child protection, family services, and community caring systems.* Toronto: University of Toronto Press.

Campbell, J., Jones, A. S., Dienemann, J., Kub, J., Schollenberger, J., O'Campo, P., ... & Wynne, C. (2002). Intimate partner violence and physical health consequences. *Archives of Internal Medicine, 162*(10), 1157.

Caragata, L. (2008). Lone mothers and the politics of care. *Journal of the Association for Research on Mothering, 10*(1): 66–81.

Caragata, Lea, and S. Cumming. (2011). Resilience among at-risk groups in Canada: A qualitative analysis of lone mother-led families. Prepared for Human Resources and Skills Development Canada.

Catalyst. (2012). *Catalyst quick take: Canadian women.* New York: Catalyst.

Cleveland, G., & Krashinksy, M. (2001). What special arrangements are necessary for lone-parent families in a universal childcare program? In G. Cleveland & M. Ramesh (Eds.), *Our children's future: Childcare policy in Canada* (pp. 315–334). Toronto: University of Toronto Press.

Collin, C., & Jensen, H. (2009). *A statistical profile of poverty in Canada.* Library of Parliament. Parliamentary Information and Research Services. PRB 09-17E.

Conference Board of Canada. (2013). *How Canada performs: Child poverty.* Retrieved from http://www.conferenceboard.ca/hcp/details/society/child-poverty.aspx#_ftn2

CRIAW. (2003). Immigrant and refugee women. Canadian Research Institute For Women Fact Sheet, No. 5. Retrieved fromhttp://www.criaw-icref.ca/sites/criaw/files/Immigrant%20%26%20Refugee%20Women%20Factsheet.pdf

Cumming, S. J., & Cooke, M. (2009). "I work hard for no money": The work demands of single mothers managing multiple state provided benefits. *Canadian Review of Social Policy, 60*: 75–99.

Diocson, C. & Sayo, C. (2001). *Filipino nurses doing domestic work in Canada: A stalled development.* Vancouver: Philippine Women's Centre of B.C.

Ehrenreich, B. (2001). *Nickel and dimed: On (not) getting by in America.* New York: Henry Holt.

Evans, P. (1997). Divided citizenship? Gender, income security and the welfare state. In P. Evans & G. Wekerle (Eds.), *Women and the Canadian welfare state: Challenges and change* (pp. 91–116). Toronto: University of Toronto Press.

Evans, P. (2007). (Not) Taking account of precarious employment: Workfare policies and lone mothers in Ontario and the UK. *Social Policy and Administration, 41*(1): 29–49.

Fleras, A. (2011). *Unequal relations: An introduction to race, ethnic, and aboriginal dynamics in Canada* (7th ed.). Toronto: Pearson Education Canada.

Fleury, D. (2008). Low-income children. *Perspectives on Labour and Income.* Statistics Canada, Catalogue no. 75-001-X. Retrieved from http://www.statcan.gc.ca/pub/75-001-x/2008105/pdf/10578-eng.pdf

Fraser, N. (2000). Why overcoming prejudice is not enough: A rejoinder to Richard Rorty. *Critical Horizons, 1*(1): 21–28.

Freire, P. (1970). *Pedagogy of the oppressed.* New York: Herder and Herder.

Frenette, M. (2007). *Why are youth from lower-income families less likely to attend university? Evidence from academic abilities, parental influences, and financial constraints.* Ottawa: Statistics Canada.

Gavigan, S., & Chunn, D. (2007). From mothers' allowance to mothers need not apply: Canadian liberal and neoliberal reforms. *Osgoode Hall Law Journal, 45*(4): 734–771.

Gorlick, C.A., & Brethour, G. (1998). *Welfare-to-work programs: A national inventory.* Ottawa: Canadian Council on Social Development.

Grandea, N., & Kerr, J. (1998). "Frustrated and displaced": Filipina domestic workers in Canada. *Gender and Development, 6*(1): 7–12.

Heise, L., & Garcia-Moreno, C. (2002). Violence by intimate partners. In Krug, E. G., Dahlberg, L. L., Mercy, J. A., Zwi, A. B., & Lozano, R. (Eds.), *World Report on Violence and Health* (pp. 87–121). Geneva: World Health Organization.

Heisz, A., Jackson, A., & Picot, G. (2002). *Winners and losers in the labour market of the 1990s*. Ottawa: Analytical Studies Branch, Statistics Canada.

Herd, D., Mitchell, A., & Lightman, E. (2005). Rituals of degradation: Administration as policy in the Ontario Works Programme. *Social Policy and Administration, 39*(1): 65–79.

Holzer, H., Schanzenbach, D., Duncan, G., & Ludwig, J. (2007). *The economic costs of poverty in the United States: Subsequent effects of children growing up poor*. Washington, DC: Center for American Progress.

Kaus, Mickey. (1995). *The end of equality* (2nd ed.). New York: Basic Books.

Leserman, J., Drossman, D.A., Zhiming, L., Toomey, T.C., Nachman, G., & Glogau, L. (1996). Sexual and physical abuse history in gastroenterology practice: How types of abuse impact health status. *Psychosomatic Medicine, 58*: 4–15.

Little, M. J. (1998). *No car, no radio, no liquor permit: The moral regulation of single mothers in Ontario, 1920–1997*. Toronto: Oxford University Press.

Logan, T. K., Shannon, L., & Walker, R. (2005). Protective orders in rural and urban areas. *Violence Against Women, 11*(7): 876–911.

Macdonald, D., & Wilson, D. (2013). *Poverty or prosperity: Indigenous children in Canada*. Ottawa: Canadian Centre for Policy Alternatives (CCPA) and Save the Children Canada. Retrieved from http://www.policyalternatives.ca/publications/reports/poverty-or-prosperity

McQuaig, Linda. (1995). *Shooting the hippo: Death by deficit and other Canadian myths*. Toronto: Penguin.

McQuaig, Linda. (1998). *The cult of impotence: Selling the myth of powerlessness in the global economy*. Toronto: Penguin.

Mahon, R. (2002). What kind of "social Europe"? The example of child care. *Social Politics, 9*(4), 409–418.

Maume, D. J. (2004). Is the glass ceiling a unique form of inequality? *Work and Occupations, 31*: 250–274.

Mead, L. (1986). *Beyond entitlement: The social obligations of citizenship*. New York: Free Press.

Millar, J. (2008). "Work is good for you": Lone mothers, children, work and well-being. *Social Security and Health Research: Working Papers, 60*: 1–18.

Moe, A. (2007). Silence voices and structural survival: Battered women's help seeking. *Violence against Women, 13*(7): 676–699.

OECD (2010). *Gender pay gaps for full-time workers and earnings differentials by educational attainment*. Organisation for Economic Co-operation and Development–Social Policy Division–Directorate of Employment,

Labour and Social Affairs. Retrieved from http://www.oecd.org/els/soc/ LMF1.5%20Gender%20pay%20gaps%20for%20full%20time%20workers% 20-%20updated%20290712.pdf

Picot, G., Hou, F., & Coulombe, S. (2007). *Chronic low income and low income dynamics among recent immigrants.* Statistics Canada.

Plichta, S. B. (2004). Intimate partner violence and physical health consequences: Policy and practice implications. *Journal of Interpersonal Violence 19*(11): 1296–1323.

Portes, A. (1998). Social capital: Its origins and applications in modern sociology. *Annual Review of Sociology, 24*: 1–24.

Putnam, R. D. (2000). *Bowling alone: The collapse and revival of American community.* New York: Simon and Schuster.

Robinson, L. M., McIntyre, L., & Officer, S. (2005). Welfare babies: Poor children's experiences informing healthy peer relationships in Canada. *Health Promotion International, 20*(4): 342–350.

Sefa Dei, G. (1995). Examining the case for "African-centered" schools in Ontario. *McGill Journal of Education, 30*(2): 179–199.

Sen, A. (2000). Social exclusion: Concept, application, and scrutiny. *Social Development Papers* (No. 1). Manila: Office of Environment and Social Development, Asian Development Bank.

Social Assistance Reform Act, Statutes of Ontario (1997, c. 25).

Statistics Canada (2012a). *Census snapshot of Canadian families.* Ottawa: Author.

Statistics Canada (2012b). *Economic well-being.* Ottawa: Author.

Statistics Canada (2011). *Portrait of Families and Living Arrangements in Canada.* Ottawa: Author

Statistics Canada (2010). *Educational Indicators in Canada: An international perspective.* Ottawa: Canadian Education Statistics Council.

Tjaden, P., & Thoennes, N. (2000). *Extent, nature, and consequences of intimate partner violence: Findings from the National Violence against Women Survey.* Publication No. NCJ 181867. Washington, DC: Department of Justice.

Torjman, S. (1996). *Workfare: A poor law.* Ottawa: Caledon Institute. Retrieved from http://www.socialpolicy.ca/52100/m9/full67.htm

Van Parijs, P. (1995). *Real freedom for all: What (if anything) can justify capitalism?* London: Oxford University Press.

Vosko, L. F. (2002). Re-thinking feminization: Gendered precariousness in the Canadian labour market and the crisis in social reproduction. *Robarts Canada Research Chairholders Series, 11.*

Vosko, L. F. (2005). *Precarious employment: Understanding labour market insecurity in Canada.* Montreal: McGill-Queen's University Press.

Vosko, L. F., Zukewich, N., & Cranford, C. (2003). Precarious jobs: A new typology of employment. *Perspectives, 4*(10): 16–26.

Wendell, S. (1990). Oppression and victimization; Choice and responsibility. *Hypatia, 5*(3): 15–46.

Williams, C. (2010). *Corporate power in a globalizing world.* Toronto: Oxford University Press.

Woolcock, M. (2001). The place of social capital in understanding social and economic outcomes. Retrieved from http://www.oecd.org/edu/educationeconomyandsociety/1824913.pdf

Books in the Life Writing Series
Published by Wilfrid Laurier University Press

Haven't Any News: Ruby's Letters from the Fifties edited by Edna Staebler with an Afterword by Marlene Kadar • 1995 / x + 165 pp. / ISBN 0-88920-248-6

"I Want to Join Your Club": Letters from Rural Children, 1900–1920 edited by Norah L. Lewis with a Preface by Neil Sutherland • 1996 / xii + 250 pp. (30 b&w photos) / ISBN 0-88920-260-5

And Peace Never Came by Elisabeth M. Raab with Historical Notes by Marlene Kadar • 1996 / x + 196 pp. (12 b&w photos, map) / ISBN 0-88920-281-8

Dear Editor and Friends: Letters from Rural Women of the North-West, 1900–1920 edited by Norah L. Lewis • 1998 / xvi + 166 pp. (20 b&w photos) / ISBN 0-88920-287-7

The Surprise of My Life: An Autobiography by Claire Drainie Taylor with a Foreword by Marlene Kadar • 1998 / xii + 268 pp. (8 colour photos and 92 b&w photos) / ISBN 0-88920-302-4

Memoirs from Away: A New Found Land Girlhood by Helen M. Buss / Margaret Clarke • 1998 / xvi + 153 pp. / ISBN 0-88920-350-4

The Life and Letters of Annie Leake Tuttle: Working for the Best by Marilyn Färdig Whiteley • 1999 / xviii + 150 pp. / ISBN 0-88920-330-x

Marian Engel's Notebooks: "Ah, mon cahier, écoute" edited by Christl Verduyn • 1999 / viii + 576 pp. / ISBN 0-88920-333-4 cloth / ISBN 0-88920-349-0 paper

Be Good Sweet Maid: The Trials of Dorothy Joudrie by Audrey Andrews • 1999 / vi + 276 pp. / ISBN 0-88920-334-2

Working in Women's Archives: Researching Women's Private Literature and Archival Documents edited by Helen M. Buss and Marlene Kadar • 2001 / vi + 120 pp. / ISBN 0-88920-341-5

Repossessing the World: Reading Memoirs by Contemporary Women by Helen M. Buss • 2002 / xxvi + 206 pp. / ISBN 0-88920-408-x cloth / ISBN 0-88920-410-1 paper

Chasing the Comet: A Scottish-Canadian Life by Patricia Koretchuk • 2002 / xx + 244 pp. / ISBN 0-88920-407-1

The Queen of Peace Room by Magie Dominic • 2002 / xii + 115 pp. / ISBN 0-88920-417-9

China Diary: The Life of Mary Austin Endicott by Shirley Jane Endicott • 2002 / xvi + 251 pp. / ISBN 0-88920-412-8

The Curtain: Witness and Memory in Wartime Holland by Henry G. Schogt • 2003 / xii + 132 pp. / ISBN 0-88920-396-2

Teaching Places by Audrey J. Whitson • 2003 / xiii + 178 pp. / ISBN 0-88920-425-x

Through the Hitler Line by Laurence F. Wilmot, M.C. • 2003 / xvi + 152 pp. / ISBN 0-88920-448-9

Where I Come From by Vijay Agnew • 2003 / xiv + 298 pp. / ISBN 0-88920-414-4

The Water Lily Pond by Han Z. Li • 2004 / x + 254 pp. / ISBN 0-88920-431-4

The Life Writings of Mary Baker McQuesten: Victorian Matriarch edited by Mary J. Anderson • 2004 / xxii + 338 pp. / ISBN 0-88920-437-3

Seven Eggs Today: The Diaries of Mary Armstrong, 1859 and 1869 edited by Jackson W. Armstrong • 2004 / xvi + 228 pp. / ISBN 0-88920-440-3

Love and War in London: A Woman's Diary 1939–1942 by Olivia Cockett; edited by Robert W. Malcolmson • 2005 / xvi + 208 pp. / ISBN 0-88920-458-6

Incorrigible by Velma Demerson • 2004 / vi + 178 pp. / ISBN 0-88920-444-6

Auto/biography in Canada: Critical Directions edited by Julie Rak • 2005 / viii + 264 pp. / ISBN 0-88920-478-0

Tracing the Autobiographical edited by Marlene Kadar, Linda Warley, Jeanne Perreault, and Susanna Egan • 2005 / viii + 280 pp. / ISBN 0-88920-476-4

Must Write: Edna Staebler's Diaries edited by Christl Verduyn • 2005 / viii + 304 pp. / ISBN 0-88920-481-0

Pursuing Giraffe: A 1950s Adventure by Anne Innis Dagg • 2006 / xvi + 284 pp. (photos, 2 maps) / 978-0-88920-463-8

Food That Really Schmecks by Edna Staebler • 2007 / xxiv + 334 pp. / ISBN 978-0-88920-521-5

163256: A Memoir of Resistance by Michael Englishman • 2007 / xvi + 112 pp. (14 b&w photos) / ISBN 978-1-55458-009-5

The Wartime Letters of Leslie and Cecil Frost, 1915–1919 edited by R.B. Fleming • 2007 / xxxvi + 384 pp. (49 b&w photos, 5 maps) / ISBN 978-1-55458-000-2

Johanna Krause Twice Persecuted: Surviving in Nazi Germany and Communist East Germany by Carolyn Gammon and Christiane Hemker • 2007 / x + 170 pp. (58 b&w photos, 2 maps) / ISBN 978-1-55458-006-4

Watermelon Syrup: A Novel by Annie Jacobsen with Jane Finlay-Young and Di Brandt • 2007 / x + 268 pp. / ISBN 978-1-55458-005-7

Broad Is the Way: Stories from Mayerthorpe by Margaret Norquay • 2008 / x + 106 pp. (6 b&w photos) / ISBN 978-1-55458-020-0

Becoming My Mother's Daughter: A Story of Survival and Renewal by Erika Gottlieb • 2008 / x + 178 pp. (36 b&w illus., 17 colour) / ISBN 978-1-55458-030-9

Leaving Fundamentalism: Personal Stories edited by G. Elijah Dann • 2008 / xii + 234 pp. / ISBN 978-1-55458-026-2

Bearing Witness: Living with Ovarian Cancer edited by Kathryn Carter and Lauri Elit • 2009 / viii + 94 pp. / ISBN 978-1-55458-055-2

Dead Woman Pickney: A Memoir of Childhood in Jamaica by Yvonne Shorter Brown • 2010 / viii + 202 pp. / ISBN 978-1-55458-189-4

I Have a Story to Tell You by Seemah C. Berson • 2010 / xx + 288 pp. (24 b&w photos) / ISBN 978-1-55458-219-8

We All Giggled: A Bourgeois Family Memoir by Thomas O. Hueglin • 2010 / xiv + 232 pp. (20 b&w photos) / ISBN 978-1-55458-262-4

Just a Larger Family: Letters of Marie Williamson from the Canadian Home Front, 1940–1944 edited by Mary F. Williamson and Tom Sharp • 2011 / xxiv + 378 pp. (16 b&w photos) / ISBN 978-1-55458-323-2

Burdens of Proof: Faith, Doubt, and Identity in Autobiography by Susanna Egan • 2011 / x + 200 pp. / ISBN 978-1-55458-333-1

Accident of Fate: A Personal Account 1938–1945 by Imre Rochlitz with Joseph Rochlitz • 2011 / xiv + 226 pp. (50 b&w photos, 5 maps) / ISBN 978-1-55458-267-9

The Green Sofa by Natascha Würzbach, translated by Raleigh Whitinger • 2012 / xiv + 240 pp. (5 b&w photos) / ISBN 978-1-55458-334-8

Unheard Of: Memoirs of a Canadian Composer by John Beckwith • 2012 / x + 393 pp. (74 illus., 8 musical examples) / ISBN 978-1-55458-358-4

Borrowed Tongues: Life Writing, Migration, and Translation by Eva C. Karpinski • 2012 / viii + 274 pp. / ISBN 978-1-55458-357-7

Basements and Attics, Closets and Cyberspace: Explorations in Canadian Women's Archives edited by Linda M. Morra and Jessica Schagerl • 2012 / x + 338 pp. / ISBN 978-1-55458-632-5

The Memory of Water by Allen Smutylo • 2013 / x + 262 pp. (65 colour illus.) / ISBN 978-1-55458-842-8

The Unwritten Diary of Israel Unger, Revised Edition by Carolyn Gammon and Israel Unger • 2013 / ix + 230 pp. (b&w illus.) / ISBN 978-1-77112-011-1

Boom! Manufacturing Memoir for the Popular Public by Julie Rak + 2013 / viii + 249 pp. (b&w illus.) / ISBN 978-1-55458-939-5

Motherlode: A Mosaic of Dutch Wartime Experience by Carolyne Van Der Meer • 2014 / xiv + 132 pp. (b&w illus.) / ISBN 978-1-77112-005-0

Not the Whole Story: Challenging the Single Mother Narrative edited by Lea Caragata and Judit Alcalde • 2014 / x + 222 pp. / ISBN 978-1-55458-624-0